Other Kaplan Books
Relating to Graduate School Admissions:

GRE

GRE with CD-ROM

GRE/GMAT Math Workbook

The Yale Daily News Guide to Fellowships and Grants

Graduate School
Admissions
Adviser
2000

SELECTION • ADMISSIONS • FINANCIAL AID

by
a nationwide team
of graduate school admissions advisers

Simon & Schuster

Kaplan Books
Published by Kaplan Educational Centers and Simon & Schuster
1230 Avenue of the Americas
New York, NY 10020

For bulk sales to schools, colleges, and universities, please contact Vice President of Special Sales, Simon & Schuster Special Markets, 1633 Broadway, 8th Floor, New York, NY 10019

Project Editor: Richard Christiano
Cover Design: Cheung Tai
Interior Design: Jobim Rose
Production Editor: Maude Spekes
Database Administrator: Enid Burns
Production Manager: Michael Shevlin
Managing Editor: David Chipps
Executive Editor: Del Franz
Contributing Editor: Trent Anderson

Special thanks to Linda Volpano

Manufactured in the United States of America
Published simultaneously in Canada

July 1999
10 9 8 7 6 5 4 3 2 1

ISBN 0-684-85955-6
ISSN 1097-539X

C O N T E N T S

Part Five: FINANCING YOUR DEGREE

Appendix: UNIVERSITIES WITH GRADUATE PROGRAMS

AUTHORS

Tim Haft revised and updated chapters 2–10. Haft has more than 10 years of experience providing academic and career advisement in various settings, and is the former director of career development at New York University's Tisch School of the Arts. He is also the author of *Trashproof Resumes* and *Job Notes: Résumés*; co-author of *Job Smart*; and a contributor to *The Career Toolbox* (www.careertoolbox.com), an interactive CD-ROM and Web site for job hunters. Haft holds a B.A. in history from the University of Virginia and an M.A. in sociology from New York University.

Dianne Lake was the primary author of *Getting Into Graduate School,* upon which this book is based. Lake has developed and taught courses for Kaplan's pre-college and pre-graduate programs, and produces several of Kaplan's award-winning *Higher Score* software titles. She earned her B.A. from Rutgers College and her M.A. from Union Theological Seminary.

Alice Murphey contributed Part Five, "Financing Your Degree." She is assistant director of financial aid for systems management at the City University of New York, and is a member of the steering committee for the National Committee for Graduate and Professional Financial Aid. She also served as editor of *The Official Guide to Financing Your MBA*, published by GMAC. She received her B.A. in English from Gettysburg College and an M.Ed. in Counselor Education from Penn State University.

Roberta S. Popik contributed critiques of personal statements and advice on writing for chapter 15, "The Personal Statement." She is assistant dean for graduate enrollment services at New York University Graduate School of Arts and Science, where she manages admissions, enrollment, and financial aid services for new and continuing graduate students. Prior to joining New York University, she worked for five years at Educational Testing Service. Popik received a B.A. in Psychology from Queens College, City University of New York, and a Ph.D. in experimental psychology from Northwestern University.

Silas Purnell wrote chapter 18, "African American Students." Purnell is the director of the Educational Services Division of Ada S. McKinley Community Services in Chicago, Illinois. To date, over 40,000 African American students assisted by the program Purnell directs have enrolled in over 200 colleges and universities throughout the United States.

Chris Rosa authored chapter 19, "Yes You Can! For Students with Disabilities." Rosa is the director of the Office of Services for Students with Disabilities at Queens College, City University of New York, where he coordinates the provision of support services to more than 450 students with disabilities. A member of the Muscular Dystrophy Association's National Task Force on Public Awareness, Rosa has written several articles published in scholarly journals on the sociology of disability and is a recipient of the Muscular Dystrophy Association's National Personal Achievement Award. He received his B.A. in sociology and philosophy at Queens College, City University of New York, and is currently enrolled in a doctoral program in sociology at the City University of New York Graduate Center.

Adele Scheele contributed chapter 17, "The Re-Entry Student's Guide to Success." Scheele, an internationally recognized career strategist and consultant on change management, is the director of the career center at California State University at Northridge. She is also the author of *The "Good" Student Trap,* published by Kaplan and Simon & Schuster, as well as *Skills for Success* (Ballantine), *Making College Pay Off* (Ballantine), and *Career Strategies for the Working Woman* (Fireside/Simon & Schuster). She appears frequently as a career expert commentator on NBC's *Today,* and in other media. Scheele earned a Ph.D. from U.C.L.A. as a Change Management Fellow, a master's degree in English from California State University at Northridge, and a bachelor's degree from the University of Pennsylvania.

Joseph Sevigny contributed chapter 20, "Especially for International Students." Sevigny is director of graduate enrollment services at New York University, where he manages the international credential evaluation process for the Graduate School of Arts and Science and coordinates the Graduate School's role in international exchange programs. Sevigny is the author of several volumes in the *Country Guide Series on Education Systems of the World,* published by the American Association of Collegiate Registrars and Admissions Officers (AACRAO), and serves as Vice Chair of AACRAO's International Admissions Committee. He received an B.A. in International Relations from the University of San Diego and an M.S. in social science from Long Island University. He is currently a doctoral candidate in International Education at New York University.

Dorothy J. Umans contributed critiques of personal statements and advice on writing for chapter 15, "The Personal Statement." She is a director of admissions at George Washington University. She has 24 years of admissions experience, primarily in graduate and professional schools, and holds a master's and an Educational Specialist degree in Counseling and Personnel Services, as well as an MBA. In addition to management consulting and conducting workshops on strategic marketing, she has conducted research on doctoral student attrition and retention. She received a B.A. in art history from SUNY—Fredonia, a M.S. in counseling and personal services and an Ed.S. degree from SUNY—Albany, and an M.B.A. from Pace University. She is currently a doctoral candidate in higher education policy at the University of Maryland at College Park.

PART ONE

An Introduction to Graduate Programs

CHAPTER 1

Assessing Your Goals

You've probably heard the good news: According to recent surveys, Americans with a graduate degree earn, on average, 35 to 50 percent more than do those with just a bachelor's degree. Maybe that's one reason there are more people than ever in the United States applying to grad school. But while the rewards of advanced study can be greater fulfillment and a higher salary, the competition of getting into a good graduate school is fierce. There are a lot of people out there thinking about going to graduate school. Meanwhile, the variety of graduate programs offered by graduate institutions is also growing. And the cost of education continues to rise.

That's why, now more than ever, deciding to go to grad school means you have to realistically assess what graduate school will do for you, and exactly what program will suit you best.

Why Should You Go?

If graduate school is so much like work, and if the degree doesn't guarantee you the career of your dreams, why did over a million people enter U.S. graduate programs last year? Despite the difficulties, there are still compelling reasons to get a graduate degree.

A career in academia

To teach at two-year colleges, you'll need at least a master's degree; to teach and research at four-year colleges, universities, and graduate programs, you'll need a doctorate.

> ### No Dreamers, Please
>
> "Graduate school is not for the squeamish. It's a long haul to the Ph.D., and there is no easy, perfect road."
>
> A graduate student

Why Are You Here?

"It seems like you go to graduate school with a whole different
set of ideas from when you
leave. Your goals and motivations constantly change."

A graduate student

Professional licensing

Social workers, psychologists, therapists, and others who
directly treat or counsel clients will almost certainly need
graduate education to meet national and state licensing
requirements. The proper licensing and credentials are
essential not only for employment reasons, but also for
insurance reimbursement. There are many insurance carri-
ers who authorize payment only to practitioners who meet
certain educational and licensing standards.

Career change

Many people make the decision to return to graduate school after working in "the real world" for awhile.
Their interests and abilities have developed over the years and may have nothing at all to do with their
undergraduate education. A graduate degree is necessary training for the new field.

The switch from practitioner to administrator

After working in the trenches for awhile, and developing a strong sense of how an organization, school,
clinic, or department could be better run, you may be interested in moving up to the management level
of your field. This may also require some graduate education.

Career and/or salary advancement

The upper levels of your field may be closed to people with only a bachelor's degree, no matter how talented or industrious you are.

Because you love it

There are plenty of people who choose graduate school because they simply love the field or because
graduate school provides welcome intellectual stimulation.

Because the job market is lousy

A slow economy is a popular reason for going directly from undergraduate to graduate school. The reasoning is: Since I'm not going to get a job anyway, I might as well go to grad school now. Maybe I can
ride out the job scarcity and even come out more employable than when I went in.

Making your investment pay off

Should you go to graduate school? The simple fact that you are reading this book indicates that you have
already given this question some thought and are considering pursuing either a master's or a doctorate.
But it's a question worth considering in some detail. First, even a master's degree is a significant invest-

ment of time, money, and work. Most master's programs take two academic years to complete; at a private institution, the cost can run over $28,000. A doctorate generally takes a minimum of four years, and while true financial aid is more available at the doctoral than at the master's level, the financial strain is significant. Even if you are willing to take on loan debt to finance your degree, you may be looking at 20 or 30 years of loan payments.

Then there is the job market. In many fields, jobs in academia are hard to come by; in some industries and businesses, even an advanced degree is no guarantee of a dream job.

The bottom line is that graduate school is a huge investment. Before you take the leap, it's key that you have a pretty clear idea where your interests really lie, what grad school life is like, and whether you are compatible with a particular program and its professors. Armed with this information, you should be able to successfully apply to the right programs, get accepted, and use your graduate school time to help you get a head start on the postgraduation job search.

Real Students: Grad School Life

What your experience of graduate school is like depends a lot on the school you attend, your particular program, what you're expecting from the experience, and issues in your personal life. Here are a handful of current and recent graduate students' impressions:

Ups and downs

"Graduate school is an emotional roller-coaster. There are times when you feel really bad about it and there are times when you feel really great."

Hard day's night

"I worked full time and went to school full time for a year, and I remember crying every day when I came home. Then the next morning it was all fine, and I got up and went to work again."

Doing it by yourself

"If you are going to graduate school expecting to be taught, you're in for a rude surprise. Basically, for most of the substantial courses, they just hand you a reading list and tell you to go learn it yourself."

Brainpower

"You're at the point where if you're thinking, you're dealing with the same questions as the professors are. Your breadth of knowledge and reading in the field is certainly less, but you are not necessarily less capable of answering the same questions that they are engaged in."

Power plays

"Undergraduates are paying a lot of tuition, and it gives them a lot of power in the university. Grad students who are on fellowships or TA or whatever—you take what you can get. You really don't have much power."

Feels like . . .

"It seems like you go to graduate school with a whole different set of ideas from when you leave. Your goals and motivations constantly change. This is almost like a job for me—it feels like a job instead of school."

Getting wise

"A lot of my fellow students complain about politics—a lot of gossip and competitiveness. This program was an honor to get into, and now I realize that it's not going to be a breeze to get through; so in this sense I have to harden myself to the politics, which could make things harder for me."

Time Flies

Median time between bachelor's degree and doctorate:

1971	. . . . .7.9 years
1982	. . . . .9.5 years
1994	. . . . .11.0 years

Median time registered in graduate programs (doctorate recipients):

1971	. . . . .5.5 years
1982	. . . . .6.4 years
1994	. . . . .7.1 years

Source: National Research Council

Making a diference

"For my field placement I worked with high school students with disabilities. I was doing career, personal, and academic counseling. The first part involved working with students who had serious physical handicaps. I helped empower them—assisted many of them up to the time of their graduation. I got a lot of personal satisfaction from this as I saw my investments pay off. Watching them grow was really great."

The Basics

Master's vs. Doctoral Programs

Broadly speaking, the two most common grad school degrees awarded are master's and doctorates. Depending on your area of interest and your professional goals, one or the other may be the goal you pursue.

Master's programs: two tracks

Master's programs are two years long, and master's students generally are one of two types: those on the academic track, where the degree programs focus on classical research and scholarship, and those on the practical track, where the degree program is actually a professional training program that qualifies you to enter or advance in a field such as social work or education.

At the master's level, the operative word is probably pressure. Since master's programs generally give very little financial aid, many master's students work at least part time and attend classes either part or full time. Juggling priorities is one of the first skills a master's student needs to develop. There is usually quite a bit more assigned reading than in undergraduate school. Once you get past the introductory or foundation courses, you're usually evaluated on the basis of your papers and your in-class or practical work. You'll be expected to maintain at least a "B" average, and will need considerably higher grades if you plan to move on to a doctoral program. If you're on an academic track, you'll almost certainly write a thesis, a 50- to 150-page paper demonstrating your grasp of scholarship and research in your field, before you are graduated. If you're on the practical track, fieldwork or additional coursework will take the place of the thesis. And in many programs, you'll be managing the whole thing more or less on your own. While on the practical track, advisers tend to be more involved, evaluating your fieldwork as well as approving your course selection and other academic matters; on the academic track, master's students tend to take a back seat to the doctoral students.

> ### Some Advice on Advisers
>
> "Choose your adviser wisely. You will be working for you adviser like you would work for a boss at a company. It's most important that you get along well with this person, and that he or she is a good manager."
>
> A graduate student

Doctoral programs: apprenticeships

A doctoral program is an entirely different world. Doctoral programs are designed to create scholars capable of independent research that will add new and significant knowledge in their fields. From the first, you will be regarded as an apprentice in your field. Your first year or two in the program will be spent on coursework, followed by "field" or "qualifying" exams. Once you've passed those exams, demonstrating that you have the basic factual and theoretical knowledge of your field down cold, you will then be permitted to move on to independent research, in the form of your doctoral dissertation. During most of this time you can get financial aid in the form of teaching or research assistantships; in exchange for assisting professors in the classroom or the lab, you get a small stipend and/or tuition remission. Doctoral programs see themselves as one of the most, if not the most, rigorous professional training programs.

Your Adviser

The person responsible for overseeing your transformation from apprentice to professional is your adviser, and the person responsible for finding the right adviser is you. You will choose your adviser no later than the end of your first year in the program. This person will be your mentor, working closely with you not only on your academic progress, but most likely employing you as a research or teaching assistant, helping you shape your dissertation proposal, steering you through the writing and defense of your dissertation, and, you hope, recommending you for jobs when you have your degree. To put it quite bluntly, your relationship with your adviser will make or break your program.

Politics, Politics

You'll need to maintain working relationships with other professors as well, since you'll need a committee of at least five faculty members to review your dissertation. In fact, you'll discover that graduate departments are quite political, and a strong adviser can help you negotiate many difficulties. The relationship with your adviser is so crucial to success in a doctoral program that as we discuss school selection and admissions, we'll constantly show you how to get a head start on the adviser selection process and what an influential role it plays in choosing a doctoral program.

Research vs. Teaching

Over the last couple of decades, "publish or perish" has been the dominant way of life in academia. Even more important than teaching has been research and publication, to the point where the conventional wisdom among grad students became, "Don't think about teaching; publish. If you're not a star in the first five years, you can kiss your career goodbye, and you're not going to become a star teaching all the classes that the senior faculty don't want." However, there seems to be a shift beginning in the other direction, as departments recognize how difficult the job market has become and how every experience may ultimately contribute to your ability to get a job.

What Degree Do You Need?

What degree you need basically depends on what kind of job you want to get. If you want to join academia and teach or research at the university level, you will need a doctorate, no matter what field you're in. It's also virtually impossible to work as a clinical or research psychologist without the doctorate. If you're considering social work, health care, education, or engineering, the master's degree usually provides the professional qualifications you need to move past the entry-level jobs.

If you want to make more money, the choice largely depends on your field. In industry, science Ph.D.'s can make significantly higher salaries than those who hold master's degrees; in English, on the other hand, a Ph.D. mostly qualifies you for university teaching, and these jobs are so scarce

In Demand

Over 1,000 doctorates are granted each year in each of the following fields: clinical psychology, electrical engineering, and educational administration.

that many new Ph.D.'s cannot find work. The alternative is usually work in publishing or related fields, which are not always the most lucrative professions either.

Real Students: Advice from the Trenches

We asked graduate students what advice they would give to someone considering graduate school. Here are their Top 10 pointers:

1. Know why you're going, otherwise you'll flounder.

2. Focus your study as quickly as you can. It will simplify your research and decrease your time in the program.

3. Get to know the professors in the programs that interest you. It's the quickest way to get a TA or RA.

4. Investigate departments in terms of the student success rate.

5. Think for yourself.

6. Read as much in your field as possible.

7. Learn how to sell yourself in a substantial, credible way.

8. Know the history of your field and the basic theories. It's dull but invaluable.

9. Don't do it if money is your main motivation.

10. Make sure you're devoted—it's a long haul.

Master's Degrees

There are two kinds of master's degrees: those awarded on the way to the doctorate, and those designated "terminal." This rather ominous title simply means that getting this degree does not automatically launch you into a Ph.D. program. In some fields, this is because the master's degree is considered the "terminal professional degree"—that is, the master's provides the knowledge and training you need to join a profession. As a rule, the Ph.D. in these fields is reserved for those who want to teach rather than practice. In other fields, the master's degree is preliminary to the doctorate, and master's degree holders usually cannot expect

Check 'Em Out

"Do as much research on your potential adviser as possible, as well as the other professors in your department."

A grad student

Joining the Ranks

"My program—Russian studies and publishing studies—is interdisciplinary. I did this because I wanted to direct my love of Russian culture into a practical network, publishing. But I have found, rather unfortunately, that straddling two majors creates a certain amount of fickleness. Both departments have looked upon me with a certain amount of cynicism—as I'm not 100 percent loyal to what they're doing, I'm kind of the thorn in their sides—so I've come to find out with a great deal of disdain that politics is really an integral part of being a grad student."

A graduate student

to advance professionally or financially as far as doctorate holders can.

Terminal master's degree programs are usually a lot like undergraduate school, only this time it's the program and not your parents that expects you to maintain at least a "B" average. Academic programs focus on coursework, research, and papers; many require a thesis for graduation. Programs in social work and education also have a practical dimension, requiring candidates to work in classrooms, clinics, and other professional settings. Most programs are two or three years long, although completing the thesis can stretch that out an extra year or two.

Master's degrees are generally seen one of three ways. First, as "practical" degrees: they provide professional training or advancement. Second, as "entry" degrees: people may choose to get a master's first to make getting into a doctoral program more likely, with a stellar master's performance. Third, as the "consolation prize" awarded to those who are not admitted to Ph.D. programs.

Variations on a Theme

In the humanities and social sciences especially, there are some interesting variations on the traditional M.A. or M.S.

Cooperative and dual- or joint-degree programs

An increasing number of graduate schools offer cooperative programs and joint- or dual-degree programs. In cooperative programs, you apply to, answer to, and graduate from one school, but you have access to classes, professors, and facilities at a cooperating school as part of the program. In some cases faculty from the cooperating school may even sit on your thesis committee. When you graduate, you receive one degree, from the school offering the program.

In joint- or dual-degree programs you work towards two degrees simultaneously, either within the same school or at two neighboring schools. You may be registered at two schools and be subject to two sets of graduation requirements. These programs are generally less expensive and quicker than earning the two degrees separately, because at least some of the coursework, research, or clinical or field work is applied to both sets of degree requirements simultaneously.

Interdisciplinary programs

This type of program is generally run by a faculty committee from a number of different departments. You apply to, register with, and are graduated by only one of the departments; for example, in an interdisciplinary program in women's studies, you would apply to the sociology department and graduate with a M.S. in sociology. But the program you actually follow is designed and administered by the interdepartmental faculty group, and you.

Doctoral Degrees

There are two basic ways to enter into the doctorate system. One is to get a terminal master's degree and reapply to Ph.D. programs; the other is to go directly to the doctoral program.

Starting with a Terminal Master's

This has good points and bad points. The terminal master's gives you flexibility. If you are not happy with the school or the faculty, or if your interests shift over the course of earning your degree, you have the freedom to change schools and programs, no questions asked. The terminal master's can also give you a taste of your chosen field and of graduate school life before you commit yourself to the doctorate. If you decide against the doctorate, you graduate, not quit. The terminal master's can also be a way into doctoral programs that might not accept you on the basis of your undergraduate record. This works better in some fields and programs than others; before you decide on this course, check with doctoral programs that interest you to be sure that master's grades are seriously considered in the admissions process.

On the other hand, continuing for the doctorate means reliving the application process, sometimes even retaking the GRE, and pulling up stakes both academically and personally if you decide on a different school. Starting in a terminal master's program will probably cost more. Master's students generally receive less financial aid than do doctoral students, and com-

---

What's Up, Doc?

1996 doctorates, by field:

Anthropology	396
Chemistry	2,148
Computer Science	921
Earth, Atmospheric, Marine Science	807
Economics	979
Education	6,772
Engineering	6,305
English	699
History	857
Mathematics	1,122
Music	699
Philosophy	369
Physics, Astronomy	1,677
Political Science	621
Psychology	3,340
Religion	213
Social Work	256
Sociology	516

Source: National Research Council

Who Do You Know?

"It's not the smartest people who get the jobs, it's the people with connections that get jobs. You have to get in with a professor that has some prestige in the field."

A grad student

pleting a master's degree followed by a doctoral program will probably take longer than earning the master's on the way to a doctorate. Some Ph.D. programs will give you advanced placement if you have already earned your master's, but the total time and cost will probably be greater than if you earn your master's on the way to the Ph.D.

Going Directly for the Doctorate

In many Ph.D. programs, there is no terminal master's degree; the master's is simply the first stage of Ph.D. completion. A specified amount of coursework is followed by a thesis and qualifying examinations. The master's is awarded after "satisfactory completion" of these requirements.

Though many students who enter doctoral programs continue on to get their degrees, admission to this type of program is no guarantee that you will actually go on to earn the Ph.D. Consider this typical warning from one prestigious university's sociology department: "The department retains the right to award a terminal master's degree to students whose performance on the preliminary examination or on the A.M. research paper gives insufficient promise of success in the doctoral program." Meaning that after this initial phase, you can be asked to leave the program if, in the opinion of the department, you are not the stuff of which Ph.D.'s are made. The master's degree is a sort of consolation prize (if you have met the requirements).

Ph.D. candidacy is tough to earn. In most programs in humanities and social sciences, for example, those who successfully clear this first hurdle have to meet other requirements, including:

- Approval of the dissertation proposal

- Demonstration of foreign language proficiency

- Completion of coursework, qualifying or field examinations, and practical/field training

- Approval by your department as "competent to write the dissertation"

Part-Time vs. Full-Time Study

Although there are many factors to consider before deciding how much time you can allot to graduate study, the decision itself is usually obvious to most people. A single mother with a career job and children, for example, will probably not have enough hours in each day to pursue a full-time graduate program. Likewise, there's no compelling reason why a freshly graduated B.A. who has the financial resources and the time to devote to full-time study would choose a part-time program. Most graduate schools offer some flexibility in how long you may take to complete your degree.

Part-time programs

If you will have to work while you are in school, particularly while you're in the course-work stage of your studies, see if part-time study is an option of the program you're considering. These programs typically involve the completion of six to nine credits per semester. They are ideal for people who have already begun their careers and who would like to continue gaining professional experience while earning the degree that will allow them to move on to the next level. While part-time study sometimes costs more in the long run, the lower tuition per semester and the free time to pursue other interests and responsibilities are the main incentive in these programs. This can make all the difference in the course-work years, where carrying two classes per semester instead of four can make balancing work and study possible. Most part-time students take two to three years to earn their master's, and have been known to take several more to reach their doctorates. Part-time programs are slow, however, which can be discouraging, especially when licensure or salary increases are at stake.

Are there night or weekend classes? When is the library open? The lab? Talk to students who are currently in the program, especially those who work. Professors can be intolerant of working students' limited study time and work obligations (especially when that means missing class). If you are in a master's program for specific training or job advancement, this may be annoying but will cause no permanent damage to your career. If you plan to apply to a doctoral program, though, in which relationships with professors are more crucial to your progress and success, the burden of pleasing a boss and an adviser at the same time may be unmanageable.

Full-time programs

Although many students in full-time graduate programs support themselves with part-time work, their primary allegiance is to the graduate degree. It will become the focus of your life, but if there is any way that you can manage full-time, or nearly full-time, studies at the higher levels, do it. You can graduate quicker and start picking up the financial pieces that much sooner—and often with a more secure base for your job search in the form of good support from your adviser.

Nondegree or Nonmatriculated Programs

Want to go to graduate school without really applying? Some programs offer nondegree or nonmatriculated status, meaning that you apply, pay tuition, register for classes, stay up all night writing papers, and generally do everything that "matriculated" students do—except earn a master's or doctorate. Why do schools have this option, and who would put herself through it when there's no degree at the end? A nondegree program might be for you if you are not quite sure what degree you do want to pursue, or if you have been out of school for a long time and want to get back into the academic world. It also can be appealing if you're a professional who wants a bit of additional graduate education without the burden of a full graduate program.

If you're not accepted into a degree program, can you get into a graduate school this way? Possibly. According to one grad school admissions officer, it pays to honestly ask the admissions office if taking classes gives you an edge.

Know Thyself

The first step in the graduate school selection process is to take an objective look at yourself as a candidate. You may hate this step because it forces you to look at your weaknesses as well as your strengths; however, bear in mind that nearly every graduate school applicant has at least one major weakness in her application. A common one is an undergraduate GPA that doesn't reflect your ability; another is lack of background knowledge or experience in the field you hope to enter. And although it's possible for you, the applicant, to rationalize that mediocre GPA, you can be sure that the admissions committee won't.

A much better strategy is to make an honest evaluation of your candidacy, then create your application in a way that convinces the admissions committee that your weaknesses are irrelevant and that your strengths, as demonstrated on your application, make you such a great asset to the department that they can't possibly turn you down. Use the worksheet on the next pages to figure out where you stand in the basic areas of any graduate school application.

School Selection Worksheet

The Numbers

Undergraduate GPA

Undergraduate major

GPA in major

Undergraduate minor

GPA in minor

Graduate GPA

Graduate degree

GRE Verbal score

GRE Quantitative score

GRE Analytical score

GRE Subject Test score

Professional Experience

Related work experience

Related volunteer experience

Research experience

The Numbers

Academic contacts

Professional contacts

Connections

Faculty in my field that I've contacted

Professional association memberships

Journals/field literature I've been reading

CHAPTER 2

Social Work

The Employment Picture

Many people who pursue social work as a career are driven by a strong sense of altruism and a desire to help the poor, oppressed, or vulnerable to achieve general well-being. Job satisfaction is often derived from contributing directly to the welfare of others and by serving as an agent of change.

Social workers—roughly one third of whom are employed by federal, state, or local governments—practice in a wide variety of settings, including schools, hospitals, community agencies, prisons, corporations, mental health facilities, and private practice. Clinical social workers help clients cope with such obstacles as inadequate housing, unemployment, child care, death, illness, physical disabilities, aging, domestic disputes, and substance abuse. Administrative social workers tend to have less client contact, and focus more on "big picture" issues. They may be involved in a variety of activities including, managing a social service agency, community planning, and/or policy making.

Currently, the demand for social workers is relatively strong, particularly for those with a specialization in gerontology. Given the vast increase in the numbers of the elderly in the population at large, there is a strong need for both clinicians and administrators who have experience locating affordable short- and long-term nursing care, working with Alzheimer's patients and their families, and generally helping older individuals to adjust to the later stages of life.

M.S.W., M.S.S., or M.S.S.W.?

The letters in your degree don't really make a difference. What matters is that the program you attend is accredited by the Council on Social Work Education.

Who's Who in Social Work*

Women	79.0%
Men	21.0%
Asian	1.8%
African American	5.7%
Caucasian	87.9%
Latino	2.8%
Mixed Heritage	1.2%
Native American	0.6%

Source: National Association of Social Workers.
*Figures are for members of NASW.

The rising cost of health care should also result in an increase of jobs for hospital-based social workers who will be instrumental in facilitating "early discharge planning"—increasingly the strategy of choice for hospitals struggling to meet their bottom line. Social workers will help free up beds and cut costs by arranging for delivery into the home of medical services that had been previously provided in hospitals.

In addition, since the turnover rate for social workers is relatively high—particularly in the largest cities where enormous case loads, low pay, and impossible challenges are often the norm—job opportunities will continue to surface, especially for those just entering the profession.

Getting In

Academics

No specific undergraduate major is required for those applying to a master's program in social work, although many admissions committees look kindly upon a traditional liberal arts curriculum and expect candidates to have taken some courses in the social sciences. Some programs may also require coursework in statistics and biology. Candidates who are deficient in a given area may still be able to enroll in a graduate program with the proviso that they make up the necessary credits in their first year. Often applicants are expected to have an undergraduate GPA of 3.0 or above, although academic deficiencies can be compensated for with strong recommendations, experience in the field, and a personal statement that reflects a thoughtful and serious commitment to social work.

Experience

Before applying to a social work program it's a good idea to gain some paid or volunteer experience in the social services. Admissions committees will review your real-world involvement in activities related to social work to determine your level of commitment and potential for contribution to the field.

Personal Statement

Keep the focus on why you want to be a social worker and what you plan to do in the field. You can discuss both personal and professional experiences including the following:

- Personal and family relationships and experiences, particularly how your ethnic, racial, economic, and religious backgrounds have influenced your decision to pursue social work.

- Societal and political issues that affect you or your community. Make sure you propose solutions to the problems you raise and connect them to your goals as a social worker.

- Educational and professional experiences that demonstrate your ability to use sound judgment, solve problems, confront an ethical dilemma, or assist a client with a difficult situation.

Your personal statement can be very personal, but should connect your own situation to a larger context, and demonstrate how you hope to have an impact on social issues through your work. If the program to which you are applying has a strong academic bent, show through your statement that you have the capacity for analytical and abstract thinking.

Recommendations

Try to get letters from those who have supervised you on jobs or volunteer activities that pertain to social work. Social work or social science professors are also good choices for recommenders. Ideally, the letters sent to the admissions committee should reveal that you possess emotional maturity, sensitivity to others, sound judgment, responsibility, leadership, and critical thinking skills.

Standardized Tests

The GRE General Test is usually not required, but check with programs in which you are interested.

Advanced Standing

Applicants who already hold a Bachelor's of Social Work degree will probably have the opportunity to place out of some of the foundation-level courses in the master's program, enabling them to either graduate sooner or at the very least to have more flexibility in their course selection.

Financial Assistance

Unfortunately, teaching and research assistantships are generally scarce for M.S.W. students. Some programs have a limited number of paid fieldwork positions, and of course for those who show need, work-study is an option.

On the Money

	M.S.W.'s	Ph.D.'s
< $15,000	1.4%	1.0%
15,000–19,999	2.6%	.4%
20,000–29,999	26.6%	8.3%
30,000–39,999	38.0%	25.5%
40,000+	31.5%	64.7%

Program Options

Master's Level

Full-time M.S.W. programs are typically two years in length. The curriculum consists of a series of core courses and electives, plus supervised field experiences. Most schools also offer a part-time version of their program to accommodate students who work full time. Keep in mind, however, that part-time programs may have more limited practicum opportunities than those that are full-time. Students who are already working in the field of social work may be able to use their current job to satisfy a program's practicum requirements. Also note that some programs offer advanced standing to students who hold a B.S.W. from an accredited program, and may allow for the completion of the master's in a single year.

Students normally choose to pursue either an administrative or clinical track along with an area of specialization such as child and family services, gerontology, school social work, mental health, and community social work. The first year consists primarily of foundation courses, while electives and fieldwork in your area of concentration generally flesh out the remainder of the curriculum.

Fieldwork

Find out how many opportunities are available in your intended area of specialization, the type of competition you are likely to face in earning a slot, and how the placement procedure works. Also, be sure to investigate practical issues such as whether you'll need a car to get to your field site. Your practicum could be severely compromised if you're riding a bike to work when it's ten degrees below zero. If you have no intention of seeking employment near campus after completing your degree, check to see if practicum opportunities are available in the areas where you hope to eventually settle.

Because your practicum can in many cases have a profound effect on post-graduation employment opportunities, try to obtain as much information as possible on how each of the schools you are considering addresses this segment of the graduate program. Ask current students and faculty about the nature and degree of supervision, as well as the review and evaluation process.

Doctoral Level

Since so few doctorates in social work are awarded each year, there is some concern that there may be a shortage of social work researchers and university-level instructors in the near future. In any case, if you want to teach or conduct research in the field of social work at the university level, you'll need a Ph.D. Note that many social work doctoral programs require appli-

---

What's Hot in Social Work

- Gerontology

- Gay issues, particularly adolescents and AIDS issues

- Death and dying, especially hospice care

KAPLAN

cants to hold an M.S.W. degree and have some experience in the field as a prerequisite for admission.

Dual-Degree Programs

These programs enable you to earn two graduate degrees at once, usually in less time than it would take to earn each degree consecutively. Two of the more common social work dual-degree programs are the:

J.D./M.S.W.

This program, which typically takes four years to complete, is ideal for those who want to practice social work and simultaneously work within the legal system.

M.S.W./M.B.A.

A good choice if you ultimately plan to manage a social service agency.

An M.S.W. can also be combined with graduate degrees in urban planning, public policy and administration, public health, theology, and dance therapy.

Licensure

This is a critical issue for social workers, particularly those who hope to open a private practice, since appropriate licensure largely determines whether one's clients can be reimbursed for mental health services by their insurance companies. Find out the licensing requirements in the state(s) where you plan to practice, and be sure that your prospective program will prepare you to meet them.

Words of Wisdom

If you've just completed your undergraduate degree, consider taking a break before beginning a graduate social work program. There can be so much hoop jumping involved in finishing the program that some experience gained in the working world before returning to academia is invaluable. Students in M.S.W. programs will need to advocate for themselves to make sure their educational needs are met.

Investigate the research interests of the faculty. If you want to pursue death studies but no faculty members are researching that area, you'll probably need to go elsewhere.

Don't ever hint during the admissions process that you are pursuing an M.S.W. as a shortcut to becoming a therapist. It's not much of a shortcut, for one thing, and this type of comment is not likely to win you any brownie points.

Who's Really Doing the Work?

The majority of the nation's mental health and therapy services are provided by social workers, not by psychologists and psychiatrists.

Source: National Association of Social Workers

For More Information

American Association of State Social Work Boards, www.aasswb.org. AASSWB develops and maintains the social-work licensing examination used nationwide. They can help answer questions that social workers and social-work students have about licensing and social-work examinations.

Council on Social Work Education, 1600 Duke Street, Alexandria, VA 22314-3421; (703) 683–8080; www.cswe.org. Publishes the annual *Summary Information on Master of Social Work Programs*, which lists all accredited master's programs and the concentrations they offer.

National Association of Social Workers, 750 First Street NE, Suite 700, Washington, DC 20002-4241; (800) 638-8799; www.naswdc.org

New Social Worker, PO Box 5390, Department WWW, Harrisburg, PA 17110-0390; www.socialworker.com. Quarterly magazine devoted to the concerns of social work students and recent graduates.

Social Work Resources Directory; http://hav54.socwel.berkeley.edu/resource.htm. Offers a complete list of CSWE-accredited M.S.W. and doctoral programs as well as social work programs abroad. Links to numerous sites, including those dealing with mental health, health, gerontology, and child welfare, as well as to nonprofit organizations and government agencies.

CHAPTER 3

Education

Why Study Education?

The graduate students we spoke with offered a wide variety of reasons as to why they decided to pursue a graduate degree in education. For some the motivation was entirely personal, and for others exclusively professional.

Coming to this particular field of study was . . . a long, personal journey for me. It began . . . as a result of being the butt of a lot of racism in high school; I am of mixed Italian and Korean blood and I grew up in a predominantly white neighborhood. From my youth the concept of having to 'change yourself to fit' really bothered me.
—M.A. candidate, multicultural education

I chose graduate school over just dancing as I was greatly interested in the applications of dance on the practical level . . . . I also wanted to have a home base such as my own studio or company from which to work. I knew academia would help me facilitate this goal.
—Ph.D. candidate, dance education

I taught fourth grade for three years as well as took some courses in teaching English as a second language. I felt that I had become stagnant both professionally and socially. I chose grad school to network and get a new perspective on teaching.
—M.A. candidate

Welcome to the Horde

There are nearly 4,000,000 teachers in the United States, and roughly 80 percent of those work at the elementary and secondary school levels.

The bottom line is that a master's degree can prepare those without an undergraduate degree in education for a teaching career, or enable those who are already working in education to change their focus, assume supervisory responsibilities, or become eligible for a salary increase. While a career in education, with the exception of high level administrative positions, is not particularly lucrative, many of those in the field nevertheless derive satisfaction from serving as a role model and contributing to the intellectual, social, and emotional growth of future generations.

The Employment Picture

There are nearly 4,000,000 teachers in the United States—roughly 80 percent of those work at the elementary and secondary school levels. Teachers create lesson plans, motivate students, grade papers and exams, confer with parents, and if that's not enough, also frequently handle administrative tasks.

Counselors working within education have the daunting task of helping students cope with the maturation process and finding their way in the world. They may have to deal with career or academic issues, family crises, drug and alcohol abuse, and sometimes even suicide. There is a great deal of personal contact with students, and in some cases with parents, but a substantial amount of time is also devoted to the administration and interpretation of tests, and the submission of paperwork. Prospective counselors should be excellent listeners, be nonjudgmental, and truly enjoy working with students. At the present time, the supply and demand of counselors is fairly balanced.

Administrators are a fixture at all levels of education, from preschool through professional school. Unlike teachers, they work year-round and are engaged in a wide variety of tasks, including hiring teachers, overseeing maintenance, enforcing disciplinary actions, and managing student affairs. Most administrators arrive at their posts with some relevant experience and at least one advanced degree.

Jobs for preschool and kindergarten, elementary, and secondary school teachers are expected to increase over the next decade, although the two latter groups should enjoy the healthiest job market because of demographic shifts. Demand will be especially strong for those in special education due to legislation emphasizing training and employment for individuals with disabilities, and technological advances resulting in higher survival rates for victims of serious accidents and illnesses. Despite the fact that jobs in their field are plentiful, many special education teachers continue to make the transition to "mainstream" teaching or change careers altogether. They cite unusually high stress on the job, the need to complete excessive

Doctorates Earned

Nonteaching fields

Educational administration,
supervision 1,170

Curriculum, instruction 896

Higher education/evaluation
and research 481

Teaching fields

Physical education, coaching 101

Health education 90

Music education 91

Source: Survey of Earned Doctorates

amounts of paperwork, and lack of support from school administrators as major reasons for leaving the field. Finally, job opportunities will continue to be abundant for bilingual and ESL teachers (Spanish, Vietnamese, Cambodian, Laotian, Chinese, Hmong, Korean, or Russian speakers are especially in demand), teachers from minority backgrounds, and for those willing to work in inner cities or rural areas.

> ### Part-Timers Rule!
> Almost three-quarters of grad students in education attend school part time.

Mathematics, science, and computer teachers remain in short supply, and will continue to be highly sought after as the nation ponders how to address widespread deficiencies among students in these disciplines. A number of jobs should also become available for school counselors as many of those currently employed are close to retirement age. On the other hand, competition for jobs in educational administration will continue to be fierce as a result of tight school budgets at the state and local levels, along with parents' demands for better classrooms not more administrators. If you have your sights set on a career in administration, consider obtaining a doctoral degree to make yourself as marketable as possible.

Getting In

Keep in mind that some education graduate programs have a strong "humanist" orientation, viewing a career in education as a calling rather than merely a vocational choice. These programs tend to be as interested in your personal qualities, values, and experiences as they are in your grades, and will probably place a strong emphasis on your personal statement and letters of recommendation. In fact, for these schools, you may want to include in your application package at least one letter from a family member or close friend that discusses how your values relate to your desire to pursue a career in education.

Experience

Note that some programs accept only those applicants who are already certified and/or experienced in the field they plan to study. Other programs have stringent coursework requirements, but might admit "deficient" applicants with the provision that they satisfactorily complete the necessary classes within a specified period of time.

Program Options

Master's Level

Although the traditional Master's of Education program is two years in length, many graduate students are employed full-time as teachers, and thus pursue the degree on a part-time basis at a relatively slow pace—

> ### Who's Who in Education
> Men: 38 percent
>
> Women: 62 percent
>
> Source: Survey of Earned Doctorates

Out of Date

Most schools of education will grant credit for courses earned through other programs only if they were completed within the last 10 years. If you are counting on coursework more than ten years old to qualify you for certain programs, first check with a program adviser.

some sources estimate that nearly 75 percent of graduate education students are part timers.

For those who plan on entering the teaching profession, the graduate curriculum—in this case called a "preservice" program—consists of a supervised teaching internship in addition to foundation courses and electives in one's area of specialization (e.g., secondary school math). Veteran teachers who are obtaining their master's as part of their professional development ("in-service" program) may be required to conduct a research project or write a thesis instead of student teaching.

Fieldwork

If a program you are investigating requires student teaching or a counseling internship, find out how and when these will be arranged. In some graduate programs, fieldwork must be done on a full-time basis, even though coursework and other aspects of the program can be done part-time. Other programs allow in-service students—those that are already teaching—to satisfy the fieldwork requirement with their current job.

Doctoral Level

The doctorate is usually the degree of choice for individuals who plan to work in educational administration, research, and, of course, academia—though some universities hire education faculty who only hold a master's degree. Doctoral programs consist of roughly two years of coursework, followed by independent research and a dissertation. Most require applicants to have a master's degree in their area of specialization, and some have work experience requirements in addition. Students pursuing a doctorate in educational psychology or school counseling will also generally be required to complete a supervised internship.

Certification

Find out the certification requirements for the state where you plan to teach before you commit yourself to a graduate program. You may be surprised to learn that a master's degree is not always necessary. Many states offer alternative teacher certification programs for individuals who have college training in the subject they plan to teach, but not the requisite education courses.

Words of Wisdom

You may want to delay full-scale graduate work until you've had a chance to work in the field for a while and have a better sense of your interests and aspirations.

Become well rounded in all areas of academics. Feel competent in math, science, etcetera. Take courses if you don't; the knowledge makes you a better teacher.

Try to develop your writing skills as much as possible; you're going to need them, especially when it comes time to write your thesis or dissertation.

Remember that maturity definitely gives you an advantage when it comes to politics, both in your graduate program and in your school.

Get some practical experience in the field you plan to study, such as working as a teacher's aide or substitute before deciding to become a teacher.

> ### What's Hot in Education Administration
>
> Affirmative action
>
> Diversity issues
>
> Restructuring and reallocation of resources
>
> Campus safety

For More Information

American Association for Employment in Education, 820 Davis Street, Suite 222, Evanston, IL 60201-4445; (847) 864-1999. Publishes the annual *Job Search Handbook for Educators*.

American Association of Colleges for Teacher Education, 1307 New York Avenue NW, Suite 300, Washington, DC 20005-4761; (202) 293-2450; www.aacte.org

American Association of School Administrators, 1801 North Moore Street, Arlington, VA 22209; (703) 528-0700; www.aasa.org

American Federation of Teachers, 555 New Jersey Avenue NW, Washington, DC 20001; (202) 879-4400; www.aft.org

American School Counselor Association, 5999 Stevenson Avenue, Alexandria, VA 22304; (800) 347-6647

National Association of Secondary School Principals, 1904 Association Drive, Reston, VA 22091; (703) 860-0200; www.nassp.org

National Association of Student Personnel Administrators, 1875 Connecticut Avenue, NW, Suite 418, Washington DC, 20009; (202) 265-7500

National Education Association, 1201 16th Street NW, Washington, DC 20036; (202) 833-4000; www.nea.org

CHAPTER 4

Psychology and Counseling

The Employment Picture

A desire to be of service to those in need, along with a fascination with the human mind and behavior, typically leads most psychologists and counselors into their respective fields. Interviewees also cited as reasons for their career choice the opportunity to be their own boss, or at least work in relative autonomy, and the chance to earn a reasonably high income—particularly as a therapist in private practice.

Psychologists and counselors work in an incredibly wide array of settings and with every conceivable population. Both professions are expected to grow faster than average through the next decade. At present, nearly 70 percent of salaried psychologists are employees of health care facilities or educational institutions while approximately 15 percent work for government agencies, and the remainder are affiliated with corporations and various nonprofit organizations. Over 40 percent of all psychologists are self-employed.

The American Psychological Association is split into over 50 different divisions representing such areas as developmental psychology, exercise and sport psychology, health psychology, peace psychology, and school psychology . . . just to name a few. Clinical psychologists make up the largest subgroup of professionals in the field of psychology. They spend their days interviewing patients, administering diagnostic tests, and pro-

It's Not Academic

Did you know that 50 percent of researched-trained psychologists work outside of academia? They do everything from design cockpits for NASA to study the perception of dental pain.

Source: American Psychological Association

Ph.D., Psy.D., or Ed.D.?

The Ph.D. affords the broadest range of career opportunities and includes a strong research component, whereas the Psy.D. is most appropriate for those who strictly want to become clinicians. The Ed.D. curriculum is similar to that of the Ph.D. but is often pursued by those who want to work in an educational setting. Consider where you want to end up before you start applying to programs, because transferring is no easy feat—not to mention that you may lose time, money, and course credits.

viding individual, family, and group therapy. Other major subgroups include developmental psychologists who study the development of human behavior over the course of the lifespan, counseling psychologists who help clients adapt to change or initiate lifestyle changes, and experimental psychologists who conduct research on both humans and animals in order to assess a number of variables including motivation, learning and retention, and sensation and perception.

Counselors are also spread out across a number of specialty areas including school counseling, gerontology, marriage and family counseling, substance abuse counseling, rehabilitation counseling, career counseling, and multicultural counseling. In general, counselors help their clients make decisions, adapt to change, and work through the full range of personal, social, educational, and vocational problems that arise in day-to-day living.

School counselors focus their energy on helping elementary and secondary students deal with academic and personal problems, whereas rehabilitation counselors work with clients who are physically challenged to help them become more self-sufficient. They may be involved in developing and implementing a rehabilitation program, as well as arranging for vocational training and job placement. Career counselors assist individuals with the process of finding and exploring a suitable occupation. They also help these people acquire job-seeking skills.

The job market is tight in academia, and recent doctorate holders are finding themselves competing fiercely for limited openings. As a result, some are gravitating to industry and finding employment in areas such as market research, advertising, product development, and human resources. Outside of academia, however, opportunities for both psychologists and counselors should be excellent. The increased emphasis on combating drug and alcohol abuse and family violence is leading to the creation of many new jobs in health care organizations. The rise in school enrollments, particularly at the secondary level, bodes well for those pursuing a career as a school counselor or psychologist. Rehabilitation counselors also have reason to be optimistic—insurance companies are increasingly providing reimbursement for their services, improvements in medical technology are leading to higher accident/illness survival rates, and corporations are seeking more and more assistance with both recruiting and managing physically challenged employees. Jobs should also be plentiful for employment counselors, particularly those who provide skills training to welfare recipients seeking to reenter the work force. Other growth areas include gerontology, health maintenance psychology, and child psychology.

Getting In

Academics

Many programs will take a close look at your GPA and most expect applicants to have at least some background in psychology and exposure to statistics. Doctoral programs generally prefer those with a psychology major and some coursework in the natural sciences and mathematics. You should be aware that doctoral programs are extremely competitive—at some, the acceptance rate is less than 2 percent—about the lowest acceptance rate of any graduate program in any discipline. Also, note that your chances of getting into a program will be greater if you take the time to locate departments whose research orientation is similar to yours, even if you're not planning on a full-time research career. To find out what type of research projects the faculty are engaged in, just take a look at the program catalog—they are usually listed there.

Experience

Clinically oriented programs will be most interested in your relevant volunteer, internship or work experiences, whereas programs that emphasize research will look more closely at your track record as a researcher. A social psychology Ph.D. candidate on the academic research track told us, "All the schools I applied to wanted to see that the applicant had done prior research."

The Interview

As one clinical psychology student put it, "Basically, they want to see if you're crazy or just a normal person with a great interest in psychology." If you're under serious consideration by a clinical psychology program expect to be interviewed. Some programs consider the interview a key factor in making the admissions decision.

Your interview may simply be a one-hour chat with the chairperson of the department, but don't count on something so traditional. One candidate we spoke with received a surprise call from a program she had applied to, and was asked to give a phone interview on the spot. This same candidate was interviewed at another school over the course of three days by three students and three professors, and actually shared a room with a student member of the admissions committee.

Stiff Competition

Acceptance rates in some doctoral programs in psychology are among the lowest for all graduate programs, bottoming out at 2 percent for the most competitive schools.

We're Psyched!

"I switched to psychology as an undergraduate because I was tired of the remoteness of engineering—solving calculus problems all the time. My field, social cognition work, which explores the mechanisms by which we think, fascinated me. I liked the high degree of applicability it had to other areas, business and medicine particularly."

Ph.D. candidate, social psychology

No matter what the situation, you can make your interviews go more smoothly by keeping the following in mind:

Carefully read the program catalog, and become familiar with the work of the faculty—especially those with whom you might want to collaborate. Read at least some articles or books that they have published.

Be ready to talk in detail about your own professional interests and goals.

Realize that you'll be evaluated on your social skills as well as your academic and professional potential. Try to put yourself at ease, and likewise make those around you feel comfortable.

Don't forget to ask intelligent questions.

Recommendations

These tend to be weighed heavily regardless of which track you're pursuing. Try to obtain strong recommendations from professors or supervisors with whom you have done research, clinical, or other relevant work.

Standardized Tests

Most programs require the GRE general test and some also require the GRE Psychology Subject Test. In certain cases a high GRE score will be accepted in lieu of an undergraduate background in the field.

Program Options

Master's Level

At the master's level, a psychology or counseling program generally requires two years of study, although many students take up to four years to finish. Some programs require you to write a thesis based on original research, while others incorporate a supervised field experience. There is virtually no distinction between an M.A. and M.S. degree, although you should know that some master's programs are considered terminal—that is, they are designed to prepare you for a specific occupation—while others are simply a prelude to the Ph.D. If you have an inkling that you might want to pursue the doctorate, you will be best off not enrolling in a terminal master's program as many doctoral programs will not accept those credits. With a master's degree, your employment options will be somewhat limited and you will often carry out your

---

Flying Solo

"There are virtually no female professors in my department, a fact that really distresses me because I have no role models. It especially bothers me because many of my research interests are focused on feminist issues. My professors, largely inaccessible white males, don't seem too keen on these ideas."

A graduate student

responsibilities under the supervision of a doctoral-level psychologist. Data collection and analysis, survey research, counseling, training, and personnel administration are all viable options.

Doctoral Level

The doctorate is the standard degree for those who want to practice psychology since many jobs and licenses require it. Most programs usually take four to seven years to complete and full-time attendance is practically mandatory. While the dissertation is the piece de resistance of the Ph.D. or Ed.D., a supervised practicum and doctoral exams are the icing on the cake of the Psy.D. An extended internship is also required for those pursuing the doctorate in counseling, school, or clinical psychology. For students on the research track, coursework requirements tend be flexible, allowing them to focus almost immediately on their area of interest and begin research early in the program. Although research-oriented programs do not require internships, students are expected to teach, in preparation for a possible academic career.

Internships and Research Opportunities

In psychology, the best choice is an APA-approved internship. In both psychology and counseling, make sure the program you are considering offers internships that dovetail with your interests. Consider lifestyle and financial issues as well. Will off-campus travel be necessary to gain access to clinical opportunities? Is safe, affordable public transportation available, or will you need a car?

When it comes to research, many catalogs claim that you'll have access to specialized populations. Try to find out which ones and what type of access is provided. Also investigate which professors have the best track records at securing and maintaining research funding—odds are you'll want to work with them.

On the Money

Median Starting Salaries for Psychology Ph.D.'s

Human Services
Administrator $44,000

School Psychologists . .$42,000

Clinical Psychologists . .$40,000

Research $40,000

Assistant Professors . . .$35,000

Source: American Psychological Association

Degrees Earned

Clinical 1,325

Counseling 464

General 279

Developmental/
Child Psychology 188

Social 170

Source: Survey of Earned Doctorates

Who's Who Among New Psychology Ph.D.'s

Women	66%
Men	34%
Caucasian	78%
Hispanic	5%
Asian	4%
African American	4%
Native American	5%
Other	1%

Source: Survey of Earned Doctorates

Special Issues

Licensing

The 50 States plus the District of Columbia are responsible for determining certification and licensing requirements for psychologists and counselors, and also oversee the examinations for which applicants must sit. Laws vary according to the State and the position in question, but most licensing boards agree with the spirit of the American Psychological Association's 1978 resolution that states that "only those who have completed a doctoral training program in psychology in a university, college, or professional school of psychology that is APA or regionally accredited are qualified to independently provide unsupervised direct delivery of professional services." Many counselors also choose to become nationally certified by the National Board for Certified Counselors (NBCC). Be sure that any program you choose will prepare you to meet the national or state licensing/certification requirements.

Respecialization

Practicing psychologists and counselors who want to make the transition into a new area of specialization are generally required to take additional graduate courses. Some programs have specific respecialization diploma programs while others admit respecialization students into their regular master's or doctoral program. You can get more information by contacting the APA (see the resources at the end of this chapter).

Words of Wisdom

Take time off between undergraduate and graduate school. Psychology and counseling programs are very intense programs—let yourself rest and mature before you take the plunge.

If you're applying to clinical programs, ask a professor or professional in the field to do some practice interviewing with you. How you do on the interview will be critical to whether or not you are accepted.

Evaluate the job opportunities a program provides to its graduates, as well as the quality of the professors, and the cost of the program. Since you are not going to make a fortune as a counselor right away, you don't want to burden yourself with undue debt.

Know what you want to do—be a researcher or practitioner, as well as what areas or populations you want to specialize in—before you apply.

Get a good background in statistics.

Consider getting into therapy. The process facilitates self-understanding and will make you a better clinician.

For More Information

American Counseling Association, 5999 Stevenson Avenue, Alexandria, VA 22304; (703) 823-9800; www.counseling.org

American Psychological Association, 750 First Street NE, Washington, DC 20002-4242; (202) 336-5500; www.apa.org. Provides information on educational requirements, financial assistance, and licensing in all fields of psychology. Publishes an annual directory, *Graduate Study in Psychology,* which lists the more than 600 doctoral and master's programs in psychology; and the booklet, *Careers in Psychology.*

Association of State and Provincial Psychology Boards, P.O. Box 4398, Montgomery, AL 36103; (334) 832-4580; www.asppb.org. Provides information on state licensing requirements.

Counselor Preparation: Volume 1, Programs and Personnel, Accelerated Development, 1900 Frost Road, Suite 101, Bristol, PA 19007-1598; (215) 269-0400. Describes approximately 500 colleges and universities offering over 1,000 graduate programs in counselor preparation.

National Board for Certified Counselors, 3-D Terrace Way, Greensboro, NC 27403-3660; (336) 547-0607; www.nbcc.org

CHAPTER 5

Nursing

The Employment Picture

"Getting an advanced degree in nursing has greatly increased my overall understanding of the science of nursing. This means I can provide my patients with a clear idea of how to prevent or cope with illness. The degree has also increased my ability to earn a good salary."— A professional nurse

The sentiments of this M.S. degree holder are echoed by many of the nurses we spoke with. An advanced degree in nursing not only significantly improves one's chances of obtaining lucrative employment in the field, but also increases one's knowledge base, opens up possibilities to take on more challenging and autonomous positions, and elevates one's status in the field. Despite the long shifts (sometimes up to 12 hours) and extreme pressure, many nurses found their increasingly specialized roles as both preventive and reactive health care professionals to be extremely rewarding. Major frustrations, on the other hand include job instability due to the specter of budget cuts and bureaucratic red tape.

The old days of nurses strictly playing the role of assistant to physicians is a relic of the past. Advanced practice nurses (APNs), all trained at the graduate level, are increasingly taking over some of the duties that previously fell into the physician's sole domain such as conducting diagnostic exams, writing prescriptions, administering anesthesia, and treating common ills. The work of a nurse has also become more and more specialized. You'll find nurse practitioners and clinical nurse specialists

Paying Top Dollar

Top-tier private graduate nursing programs can cost up to $29,700 per academic year.

Mr. Nurse

"As a man in a graduate program, I've never encountered any prejudice from my classmates. Though I'd heard that it would be smart for me to keep my mouth shut in class, I didn't follow that advice and everything has worked out fine. I'm comfortable here."

M.S.N. candidate

working in a variety of areas including: primary care, neonatal health, adult health, acute care, child care, emergency care, gerontology, oncology, community health, as well as pediatric, surgical, maternity, psychiatric, and women's health nursing. Finally, nurse administrators, trained in nursing, management, and business, are another growing breed within the profession.

While nurses with master's degrees, particularly family nurse practitioners, are in great demand nationwide, their counterparts with associate's or baccalaureate degrees are having a tough time finding work. Starting salaries for nurse practitioners are nearly twice those of nurses at the bachelor's level. Nurses in middle management, on the other hand, are witnessing a decline in job opportunities due in part to the trend toward abbreviated hospital stays. In fact, many nurses have returned to school to obtain the training necessary to qualify for nurse practitioner status. It is estimated by the American Nurses Association that there is a need for 300,000 more advanced practice nurses in the United States by the end of the millennium. Another growth area for nurses is home health care. As the average age of the population continues to soar, there will be a great need for nurses to care for the elderly.

Getting In

Academics

Most master's nursing programs require applicants to hold a bachelors' degree from a school accredited by the National League for Nursing, along with a state RN license. Doctoral programs generally expect applicants to have a master's degree in nursing, an RN license, and at least a year of clinical experience.

Recommendations

Letters of reference are important—in fact, some schools require as many as five. Each letter should address the student's potential for graduate work. Good choices for recommenders are professors, deans, recent employers, and mentors in the field.

Personal Statement

A personal statement is required by most graduate programs. The questions asked typically deal with clinical or research interests, personal strengths and weaknesses, and issues in contemporary nursing.

Standardized Tests

Almost all graduate nursing programs require applicants to take either the Graduate Record Exam (GRE) or the Miller Analogies Test (MAT).

Program Options

Master's Level

The most commonly pursued master's degrees include the M.N., M.S., or M.S.N. All can prepare you to become an advanced practice nurse and to pursue such occupations as nurse practitioner, certified nurse midwife, certified clinical nurse specialist, certified nurse anesthetist, nurse administrator, and nurse educator. The typical program requires two years of full-time study and includes a core of foundation courses such as statistics, health policy, health-care ethics, and nutrition—plus electives, a clinical field component, and a thesis or other type of culminating experience. Combined seminar/laboratory courses offer direct experience in the application of theory to nursing practice.

Doctoral Level

Doctoral programs in nursing, which generally take four years of full-time study to complete, are designed to prepare scholars to teach, conduct research, practice nursing, and work in health administration. Degrees at the doctoral level include the Ph.D., D.N.S. (Doctor of Nursing Science), D.S.N. (Doctor of Science in Nursing), N.D. (Doctor of Nursing), or Ed.D. (Doctor of Education). Students typically study the history, philosophy, development, and testing of nursing; data management and research methodology, and health care ethics. Research projects and a dissertation are required.

Accelerated Programs

In the past 10 years, many former stockbrokers, lawyers, electricians, accountants, and scientists have chosen to enter nursing through accelerated programs at the postbaccalaureate level. Accelerated programs also exist for RNs (registered nurses), and nurses with nonnursing degrees.

Distance Learning

A number of programs allow you to obtain nursing credit by studying independently from remote sites and passing examinations provided by

From a Distance

The Regents College of the State of New York has 14,000 students studying for a variety of college credits via a unique distance-learning program.

For information, contact: Regents College Nursing Program, University of the State of New York, 7 Columbia Circle, Albany, NY 12203-5159; (518) 464-8500 the institution. Some require you to pass an intensive, weekend-long clinical nursing practicum test on site at the college. Some schools also require a local mentor and a two-week, two-summer, residency requirement. If you are considering a distance learning program, make sure it is accredited by the National League for Nursing and that the degrees it awards are recognized by the State Board of Nursing for eligibility for the nursing licensing board exam (RN exam).

Dual Degree Programs

Applicants must generally apply separately to the two programs. Often, some coursework in one program is recognized for credit in the other. The student must meet all requirements for both programs in order to graduate. Some of the most popular dual degree programs involving nursing are:

Nursing and Public Health (M.S./M.P.H.)

Prepares nurses to be both practitioners and public health administrators in community settings.

Nursing and Business (M.S./M.B.A. or Ph.D./M.B.A.)

Prepares advanced clinical practitioners to take on the role of business manager, and is especially appealing to those interested in establishing nursing-related businesses.

Nursing and Theology (M.S./M.Div.)

This training is useful to those who wish to combine advanced clinical care with spiritual counseling services, often within religious agencies or hospitals.

Financial Assistance

Other than the standard grants, fellowships, scholarships, teaching assistantships, and loans, tuition reimbursement is available through some hospital benefit programs. This is an excellent way for practicing nurses and other hospital workers to finance their graduate education.

Men in Nursing

Men are very much the minority in both undergraduate and graduate nursing programs—comprising less than 10 percent of the student body. Yet as salaries for nurses with graduate degrees continue to rise, more men are looking at nursing as a viable career alternative—often as a second career. While some male students report discomfort at being the minority in a distinctly female-dominated field, others say they are extremely comfortable in both the classroom and on the job, and find their fellow students very supportive. One male nurse we spoke to said that he's found that men make great nurses: Since they have to overcome a certain stigma in their career choice, they tend to be extremely committed to their studies as well as their jobs.

Words of Wisdom

Get a good clinical background before you start.

Look for a program with faculty members who are well-suited to helping you build on your strengths and interests. Just because a program is highly rated in general, that doesn't mean it's the best one for you. Read what the faculty have published, visit the schools that interest you, and ask a lot of questions.

It is essential to know what you want to specialize in before entering a master's program. The extent of your imagination is the only restriction.

Take a course in cost-benefit analysis. This should serve you well, since health-care professionals in today's era of managed care are increasingly being asked to justify a treatment's expense as well as its effectiveness.

Work on building solid interpersonal and communication skills. The better you can understand your patient, the more effective and satisfied you are likely to be in your role.

On Leading a Double Life

"You can work while you're in school. It takes a flexible program, good time management on your part, and an aggressive approach to your thesis and your advisers."

A nursing student

For More Information

American Association of Critical Care Nurses, 101 Columbia, Aliso Viejo, CA 92656; (949) 362-2000; www.aacn.org

American Association of Nurse Anesthetists, 222 South Prospect Avenue, Park Ridge, IL 60068; (847) 692-7050; www.aana.org

American College of Nurse Midwives, 818 Connecticut Avenue NW, Suite 900, Washington, DC 20006; (202) 728-9860; www.acnm.org

American Nurses Association, 600 Maryland Avenue SW, Suite 100 West, Washington, DC 20024-2571; (800) 274-4262; www.nursingworld.org

National League for Nursing, 61 Broadway, New York, NY 10006; (800) 669-1656; www.nln.org

National Student Nurses Association, 555 West 57th Street, Suite 1327, New York, NY 10019; (212) 581-2211

Sigma Theta Tau, International Honor Society of Nursing, 550 West North Street, Indianapolis, IN 46202; (888) 634-7575; http://stti-b.iupdu/

CHAPTER 6

Humanities and Social Sciences

Because the humanities and social sciences encompass so many programs—too many to cover in a single chapter—we've decided to focus on three of the most popular disciplines—English, history, and sociology. Fortunately, much of the discussion will be applicable to other areas of study as well. For more information on your specific field of interest, see the end of this chapter for a listing of relevant professional associations and other resources.

The Employment Picture

Most students pursue graduate studies (especially doctoral studies), in the social sciences and humanities (e.g., English, economics, geography, history, anthropology, sociology, languages, and literature) because they are hoping to launch a career in academia. Sadly, the academic job market is extremely tight these days—so tight, that the English Department at Indiana University sent out a form letter to prospective graduate students which stated, "In short, the job market for Ph.D. holders in the humanities is very rough indeed." Sadly, it would be hard to exaggerate the fragile state of the job market for English Ph.D.'s. College teaching jobs in English are so scarce that schools are flooded with literally hundreds of applications for a single associate professorship. Many schools in difficult financial straits are not even trying to replace retiring professors with permanent faculty. It is much less costly to hire a newly graduated Ph.D. for a short-term contract at a low salary.

Mmm, Mmm, Good!

"The study of history will put little food in your stomach, but it will enrich the soul."

A graduate student

The academic job market for history Ph.D.'s is not much better. In 1995, fewer Ph.D.'s were employed by four-year colleges or universities than ever before. As a result, some would-be history professors are now turning to museums, historical societies, and even national, state, and city parks to find work. The employment prospects for sociology Ph.D.'s, on the other hand, are not quite as dismal, particularly outside academia. Sociologists are finding positions in diverse fields such as marketing, advertising, consulting, public opinion research, personnel, criminal justice, and policy making. Many sociologists are also employed by local, state, and federal government. In fact, the federal government employs sociologists in the following departments: Health, Human Services, Agriculture, Education, Commerce (Bureau of the Census), Defense, General Accounting Office, Peace Corps, National Institute of Health, National Institute of Aging. Sociologists specializing in demography, economic development, or health may find work at such prestigious international organizations as the World Bank, the United Nations, and the World Health Organization. Sociologists with solid training in math and statistics, and quantitative and qualitative research methodology, as opposed to pure theory, will probably have the best job opportunities over the next decade or so.

If, in spite of the caveats above, you still want to build a career in the classroom, you may need to consider alternatives to the tenure-track professorship that most graduate students fantasize about. Teaching as an adjunct faculty member, at a junior college, or even at the high school level are all viable options, and can be quite rewarding and satisfying in their own right.

Getting In

Academics

Most programs expect candidates to have a strong academic record, with a healthy background of relevant survey/introductory courses plus some advanced classes in your particular area of interest. If you're transitioning from another field (e.g., history to English) and are deficient in relevant coursework, consider taking undergraduate or continuing education courses in your prospective field before you apply to graduate school. Note that those seeking entry into social science programs

---

Degrees Earned

Social Science Ph.D.'s

Economics 979

Political science 621

Sociology 516

Anthropology 396

History Ph.D.'s

American 335

European 187

General 101

Science 37

Language and Literature Ph.D.'s

English 699

American 314

Spanish 196

French 142

German 88

Source: Survey of Earned Doctorates

---

should have some background in computer, math, statistics, and/or research methodology.

If the Ph.D. is your goal, it generally makes the most sense—and is faster and less costly—to apply directly to a doctoral program. However if your undergraduate record is less than stellar, you may benefit by first obtaining a master's degree. By taking this route (and assuming you do well at the master's level), you will probably improve your chances of being accepted to a top doctoral program.

Writing Sample

In the humanities and social sciences, applicants are generally either invited or required to submit a creative or scholarly writing sample along with their application. In fact, for some graduate programs such as an M.F.A. in poetry, your writing sample could literally make or break your application. A short paper will usually suffice as a sample, but make sure that the content is relevant to the program to which you are applying. Your grammar and spelling need to be flawless, and the actual document should be free of dog-eared corners, coffee stains, and other unsightly blemishes.

Recommendations

Most humanities and social science programs want to see two or three recommendations from faculty members who are well acquainted with your work. Recommendations from nonacademics are given little weight.

Standardized Tests

Most humanities and social science programs require the GRE general test; however, there is great variation in policy regarding the GRE subject tests.

Portfolio/Audition

If you're applying to a creative writing, fine art, dance, film, or music program, your application will be judged to a large extent on the quality of your portfolio (videotapes/audiotapes of your performances, slides of artwork, writing samples) and in some cases on a live audition. Be sure to precisely follow the directions for submitting supporting materials—for example, always use the slide carousel size, VHS format, and page binding that is specified in the application. Graduate programs in

---

What's Hot in English

Deconstruction (including theatrical work)

Gay studies

Gender studies

Minority issues and studies

What's Hot in History

Women's history

African American history

East Asian history

What's Hot in Sociology

Political sociology

Race and ethnicity

Gender studies

the arts are not only seeking talented students—they also want mature and disciplined individuals who know how to follow instructions.

Personal Statement

Most programs will be looking for a coherent statement that clearly expresses your academic and professional goals. Try to be as specific as possible about what area(s) you want to study within your prospective field. Fortunately, you need not feel locked in as most graduate departments are well aware that your interests may still be evolving at this point, and that they are likely to change as you proceed through your program. In addition, if you have some noteworthy work, extracurricular experiences, or personal circumstances that merit discussion, the personal statement is a good place to bring them up.

Program Options

Master's Level

Most master's programs in the social sciences and humanities require the full-time equivalent of two years of coursework. Many also require students to write either a thesis or pass a written or oral exam.

Those who pursue a master's as a terminal degree typically either want to teach at the secondary school level, simply love their field and want to increase their knowledge of it, or plan to enter an allied profession. For example, many graduates with an M.A. in English or M.F.A. in creative writing often seek positions in either publishing or journalism, while those with degrees in history frequently gravitate toward jobs in government. A master's in sociology is sufficient to allow one access to a variety of positions in government agencies, research firms, and nonprofit organizations—essentially wherever research, analytical, and quantitative skills are needed.

Doctoral Level

Although Ph.D. programs are generally designed to take roughly five years to complete including qualifying exams and the dissertation, in reality they often take much, much longer—on average about ten years. This is due to the fact that many students lack the funds necessary to pursue their studies full-time, and then often stall out at the dissertation stage when they become increasingly isolated from the academic environment. Also, many dissertations, particularly in the social sciences, require complex and expensive data collection efforts, which can easily take more than a year to complete.

Most Ph.D. programs are geared toward producing academics, but with the shortage of college teaching positions some are beginning to increase their sensitivity to the demands of the marketplace. In the social sciences, for example, many doctoral programs allow students to focus on applied research, which boosts their chances of finding employment upon graduation.

Special Issues

Job Placement

With the job market as tight as it is, it's crucial that you find out whether graduates of the programs you're investigating have been able to find work, and where. A program may point to the successes of a high-profile graduate who is now conducting the Chicago Symphony Orchestra, but what has happened to the others? Are they barely eking out a living, or are they well situated within their profession?

Language Requirements

Some programs require applicants to have knowledge of a foreign language (typically reading ability) as a condition of admission, while others expect candidates to pass a proficiency exam as a condition of graduation. If you have the ability to speak a foreign language, it certainly won't hurt to mention this in your personal statement, regardless of whether such knowledge is required. At the same time, if your foreign language skills are a bit rusty, it's a good idea to resume your studies as soon as possible, and certainly well before examination time.

Words of Wisdom

Investigate the jobs available to you in your field, especially those outside of academia—know what you're getting into.

Learn how to sell yourself. Keep a list of all your transferable skills and how they can be applied within different work settings.

Persistence is important above all. The Ph.D. is a very long haul. If you're not sure it's what you want, don't do it. Otherwise, you'll flounder.

Get your language exam out of the way as quickly as possible!

Once you get started in your program, try not to stop. Momentum will carry you through.

If your ultimate goal is to become a professor, make sure when you're accepted to a graduate program that getting some teaching experience is part of the deal. Once you're actually in a program is not the time to find out you won't get any meaningful college-level teaching experience.

> ### Return On Investment
>
> "If I were to continue with any graduate school courses at this point, I would want to make sure they had some type of vocational slant so that I could perhaps make sure I got a little more for my money."
>
> M.A. candidate, history

Resources

Anthropology

American Anthropological Association, 4350 North Fairfax Drive, Suite 640, Arlington, VA 22203; (703) 528-1902; www.ameranthassn.org. Offers information about careers, and grants and fellowships.

Archaeology

Archaeological Institute of America, 656 Beacon Street, 4th floor, Boston, MA 02215; (617) 353-9361; http://csaws.brynmawr.edu:443/aia.html

Art and Art History

College Art Association, 275 Seventh Avenue, 18th floor, New York, New York 10001; (212) 691-1051; fax (212) 627-2381; www.collegeart.org/

Demography

Population Association of America, PRB, 1875 Connecticut Avenue NW, Suite 520, Washington, DC 20009; (202) 462-2726

Economics

American Economics Association, 2014 Broadway, Suite 305, Nashville, TN 37203; (615) 322-2595

Geography

Association of American Geographers, 1710 16th Street NW, Washington, DC 20009-3198; (202) 234-1450; www.aag.org. Publishes *Geography: Today's Career for Tomorrow*, (free), *Careers in Geography*, ($3.00), and *A Guide to Programs of Geography in the U.S. and Canada* ($20 for prospective students).

History

American Historical Association, 400 A Street SE, Washington, DC 20003; (202) 544-2422; http://chnm.gmu.edu/aha/index.html. Publishes a guide to graduate programs in history.

Language and Literature

Modern Language Association, 10 Astor Place, New York, NY 10003; (212) 475-9500; www.mla.org

Philosophy

American Philosophical Association, University of Delaware, 31 Amstel Avenue, Newark, DE 19716; (302) 831-1112; www.udel.edu/apa

Political Science

American Political Science Association, 1527 New Hampshire Avenue NW, Washington, DC 20036; (202) 483–2512; www.apsanet.org. Provides information on careers and job listings, and publishes *Careers and the Study of Political Science: A Guide for Undergraduates,* ($3.50, plus $1.00 for postage and handling).

Sociology

American Sociological Association, 1307 New York Avenue NW, Washington, DC 20005; (202) 833-3410; www.asanet.org. Publishes the annual *Guide to Graduate Departments* ($20 for student members).

CHAPTER 7

Engineering

The Employment Picture

Engineers solve practical technical problems through the application of mathematical and scientific principles and theories. They are employed in a wide range of settings although nearly 50 percent work within manufacturing industries in areas such as production, design, development, testing, maintenance, management, and sales. The field of engineering is divided into numerous specialty areas including aerospace; architectural; chemical; civil; electrical and electronics; environmental; industrial; marine; mechanical; metallurgical, ceramic, and materials; mining; nuclear; and petroleum engineering.

First, the good news. Employment prospects should be strong for environmental, biomedical, materials, and chemical engineers—particularly for graduates with interdisciplinary training, and some experience in industry. More engineers will be needed to help manufacturers get the highest return on their investments in high tech equipment, as well as to improve the country's deteriorating infrastructure—highways, roads, bridges, and tunnels.

Now, the bad news: Defense cutbacks eliminated a number of jobs for aerospace engineers, and the market for mining engineers never quite recovered from the price drops in oil and metals in the mid-1980s. With few Americans wanting a nuclear reactor in their backyards, employment opportunities for nuclear engineers are also not expected to

Body Snatchers

Over 70 percent of all engineering job openings in the foreseeable future will be due to replacement needs—mostly as a result of engineers transitioning to other positions and fields, not as a result of their retiring.

increase in the near future. For civil engineers, the job market varies from one geographic region to another—in economically healthy areas, jobs are plentiful, whereas in depressed regions, work is hard to come by. As always, the job market for would-be professors is tight. All in all, however, employment opportunities for engineers are expected to increase at the same rate as other occupations through the beginning of the next century.

While a bachelor's degree in engineering is all that is necessary to gain entrée to the profession, many engineers choose to continue their studies to stay current with new developments in technology, as well as enhance their opportunities for promotions and salary increases.

Getting In

Academics

Most engineering graduate programs prefer applicants to have either a bachelor's degree in engineering, mathematics, or one of the sciences. Those without an undergraduate engineering degree may need to take additional courses, possibly extending their program by a full semester.

Your undergraduate record will be a major consideration. A high GPA is important, especially for the more competitive programs.

Standardized Tests

Since program policies vary regarding the GRE general and subject tests, you'll need to check with the admissions offices at the schools which interest you for their specific requirements.

Personal Statement

Those on the professional track should stress their related work experience, while those on the academic/research track should focus more on past research projects. All applicants need to clearly communicate what they hope to do with their graduate degree.

Degrees Earned 1995

Master's

Electrical and
Computer 11,910

Mechanical and
Aerospace 5,409

Civil and
Environmental 5,469

Industrial, Management,
and Manufacturing 3,281

Chemical and
Petroleum 1,403

Doctorates

Electrical and Computer . . .2,178

Mechanical and
Aerospace 1,265

Civil and Environmental 700

Chemical and Petroleum 689

Industrial, Management,
and Manufacturing 331

Source: Survey of Earned Doctorates

Program Options

Master's Level

Most master's programs in engineering take two years to complete, although the increasingly popular "professional master's degree" (M.E.) can be finished in just one year. This option, which often includes an internship component, is appropriate for those who simply want to practice engineering in a business setting. Other programs may focus more on research so it is crucial to know your long-range objective before applying. All programs typical have a culminating experience that might be a thesis, exam, or research paper.

Doctoral Level

Doctoral programs, which are designed for those who want to teach at the university level or embark on a research career, generally take four to seven years to complete. After finishing your coursework, you'll need to pass an oral or written exam, and then write a dissertation based on original research.

Interdisciplinary Options

Recently, a number of engineering programs have jumped on the "interdisciplinary bandwagon." Some blend coursework from multiple disciplines within the engineering umbrella (e.g., electrical and mechanical engineering), while others incorporate classes from outside disciplines such as physics. The prerequisites and curricula for these programs vary widely.

Many graduates of interdisciplinary programs find that they have an edge when it comes to seeking employment since they can offer a broader skill set than students who followed the traditional curriculum.

Dual Degrees

Increasingly, businesses need engineers who are not only technically competent, but who also understand and can navigate through the issues of the business world. In response to this demand, schools such as the University of Washington and M.I.T. have devised special programs that integrate courses on management, finance, marketing, leadership, and organizational behavior with the more traditional classes of the graduate engineering curriculum. Students who complete the programs are granted both a master's in engineering and an M.B.A.

No-Nonsense Approach

"There are fundamental differences between engineers and physicists. For example: a physicist describes 'a hollow conduction cylinder with infinite length,' while an engineer just calls it 'an antenna.' It's the same problem, but the attitude is totally different. The physicist makes it a math problem, the engineer simplifies the math and puts the system to work."

An engineering student

On the Money

Starting salary,
master's degree $40,200

Median salary,
master's degree $53,200

Starting salary,
Ph.D. $55,300

Median salary,
Ph.D. $62,300

Source: Survey of Earned Doctorates

Special Issues

Women in Engineering

Women are a distinct minority in the world of engineering, both in graduate school and the workplace. They comprise less than 20 percent of the graduate engineering students, and earn less than 10 percent of the doctorates granted in the field. In response, admissions committees have tried to step up their efforts to increase both gender and ethnic diversity among the engineering student body.

Funding

Always investigate what grants and funding are available at the programs that interest you. Does the faculty have a strong track record of securing and maintaining grants? Are the projects that interest you stable and secure, or could the financial rug be pulled out at any moment? What are the opportunities for becoming a research assistant?

Words of Wisdom

Given that a great deal of work in the field today is handled by teams, engineers need to learn how to communicate effectively and work well with others. Technical know-how is not enough.

Finding a good advisor is in many respects as important as being accepted to a strong program. Your advisor is in a position to serve as a mentor, help you get involved with research projects, present papers at conferences, and even find a job after graduation. Take the time to shop around for an adviser who will meet your needs.

Try to determine your career goals and research interests before applying to graduate programs. If you have an academic bent you'll be best off in research-oriented programs, whereas if you are most interested in applying your knowledge with a business setting you'll be happiest in a professionally oriented program.

For More Information

American Association of Engineering Societies, 1111 19th Street NW, Suite 403, Washington DC 20036; (202) 296-2237

American Institute of Chemical Engineers, 3 Park Avenue, New York, NY 10016; (212) 591-7338; www.aiche.org

American Society for Engineering Education, 1818 N Street NW, Suite 600, Washington, DC 20036-2479; (202) 331-3500; www.asee.org; e-mail: webmaster@ns.asee.org. Publishes the annual *Directory of Engineering Graduate Studies and Research,* which contains summaries of more than 200 engineering programs in the United States and Canada, as well as information on research funding.

American Society of Civil Engineers, 1801 Alexander Bell Drive, Reston, VA 20191; (800) 548-2723; www.asce.org

American Society of Mechanical Engineers, 345 East 47th Street, New York, NY 10017; 800-843-2763; www.asme.org

Institute of Electrical and Electronics Engineers, Inc. (IEEE), 445 Hoes Lane, Piscataway, NJ 08855; (732) 981-0060; www.ieee.org; e-mail: membership@computer.org

Institute of Industrial Engineers, 25 Technology Park, Norcross, GA 30092; (770) 449-0461; www.iienet.org

Society of Petroleum Engineers, 222 Palisades Creek Drive, Richardson, TX 75080; (214) 952-9393; www.spe.org

CHAPTER 8

Computer Science

The Employment Picture

Computers have become a permanent fixture in our lives—in fact over half of the U.S. populace uses a computer at home or at work. Organizations are constantly searching for new ways to use computers to boost efficiency and productivity. Thus, it is not surprising that jobs for computer scientists and systems analysts are plentiful. In fact, according to the U.S. Department of Labor, these should be two of the fastest growing occupations in the United States through the year 2005.

Job growth will be fueled by the demand for increased networking (i.e., the linking of computers), the expansion of the Internet, and the increase in the numbers of personal computer users who require complex technical support and assistance. Job prospects should be especially strong for graduates who have expertise in object-oriented and client-server programming, multimedia technology, networking, and database and systems design. Strong written and oral communication skills and an understanding of business will also be beneficial. Those who hold advanced degrees will fare best when competing for jobs at research facilities, academic institutions, and high technology companies. Increasingly, however, employers across the board are seeking workers with greater technical skills to help them get the most from their investment in expensive computer equipment. As a result, candidates with advanced degrees should be in an advantageous position. In

Who's Who in Computer Science

Men	.84.9%
Women	.15.1%

Source: Survey of Earned Doctorates

academia, as with all disciplines, the job market is tough. Even graduates from the top schools are struggling to land college teaching positions.

Getting In

Academics

Your undergraduate record will be a major consideration. You'll need excellent grades to have a good chance of getting into the most competitive programs. In addition, many graduate schools require that you have an undergraduate degree in computer science, although you can sometimes gain provisional admittance without it. Previous coursework in math will most certainly be an asset. If you don't have the appropriate background, first consider taking some computer science classes as a nondegree student—then you'll have a better sense of whether it will be worth applying for admission to a full-fledged graduate program.

Standardized Tests

Most programs require the GRE general test, while the subject test is often optional. Clearly the emphasis will be on your quantitative score, although verbal scores are also closely scrutinized.

Recommendations

If you're applying to an academically oriented program you'll be best off with letters from professors, whereas for a program with a professional focus you would be wise to solicit recommendations from an employer in the field.

Personal Statement

Your statement should communicate your reasons for wanting to attend graduate school, as well as your research and professional goals. Don't forget to mention relevant employment experience plus any other selling points that don't appear elsewhere on your application.

Program Options

Master's Level

The typical master's program takes two years to complete. Some require a thesis as a culminating project, while for others you may need to sit for a final exam or write a paper. Depending on the program, the curriculum may be very loosely structured and allow a great deal of individual choice, or it may be highly regimented. Programs are generally either academic or professional in orientation, although sometimes the distinction is fuzzy, and increasingly curricula are interdisciplinary.

Note that many successful and highly paid computer science professionals do not have an advanced degree, although for certain research positions the master's is often preferred. This is certainly a field where for the most part employers are more concerned with a prospect's skills and experience rather than her credentials. Before embarking on your graduate studies, do some investigative work and try to determine whether, in fact, a master's degree is really necessary to help you achieve your professional goals. You may find that one of the many professional certificate programs will do the trick.

Doctoral Level

The Ph.D. track is generally for students who want to launch a career in academia or research. If you're aiming for a doctorate, expect your program to take four to seven years to complete. After finishing your coursework you'll take an oral or written exam, and assuming you pass, you will then be able to begin work on your dissertation.

Interdisciplinary Programs

As computers increasingly become a driving force across the industrial landscape, organizations are gaining a better appreciation for an education that includes coursework in both computer science and business. As a result, a number of M.S./M.B.A. programs have sprouted up with the goal of producing graduates who can apply their technical and managerial expertise to solving the problem of today's ever more complex workplace. In addition, other dual degree programs pair computer science with medicine, architecture, and education.

Special Issues

Women in Computer Science

A recent survey revealed that women comprise about 30 percent of computer science graduate students, but only 15 percent of those who earn computer science doctorates. Virtually all graduate programs are committed to increasing the diversity of their student body, and thus welcome applications from women and minorities.

Cyber Sisters

The following universities have computer science associations for women:

Rensselaer Polytechnic Institute

California Institute of Technology

University of Wisconsin—Madison

Computer Science: Areas of Specialization

Artificial Intelligence/robotics

Architecture/hardware

Database

Design/graphics

Numerical computing

Programming

Software engineering

Software/networks

Systems

Theory

Financial Assistance

Funding for computer science research has already been cut since the end of the Cold War due to decreases in the defense budget—and now congressional plans to balance the federal budget threaten to deepen these cuts. Ask about the stability of the funding situation at the schools you're investigating. Also try to find out how successful the faculty have been at securing and maintaining grants? Fortunately, at the doctoral level, many programs are able to support most, if not all, of their students.

Words of Wisdom

Mathematics is the language of the research scientist, so if your math skills are a bit rusty, give yourself some time to get back in the saddle before taking the plunge into graduate level coursework.

Get to know your computer science professors while you're still an undergraduate. They will help you make contacts that may lead to funding opportunities at the graduate level.

Try to stay open minded about where your degree will take you professionally. Academia is far from the only option.

You need more than just technical skill to get a good job. Don't neglect your critical thinking, listening, and writing skills.

Know what you want to get out of a graduate degree. Read the professional journals and find out who is publishing in the areas that interest you. Look for a program that is strong in the field in which you want to specialize.

For More Information

Ada Project, www.cs.yale.edu/html/yale/cs/hyplans/tap/tap.html. Provides information and resources for women in computer science.

Association for Computing Machinery, 1515 Broadway, 17th floor, New York, NY 10036; (212) 869-7440; e-mail: wcarlist@acm.org. Publishes *Communications of the ACM*, a journal.

Computing Research Association, 1100 17th Street NW, Suite 507, Washington, DC 20036; (202) 234-2111; http://cra.org. Publishes the annual *Taulbee Survey,* which provides information on the production and employment of computer science faculty and Ph.D.'s in North America, and the *Forsythe List,* a directory of all Ph.D.-granting programs in computer science and computer engineering.

CHAPTER 9

Health

The Employment Picture

Employment prospects are currently good for graduates of M.P.H. programs who are finding positions as administrators, researchers, planners, and analysts in a variety of settings. While many graduates accept jobs at government agencies, other are employed at universities, nonprofit organizations, and pharmaceutical companies. Management, grant writing, fundraising, public relations, and budgeting experience and skills are all valued highly by employers.

Public health professionals are primarily involved with promoting health, community welfare, and preventing the spread of disease. They analyze and evaluate health issues, disseminate information to the public, and oversee community outreach campaigns. More specifically, epidemiologists and biostatisticians work with data discerning, analyzing, and interpreting patterns of disease and disability. Environmental health specialists deal with the health-related aspects of the relationship between humans and the environment. Health educators promote wellness by teaching people how to improve their dietary and exercise habits, reduce stress, and make other healthy lifestyle changes. Public health administrators are responsible for planning, organizing, directing, coordinating, and evaluating health services for hospitals, clinics, state and federal health care agencies, consulting firms, and insurance

Peace

Boston University's School of Public Health has a special program for M.P.H. students who are also interested in the Peace Corps. For more information, call (617) 353-6680.

companies. Finally, health economists offer consultation to hospitals, nursing homes and other health care facilities on how to most efficiently run their businesses.

The job market is also strong for individuals with a graduate degree in health administration. In fact, employment of health services managers is expected to grow much faster than the average for all occupations in the United States for the next decade as health services continue to expand and diversify. Currently, over half of those with graduate degrees in health administration work in hospitals, while another 25 percent are employed by nursing facilities and clinics, and the remainder hold jobs in home health agencies, medical and dental laboratories, and the offices of dentists and other practitioners. While it is expected that hospitals will continue to employ the greatest number of managers for the foreseeable future, job growth will actually be strongest in home health agencies, and nursing and long term care facilities due to the increase in the elderly segment of the population. Also, more job opportunities for department administrators should emerge at group medical practices and HMOs as the trend toward managed care continues and our already unwieldy healthcare system becomes larger and more complex.

New graduates with master's degrees in health services or hospital administration may start their careers as assistant hospital administrators, managers of clinical departments (e.g., emergency room, critical care unit), directors of non-health departments (e.g., finance, human resources), or as administrators with an HMO, large group medical practice, mental health facility, or nursing home. Some also find work as underwriters for insurance companies, or as sales representatives with health equipment manufacturers. Job opportunities will be most plentiful for individuals with strong business and management skills and experience.

Getting In

Academics

Most programs require a strong academic background in science, math, statistics, and/or social science, depending on your specific area of interest. Many admissions committees will be expecting to see an undergraduate GPA of 3.0 or above, and for the more competitive programs, 3.5 and above. While some M.P.H. programs will consider all applicants with a bachelor's degree in a relevant field, others are restricted to can-

Helping Hand

"I initially got interested in this field two years after I finished my undergraduate career as a business and French major. I had never really been happy in what I had majored in as an undergraduate—I only stuck with it as it seemed the practical thing to do. Working in the Peace Corps in East Africa for two years after I graduated was the deciding factor. There I worked with small groups of people, mostly women. I got to coordinate a lot of health lessons. As I taught them about such issues as nutrition, family planning, HIV prevention, and more, I saw the importance and relevance of good health for all—it's something that really makes a society work."

A graduate student

KAPLAN

didates with a prior graduate degree and/or some health or human services work experience.

Experience

You don't have to be an M.D. or R.N. to be accepted to an M.P.H. program, however, your application will certainly be stronger if you have worked in healthcare. And, as mentioned above, related work experience is required for some programs.

Standardized Tests

M.H.A. programs typically ask for either GRE or GMAT (Graduate Management Admissions Test) scores.

Personal Qualities/Skills

Health services managers are often responsible for multimillion dollar facilities and huge staffs, and must make tough decisions based on information that is not always complete or consistent. In light of this, M.H.A. programs place a high premium on decision making, leadership and motivational ability, communication and analytical skills, and tact and diplomacy.

Slim Pickings

Graduate programs in public health are accredited by the Council on Education for Public Health, while those in health administration are accredited by the Accrediting Commission on Education for Health Services Administration. Currently there are less than 125 accredited programs in public health and health administration, so your search should definitely be manageable.

Program Options

Master's Level

In most cases, the Master of Public Health (M.P.H.) and the Master of Health Administration (M.H.A.) are the terminal professional degrees of choice for individuals who want to work in the field of health management and policy. The M.S. in public health is much like the M.P.H., although its scope is sometimes narrower.

The M.P.H. is a two-year program with a curriculum that is typically broad-based, although at certain schools specialization is an option (e.g., biostatistics, international health, or mother and child health). Coursework is macro in scope—focusing on populations rather than individuals—and addresses the societal, political, and historical aspects of public health problems and public health care. Some programs require supervised employment in a health care agency or other public health setting.

The Master of Health Administration master's degree typically takes two to three years to complete. The curriculum combines classes from the disciplines of business and health and may include accounting,

Top PH/PHA Doctorates

Epidemiology 149

Public health 156

Administration 60

Environmental health 58

Source: Survey of Earned Doctorates

budgeting, finance, information systems, health economics, and hospital management. Students generally specialize at the facility level—hospitals, nursing homes, mental health facilities, HMOs, group medical or outpatient care facilities.

Doctoral Level

The Ph.D. and Doctor of Public Health degree (D.P.H.) are appropriate for students who want to launch careers in academia or research. The admissions criteria and the program requirements are similar to those of other master's/Ph.D. science programs. Applicants should have a strong academic background in the sciences and mathematics, particularly statistics, and some undergraduate research experience. Knowledge of computer programming may also be required, depending on your area of specialization.

Dual Degree Programs

The M.H.A./M.B.A. allows students to gain a deeper and broader background in business than if they simply completed the M.H.A., and prepares them to specialize in areas such as health facility marketing or finance. Other dual degree programs blend health with social work, law, medicine, dentistry, and nurse-midwifery.

Special Issues

Fieldwork

If you're planning on enrolling in an M.P.H. program, take a close look at each school's fieldwork opportunities. Your internship could help provide you with an important professional foundation and pave the way for employment after graduation. Also both M.P.H. and M.H.A. applicants should ask admissions representatives whether their programs offers assistance in locating relevant summer positions.

Placement

Ask the career planning staff how long on average it takes graduates to find jobs. How many are still searching after six months? After one year? Find out where the graduates are employed, as well as what positions they have accepted and what salaries they are earning. For those considering a dual degree program such as the M.H.A./M.B.A. you might want to interview employers in your area regarding their perception of the dual degree and whether it lends an advantage come graduation time.

Words of Wisdom

Public health is an incredibly diverse field. When you start your program, keep an open mind and explore all the potential career opportunities.

Specializing in a particular type of health care facility such as an HMO, nursing home, or mental health hospital, may enhance your marketability.

Public health is an incredibly diverse field. When you start your program, keep an open mind and explore all potential career opportunities.

Get to know the faculty and the other students. Not only are they a great network when you're looking for a job, they're also a rich intellectual resource and can offer you valuable ideas and perspectives from other areas of this broad field.

Be able to articulate why you want a graduate degree in public health or health administration, as well as what you plan to do with it. Also be prepared to explain why you have chosen a particular area of specialization.

For More Information

American College of Health Care Administrators, 325 South Patrick Street, Alexandria, VA 22314; (703) 549-5822; www.achca.org. Provides information about career opportunities in long-term care administration.

American College of Healthcare Executives, 1 North Franklin Street, Suite 1700, Chicago, IL 60606; (312)424-2800; www.ache.org. Publishes quarterly and bimonthly journals on health care management, and provides career information.

Association of University Programs in Health Administration, 1110 Vermont Avenue NW, Suite 220, Washington, D.C. 20005; (202)822-8550

Medical Group Management Association, 104 Inverness Terrace East, Englewood, CO 80112-5306; (303) 799-1111; www.mgma.com. Offers information about career opportunities in medical group practices and ambulatory care management.

CHAPTER 10

The Sciences

Since there are far too many fields that fall under the umbrella of science to consider in a single chapter, we are going to focus on three of the most popular disciplines; biology, chemistry, and physics.

The Employment Picture

Scientists with graduate degrees can entertain a number of employment options, however, increasingly the best prospects are in applied research and technology, rather than basic research or academia. Scientists with strong business and management experience are being recruited as sales representatives, consultants, and administrators, especially by companies in the growing field of biotechnology. Others opt to pursue less traditional career fields such as science journalism, engineering, and teaching at the high school level. Major employers of scientists include universities, government agencies, pharmaceutical companies, foundations, and nonprofit organizations. Although a master's degree, and in some cases a bachelor's is often sufficient for entry-level research positions, without a doctorate, one's career mobility and salary potential are severely limited.

For those who hope to launch a career in academia, pursuing a postdoctoral fellowship is often the first step. In fact, a recent survey revealed that half of all chemistry Ph.D.'s and about three-quarters of biological sciences Ph.D.'s plan on pursuing postdoctoral study immediately after graduation as opposed to seeking employment. Unfortunately, finding a

Who's Who in Biology

Men 25,450

Women 22,499

Source: National Science Foundation

Degrees Earned

Biology Doctorates

Biochemistry 825

Molecular 618

Microbiology 426

General 350

Neuroscience 305

Chemistry Doctorates

Organic 483

General 458

Physical 338

Analytical 317

Inorganic 257

Physics Doctorates

Solid state/low-temp 371

General 355

Elementary particles 183

Source: Survey of Earned Doctorates

postdoc is no easy feat, nor is landing a job as a professor. The postdoc situation is most encouraging for biological sciences Ph.D.'s. and least promising for physics Ph.D.'s.

Biologists, Physicists, and Chemists at a Glance

Of the three occupational groups, the picture is perhaps most promising for biologists, who study living things and their connection to the environment. The rise of biotechnology has resulted in the creation of numerous research positions as biochemists and molecular biologists attempt to develop new commercial applications in agriculture, and the food and chemical industries. Other jobs have sprouted up as a result of the increased interest in developing biodegradable products and preserving the environment, and because of the continued emphasis on AIDS and cancer research. Beware, however, that proposed budget cuts may limit the amount and number of federal research grants. Most biologists are employed by federal, state, or local governments, followed by pharmaceutical and biotechnology companies, universities, and research laboratories. They work across a variety of subdisciplines including aquatic biology, biochemistry, botany, microbiology, physiology, zoology, ecology, and agricultural science.

The work of physicists focuses on the creation, structure and behavior of matter and energy. Some physicists work in basic research laboratories delving into the mysteries of the universe while others apply their knowledge to more earthly concerns such as developing new materials, consumer products, and scientific equipment. Major employers include colleges and universities, laboratories, the federal government, and manufacturing companies. Budget reductions in defense-related research and the federal government, combined with an expected decrease in nonmilitary research projects means that the current job market for physicists is not particularly promising. In fact, a decline in the employment of physicists and astronomers is expected to persist through the end of the millennium. The best job opportunities are likely to be in private industry.

Chemists are responsible for developing and inspiring thousands of innovative new products, as well as numerous advances in areas such as medicine, agriculture, textiles, and food processing. Chemists typically work in teams for manufacturers in research and development or production and quality control—some are also employed by federal, state, and local government agencies, and others by universities. Jobs in chemistry are expected to grow at the same pace as the national average for all occupations. The best opportunities will likely be found at pharmaceutical and biotechnology firms due to the anticipated emphasis on drug research and development, and the creation of environmentally "friendly" products. Those trained as analytical, environmental, or synthetic organic chemists should find themselves with the largest number of employment options.

Getting In

Academics

Most programs expect applicants to have good grades, and either a major or substantial undergraduate coursework in a scientific discipline. A background in computers, math, and statistics can also prove helpful. Those lacking in the prerequisites may still be admitted provisionally with the understanding that any deficiencies will be made up early on in their graduate program.

Research Experience

Prior research experience can help compensate for a transcript that is light on science courses. Regardless of whether or not you majored in a scientific field, gaining research experience during the summer as a volunteer or intern in a lab or clinic can give your application to graduate school a big boost. If you're still an undergraduate, consider arranging an independent research project for credit. As a bonus, the professor who supervises your research will likely be an excellent reference when the time comes to submit letters of recommendation.

Standardized Tests

Programs vary as to the emphasis they place on GRE scores. Virtually all require the general test, and some require the subject test.

Black Hole

"In physics, the academic positions don't really exist any more . . . . You've got postdocs that people are still getting, but in terms of major research universities hiring professors, you've probably got one or two positions opening per year with maybe 200 to 1,000 people applying from all over the world. For all practical purposes, even if you went to Princeton or Harvard, you're not going to get any jobs. I knew by my third year that I wasn't going to teach. But I finished anyway, because I went for other reasons —mainly to gain knowledge."

Ph.D., physics

Personal Statement

Most admissions committees will expect you to address your reasons for wanting to attend graduate school, describe your research and professional goals, and discuss your relevant work experience. The emphasis, however, should be on research skills, experience, and plans.

Program Options

Master's Level

A master's program in science generally takes two years to complete. Some programs require a thesis, whereas others do not. Note that you may experience science courses at the graduate level to be a quantum leap ahead in difficulty and complexity from those you attended as an undergraduate. Frequently, students who view the master's as a terminal degree are planning to teach at either the secondary school or junior college level, although some gravitate to positions in research, sales, inspection, or management.

Doctoral Level

Doctoral programs can last anywhere from four to seven years, and sometimes longer if the program permits. Programs vary as to how early in the curriculum you can begin to focus on your area of specialization, but all include fieldwork and laboratory research. Upon completing your coursework, you will take a series of exams. Assuming you pass them, you will then move on to propose, write, and defend the dissertation.

Interdisciplinary Studies

Lately, the scientific community has realized the benefit of encouraging students at the graduate level to study across disciplines, and the fact is that interdisciplinary study makes science Ph.D.'s more employable. This is especially true in emerging fields like biotechnology, biochemistry, and materials science. At Washington University in St. Louis, for example, graduate students in the biological sciences are admitted to the Division of Biology and Biomedical Sciences, not to any specific department. The Division, in turn, oversees ten biological science programs, and students have the opportunity to work with faculty from 20 departments overall. Early lab assignments are rotational in nature, enabling students to sample various disciplines before making a decision to focus on a particular area of specialization.

The University of Chicago is another pro-interdisciplinary institution. The university recently merged its Department of Biochemistry with the Department of Molecular Genetics and Cell Biology. In their first year, students sample course from both disciplines before making a decision about which course of study they will ultimately pursue. In addition, they are permitted to work with any adviser they choose, whether she resides in their discipline or not. All students are encouraged to participate in seminars and clubs that cross disciplinary lines.

Special Issues

Funding

Some Ph.D. programs guarantee up front that every student accepted will receive tuition remission plus a stipend. In return, students typically work as teaching or research assistants. Often these awards can be renewed for the entire length of one's Ph.D. program. Unfortunately, on occasion the funding that allows this generous support dries up! Budget cuts, decisions not to renew or extend grants, the departure of a professor with her funds in tow, or the reallocation of funds are usually the culprit. This can have serious consequences for your dissertation research since without the necessary funds the completion of your project may be delayed, or in the worst case scenario, you may have to revise your topic and find a new faculty member to work with. To protect yourself, find out where the funding for your department comes from and how long it is supposed to last. Beware of grants that are about to expire—they may not be extended. The ideal situation is to locate a department with a history of long-term, stable funding, which has recently received grants that are not due to expire until your with your dissertation research is finished.

> ### Fab Lab
>
> If you expect to spend part of your graduate career as a research assistant, ask current students how the labs are maintained and whether research assistants are constantly scrounging for supplies. For example, Ohio State's catalog promises assistance in stocking and maintaining the labs so that grad students research rather than administer.

Placement

Some program catalogs proudly mention their placement records, but don't settle for a generalities. Ask for detailed information about the fates of program graduates. Where do they get hired? What are typical starting salaries? How long does the job hunt take? How extensive is the on-campus recruitment program?

Words of Wisdom

Funding, postgraduate employment opportunities, and departmental dynamics are all factors to consider when evaluating graduate programs.

If you're still an undergraduate, register for research-credit classes, volunteer to work with professors on research projects, and look for summer internship programs. Any research experience you can muster will be extremely helpful when applying to graduate programs.

Don't rule out nonacademic and nontraditional career paths. A graduate science degree opens up a host of employment possibilities besides teaching or conducting research at a university—not to mention these jobs are few and far between.

If your game plan is to go to work at a bleeding-edge biotechnology company, in addition to amassing expertise in your particular scientific discipline, don't underestimate the value of writing, speaking, and leadership skills, all of which are highly valued by today's employers.

For More Information

Biology

American Institute of Biological Sciences, 1444 Eye Street, NW, Suite 200, Washington, DC 20005; (202) 628-1500. Publishes the brochure, *Careers in Biology*.

American Physiological Society, Membership Services Department, 9650 Rockville Pike, Bethesda, MD 20814; (301) 530-7164

American Society for Biochemistry and Molecular Biology, 9650 Rockville Pike, Bethesda, MD 20814-3996; (301) 530-7145.

American Society for Microbiology, Office of Education and Training—Career Information, 1325 Massachusetts Avenue, NW, Washington, DC 20005; (202) 737-3600

Biotechnology Industry Organization, 1625 K Street, NW, Suite 1100, Washington, DC 20006; (202) 857-0244

Botanical Society of America, 1725 Neil Avenue, Columbus, OH 43210-1293; (614) 292-3519

Chemistry

American Chemical Society, 1155 Sixteenth Street NW, Washington, DC 20036; (202) 872-4414. Publishes the *ACS Directory of Graduate Research*; *Current Trends in Chemical Technology, Business, and Employment*; and *Planning for Graduate Work in Chemistry*.

Physics

American Institute of Physics, American Center for Physics, 1 Physics Ellipse, College Park, MD 20740; (301) 209-3007. Publishes *Graduate Programs in Physics, Astronomy, and Related Fields*.

PART TWO

Selecting a Program

CHAPTER 11

Getting Information

Whatever sort of program you're looking into, the more information you can gather, the better. Make sure you leave yourself enough time to study catalogs, talk to students, alumni, and professors, and visit schools if possible.

Where to Look

Information on graduate schools can come from both formal and informal sources. Once you have a good idea of what your priorities are, consider the following ways of getting both the official word and the inside scoop on grad programs.

Professional Associations

This is the best place to start. Groups like the American Psychological Association and the American Historical Association have a variety of free or fairly low-cost information on graduate programs in the field, including program directories, advice on getting into graduate school, and career information. This is the most efficient way to get information, since it's all focused on your field and you don't have to sort through a lot of extraneous information. See the individual program chapters for

---

Info Online

Yahoo's Internet site is a great place to start an online search for information on graduate school programs.

Don't miss the Financial Aid Information page, which provides access to FastWeb, a searchable database of over 180,000 scholarships, loans, and grants. Find it at: www.yahoo.com/education/financial_aid

Top Guns

A different way to identify top programs in your field is by reading the professional journals. Look for professors who publish frequently and who are quoted, referenced, or otherwise involved with other people's articles. These professors, and their departments, are almost certainly the top in the field.

addresses and some pointers to what's available from the various associations.

Commercial Guides

There are several comprehensive directories, in print, on software or CD-ROM, or online, that list every graduate program, complete with addresses and phone numbers. If you're still in undergraduate school or still have access to your undergraduate career office, you may be able to use one of these directories free. The software and CD-ROM versions are great if you have settled on your specialization areas and location, since you can usually search these according to specific criteria and come up with a list of schools that match your requirements. If you can't get access to these directories, check your local library and bookstore for the print versions. The reference section of a big university or urban library will probably have these guides. If not, they are for sale in most larger bookstores.

Use a guide that lists by program rather than alphabetically, by state, or some other way. (It's far more difficult to pick though an alphabetical list of thousands of schools looking for "bioengineering" or "French literature." Use a guide that's already done the work for you.) The best are guides that contain not only broad categories like "engineering" but a breakdown of each school's specializations, like civil or electrical engineering.

Rankings

Each year, groups publish rankings of graduate programs: *U.S. News and World Report* on American graduate programs, *McLean's* on Canadian programs, *The Gourman Report* on American and international schools, and others. These rankings are useful, up to a point. They can give you a good general sense of the nationally known programs in your field, and even if you think you don't have a snowball's chance of getting into one, you should order at least a couple of catalogs and applications from them. Reading through this information will acquaint you with the latest developments, research, and prominent faculty in the field, which will be useful as you research other programs.

Keep in mind, though, that rankings are subjective (no matter how impressively complicated the methodology looks) and of course tell you nothing about the professors, politics, job placement records, or financial aid possibilities. Rankings give you a general sense of which programs in your field will have nationally known "name value" when you go to look for a job, which is a very desirable thing, but tell you nothing about whether one of these schools is the right choice for you.

Catalogs—and More

Once you've sorted out a group of programs, it's time for a more detailed investigation. The catalog is the obvious place to start; just don't stop there. Most departments have a chairperson who is also the admissions contact; he or she can put you in touch with current students and alumni who are willing to discuss the program with you. The chair is usually willing to answer questions as well.

Getting the catalog can turn into an odyssey in itself. If you just call the school's main admissions number and ask for a catalog and application, you're likely to get a general "Graduate School Catalog" that directs you to contact the individual departments for the specifics on being admitted to that program. You may or may not be able to use that particular application. Health, nursing, social work, engineering, and education programs are usually administered separately from "the graduate school," which means that the general catalog and application may not be of any use to you at all; many of these programs have their own catalogs and applications. Science, social science, and humanities departments, on the other hand, may or may not have separate catalogs and applications. Usually individual departments have at least a brochure listing faculty and any specialized requirements of the program.

Try to contact your school or department directly on the first try. It will save you time, and it's a golden chance for you to get your name out there in the department. When you're on the phone, introduce yourself, be courteous, and be sure to ask for the name of the administrative staff member who's helping you out. Write it down. When you have to contact the department later to ask questions, follow up on your application pieces, or get in contact with faculty, students, or alumni, you'll be familiar to the department, which helps in big and small ways when it's time to consider your application. Being sincerely nice to and respectful of support staff is not only the way your mother taught you to act, it's also a way to make a friend whose influence can affect your application process at unexpected moments, like when your third recommendation writer doesn't make the submission deadline and you need just a day or two extra to get that letter in!

Current Students and Alumni

You'll find that many graduate students are quite outspoken about the strengths and weaknesses of their professors, programs, and the state of the job market in their field. Try to speak to at least one current student and one alumnus from each program you're seriously considering. Professional associations as well as graduate departments have opportunities for people considering graduate school to talk with people who actually have the degree and are out there in the working world. The American Institute of Physics World Wide Web service, for instance, sponsors a careers bulletin board with new guests each month. These master's degree and Ph.D. holders answer questions about their own

Kaplan Online

Check out Kaplan's site for up-to-the-minute info on test prep, admissions, and financial aid:

- America Online: keyword "Kaplan"

- World Wide Web: www.kaplan.com

Hot Links

Here are some graduate schools with hot Web sites:

Baylor:
www.baylor.edu

Brown:
www.brown.edu

CA Institute of the Arts:
www.calarts.edu

Carnegie Mellon:
www.cmu.edu

Cornell:
www.cornell.edu

Duke:
www.duke.edu

Emory:
www.cc.emory.edu

Rice:
www.rice.edu

Stanford:
www.stanford.edu

U. of CA at Berkeley:
www.berkeley.edu

U. of Pennsylvania:
www.upenn.edu

U. of Texas at Austin:
www.utexas.edu

grad school experiences and talk about the career paths they've carved out for themselves in an economy that holds few traditional academic/research jobs for physicists.

Online Services

Online is a very good place to gather information in general. Bulletin boards, especially on the commercial online services, are a great place for exchanging information. There are also online discussion groups and mailing lists specifically for graduate students and prospective graduate students, with lots of real-life perspectives on choosing and applying to schools.

Classes

If the programs that interest you are nearby, take a course, preferably with one of the professors you hope to study with. This will not only give you a chance to experience the professor and the academic environment, but will also help you meet students in the program, and get a look at how the school itself operates. When you apply, you can point out in your statement of purpose and interviews that you have already attended classes. This shows your interest in the program, and allows you and your interviewer to dispense with some of the more basic questions and discuss the program and the school in greater depth.

Professors

If you're still in undergraduate school, or still have contacts at your undergraduate school, ask your professors for their take on the various graduate programs. You'll often find that they have a great deal of inside information on academic and research trends, impending retirements, intellectual rivalries, and rising stars. If the professor knows you and your interests well enough, he or she may even be able to suggest some programs that might be a good fit for you.

What to Ask

Since your objective is to identify graduate programs and departments that are strong in your area of interest, with a faculty deep enough for you to find a great adviser, many of your investigative questions will concern the faculty and the department at each school. Use all your sources to get answers to these questions in as much detail as you can. Above all, talk to current students. Don't let a professor's impressive catalog profile intimidate you. A Nobel prize is nice, but what really matters to you is what kind of adviser this laureate will make. His or her current students are your greatest resource.

Faculty

Whom you study with obviously can make or break your graduate school experience. You'll want to find out not only who is in the department, but what their attitudes are towards graduate students. Start by asking the following questions:

Is there someone in the department who would make a great adviser?

Your adviser will be your guide through practical, academic, and political challenges for the next two to seven years. This one person will help you with course selection (not only academically but with an eye towards building useful relationships with other members of your department and your field), clinical, research, or field education opportunities, and can make or break the thesis/dissertation process. The focus of your faculty investigation, then, is to figure out whether there is someone you can live with for the next seven years, both personally and professionally, and the depth of the department.

Who else is in the department?

Many graduate students apply to a particular department because they know that a prominent researcher, scholar, or other figure in the field is teaching there. That's fine, but you may discover that, in spite of your plans, the professor you came to study with is unavailable, uncooperative, or not interested in working with you; if that happens, you'll need somewhere else to turn. If you're writing a master's thesis or going for a Ph.D., you'll need at least two (master's) or as many as five (doctorate) readers/committee members to review your work; a tiny department won't afford you much depth. Look for a couple of other professors who, although their interests may not coincide exactly with yours, could work with you if you need them.

Joining the Ranks

"Where you fit among your peers can have a great deal of influence on how you are seen in your department and what your opportunities are."

A graduate student

How much does the faculty actually work with students?

At the master's level, access to prominent professors is often limited to large, foundation-level lecture courses, where papers and exams are graded by the professor's graduate assistants or tutors. The professor sees only the written work that the tutors feel is outstanding; for all practical purposes, the tutor, not the professor, evaluates your work and assigns your grade.

At the doctoral level, professors are generally much more accessible; they work directly with students in small seminar classes and in research. However, that access is subject to all sorts of complications. Seminars or research opportunities may be limited in size or open only with the professor's permission. Professors take sabbaticals to work on their own research and writing. And that's just classroom time. Even more important, is the professor generous with her time outside the classroom? Plenty of graduate students have joined departments specifically to work with distinguished professors, only to discover that the extent of their interaction with the brilliant scholar in question was half an hour, once a semester.

Of course, professors have demands on their time, especially publication pressures. They cannot spend all their time hand holding; their careers depend on publication. What you're looking for are professors who are available enough and give enough guidance that there are no awful last-minute surprises, like incomplete course requirements discovered just before graduation, performance problems in your fieldwork that are not discussed until grades are due, or a dissertation that is trashed halfway through the first draft because the adviser failed to voice concerns at the outline stage.

You don't want to find yourself working as the professor's indentured servant, either. Expect to spend some time proofing articles and contributing to the professor's research instead of focusing exclusively on your own, but you do not want to spend so much time on these endeavors that you can't finish your own program. Ask about all of these issues when you speak to current or former students of any professor you're considering as an adviser.

In a program with supervised fieldwork, where your performance will be monitored and reviewed by your adviser, it's equally important to find a good one. You will put a lot of work into your field placement, and your performance there will be even more crucial to your job search than your grades will. Look for advisers who give regular criticism, who can be constructive, and who do not wait until the end of your placement to tell you everything you have done wrong.

Is the department stable or changing?

Find out whether the faculty is nearing retirement age. Impending retirements may not affect you in a two-year master's program, but this is a serious consideration in doctoral programs, which can (and often do) stretch on for over five years. If you have hopes of working with a distinguished professor, will he or she even be available for that time—and longer, if you are delayed? Will the department be large and stable enough to allow you to put together a good thesis or dissertation committee? One doctoral student wanted to drop a class taught by a well-known professor who expected an invitation to sit on her dissertation committee. He not-so-subtly tried to threaten her into staying with the class by suggesting that a drop might make him angry enough to refuse to sit on her committee. Fortunately, the department was large enough that the student did not need him on the committee, even as a well-known scholar in the field. She dropped the class—and the idea of asking him to sit on her committee.

A younger department offers more stability over the course of your program, and may be an exciting environment to work in, but also try to find out whether younger members of the department are established. Do they get sufficient funding? Have they settled into the institution enough that there are not likely to be political controversies? The last thing you want in the middle of your thesis or dissertation is open political war between two of your committee members.

Real Students: From the Trenches

Here's what some graduate students we spoke to said about finding the right adviser for you:

Pretzel Logic

"Don't make my mistake. I thought I should go to the best school I could get into. I figured I'd just find an adviser when I got there. Was that backwards."—recent Ph.D.

Can You Relate?

"Do as much research on your potential adviser as possible, as well as the other professors in your department. It's really important to have a good relationship with him or her to be able to advance in your field. Try and obtain this information as early as possible."—Ph.D. candidate

Clash of the Titans

"You can avoid personality clashes by meeting the adviser you may want to work with. You can't always tell everything about a person based on a first impression, but you can get a feeling whether you may get along with him. You also want to know how that person is viewed by others in the field, because you are going to be identified as his disciple, and if he's not well liked, that may cause you some trouble too."—M.S., political science

> ### *Read Between the Lines*
>
> A critical reading of the catalog can give you valuable information on faculty, course selection, and assistantships.

Till You Bleed . . .

"At the university where I got my M.A. there was a professor who told me and a group of other students at orientation to drop all

Worth 1,000 Words

While catalog photos tend to present a school in the most favorable light, they can also reveal valuable info on the age of the faculty, as well as the school's gender balance and ethnic mix.

our outside hobbies for the sake of our graduate work. Now I realize this man had a very distorted and negative perception of what the graduate process is all about."—Ph.D. candidate, American studies

Student Body

The student body, as well as the faculty, will have philosophical and political orientations. If you're going for the doctorate, it's important to investigate your student colleagues a bit.

What's the student body like?

The theories and perspectives that make you the house liberal in one program can be deemed conservative in another, and where you fit among your peers can have a great deal of influence on your image and your opportunities in your department.

One engineering student we interviewed told us about the department where he earned his master's, which happened to be near his hometown in a fairly conservative area of New York State. He assumed, mistakenly as it turned out, that the faculty and students would be as conservative as the people he had grown up with. "I was 'home' in a geographic sense, but not, however, in a socioacademic sense," he said. Fortunately, both he and his liberal colleagues kept a sense of humor and he graduated with a master's degree and good relationships. In a more self-important department, however, such a political schism could be a recipe for disaster. If you plan on an academic career, remember that your student colleagues will someday be your professional colleagues, and you don't want old rivalries or dislikes surfacing just as you're trying to get your first book published or receive tenure.

Program

Knowing the program's particular theoretical bent and practical selling points can help ensure that you choose a school that reflects your own needs and academic leanings.

What are the program orientations in the department?

Does one school of thought, one style of research, predominate? If so, is there anyone else working in the department with a different theoretical framework? Will you have opportunities to work within a variety of theories and orientations? Graduate education has become very specialized, and in today's job market that may actually be a disadvantage. Employers look for people who can be flexible and who have at least the base knowledge to learn new skills and fields.

What special opportunities are available?

How well are research programs funded? Do the professors have good records at rounding up grants? In field or clinical work, what are the options? Are programs available in your area of interest? Especially in social work, counseling, and psychology, this early field and clinical work may be your first step towards getting a job when you graduate. The contacts you make during your practical work, especially if your program is in the city or area in which you intend to work, can be a valuable resource after graduation.

Job Placement

Even if you're pursuing an advanced degree simply for the love of knowledge, it pays to find out what recent grads have done with their degrees. You'll also want to ask what kind of track record the program has in placing their alums.

When you graduate, what are your chances of getting a job?

What are your chances of getting your desired job? With the currently difficult job market, it's especially important to find out when and where graduates have found work. If you're considering work in business, industry, local agencies, schools, health-care facilities, or the government, find out whether these employers visit the campus to recruit. Major industries, for instance, may visit science programs to interview prospective graduates. Some will even employ graduate students summers or part time. If you're going into academia, find out whether recent grads have been able to find academic posts, how long the search took, and where they are working. Are they getting tenure-track positions at reasonably prestigious departments, or are they shifting from temporary appointment to temporary appointment with little hope of finding a stable position?

Great Stuff You Can (and Can't) Find in Catalogs

A catalog can give you a wealth of information; some of this is intended by the school, but some you can find by reading between the lines. By dissecting the catalog, you can get info on faculty, course selection, and less obvious opportunities and requirements.

Faculty

Every graduate catalog lists faculty, but as always, each school has its own way of doing things. The entire faculty, regardless of department, may be listed in alphabetical order, or each department faculty may be listed separately. Faculty titles and academic background are always listed; usually, but not always, research and teaching interests are described. It may take some work to sort through it all, but a good, critical reading of the faculty infor-

> ### *Heart's Desire*
>
> Not every course listed in the catalog is offered every year. If you have your heart set on a particular class, call to check the likelihood of its being offered when you attend.

mation can tell you a lot about a program, or raise important questions. Here's the information you want to end up with:

Faculty numbers

How many faculty members in your program/department? A quick count will tell.

Faculty focus

How many of them are working in research/teaching areas that are relevant to you? This is crucial. A large history department does you no good at all unless there is at least one person working in your particular area.

Faculty titles

What are their titles? Professor titles generally follow a hierarchy like this:

The Henry Tyler Grant Distinguished Professor of European History. This sort of title indicates an endowed position, meaning that the position is permanently funded and will not be cut in times of budgetary crisis or low enrollment. People in these titled positions are a permanent part of the institution.

Professor of European History. These titles indicate permanence; their holders will be around for a while.

Associate Professor of European History. Less senior, and also less secure. This may be a temporary position, that is, available for only three years, or subject to some other time limit.

Assistant Professor of European History. This is a less senior title and may be less secure.

Adjunct Professor of European History. This often indicates that the professor in question is not part of the faculty in that department, or in that school, at all. Because of their teaching and research interests, these professors teach courses in your area from time to time, but it is not their major interest.

Lecturer. Often someone in a related field or already out in the working world, who is a sort of guest speaker for a semester or two.

Emeritus. No longer teaching.

Faculty age

How old are they? This information, of course, isn't published in the catalogue, but if the date of the bachelor's degree is there, you can generally figure it out.

Faculty stars

Have you heard of any of these people before? Names that you recognize from your undergraduate or current work are worth investigating. They are probably the best-known faculty at the school.

Faculty mix

Are there pictures? Science departments in particular publish snazzy, four-color brochures complete with faculty and student profiles—and photographs. The photographs inadvertently tell you a lot about the department—more or less how old the faculty is, the gender balance, the ethnic mix.

Aim High
_____

Apply to a few schools that seem just beyond your reach. It's worth a try!

Sample Faculty Entry

From a simple faculty bio, you can deduce the professor's ranking in the department, as well as the likeliness of his or her being around when you enter the program. Take the following two listings:

Rolando Grassi, Associate Professor, graduated from Amherst in 1959 with the B.A., and received the Ph.D. in 1976 from University of Virginia. His field of teaching and research is medieval literature, with particular emphasis on the formative romantic traditions in European literature and on the contemporary significance of these themes in poetry.

Cynthia Leavenworth, Brodkey Professor of English Literature, graduated from Vassar College with the B.A. in 1954 and received the Ph.D. from University of Chicago in 1963. Her teaching and research are in the 20th-century: poststructuralism and the American novel.

Here's what you can deduce about these two people:

- He's an associate; she's a professor. Her title indicates that she has a very secure job and will be there permanently, unless she chooses to leave. His title indicates that his position may expire, leaving him to find another job. If you want to study with him, check around and find out whether he is about to become a full professor, or whether he is likely to leave.

- Approximate ages. Assuming they received their B.A.'s at age 21, that makes her 68 and him 63. Retirement may be an issue here; investigate their plans.

Tutors, Assistants

"Over 700 assistantships are given by our school each year." Sounds like the mother lode, doesn't it? But that's for the school as a whole. Look in your department. Are there a lot or just a couple? A small number may indicate that the department is small and/or not very well funded. It may be hard for you to get a teaching job later in your doctorate if you need one. Or it may not be—they may be glad to have someone interested in a less popular field!

Course Selection

Most graduate programs can give you a booklet describing the courses offered in each department. Look these over as well, keeping in mind the following questions:

Course Availability

What's the date on the catalog? If it covers a two-year period, for instance, 1999–2001, remember that not all courses may be offered each year, or that by the time 2001 rolls around, the professor may have decided not to teach a particular course.

Concentrations

What's the concentration of courses in your area? You will take some required courses and then select others according to your concentration and interests. Check the course listings in your specific areas of interest to see whether the department offers any depth.

Student Profiles

Some graduate catalogs contain profiles of or statements by current master's and Ph.D. students. Sometimes this is an informal blurb on a few students—it's really marketing material—and sometimes it's a full listing of graduate students. Use this as a resource both to find out what everyone else in the program is up to, and to find current students you can interview about the school and the program.

Residency Requirements

Most master's programs are flexible about part-time studies, but doctoral programs are less so. Many doctoral programs expect a minimum amount of time "in residence"—that is, enrolled as a full-time student for a certain number of consecutive semesters. This requirement is usually listed in the catalog.

Where You Stand

At this point it's time to make a preliminary estimate of where you stand in the applicant pool at each school you're interested in exploring further. Ultimately the admissions committee will judge your application not only by objective standards like GPA, but also by subjective criteria like their evaluation of your Statement of Purpose. You can't really replicate the process, but you can get a rough idea by comparing your GPA and GRE scores to those of the most recent entering class.

This information almost certainly won't be published in the bulletin; you're better off contacting the department directly and asking for it. If they can't or won't give it to you, try one of the graduate program directories available in libraries, bookstores, and career offices. In some cases less than half of graduate programs actually submit GRE and GPA numbers, but it's worth a try to see if your program is listed.

Don't overlook the section of the bulletin that lists program prerequisites. Psychology programs may expect you to have a psych undergraduate major, or score well on the GRE Psychology Subject Test; social work programs may require a strong social sciences undergraduate background. If you don't have the prerequisite academic background or knowledge base, don't automatically assume you won't get in. Look for the catalog sections on "provisional" admissions or nondegree admissions; you may be able to enter under one of these programs. Once you have some idea of where you stand in the applicant pool, you can form your application strategy. Here's how.

Select a "safe" program

First, no matter what your qualifications, it's wise to choose at least one school that is likely to accept you. Make sure it's one that fits your academic goals and economic circumstances. How do you know that a program is likely to accept you? If your GRE scores and GPA are well above the program's median scores, and you don't anticipate any serious problems with other parts of your record or application, you've probably found a "safe" program.

Broaden your program selections

Next look for two or three programs with the following criteria: Your GRE scores and GPA match the median scores, and your research, practical, or academic background seems at least average for that program. If you've made an accurate assessment of your potential, one of these is probably the program you'll attend. If your ideal program is among them, you've completed your school selection.

Aim high

If your ideal program is one that you don't seem qualified for, apply to your "dream school" anyway. GPA and GRE scores are not the only two criteria by which applications are judged, and you may discover that you are admitted in spite of your academic background. It's always worth a try.

Maybe you're very committed to one or two programs, or maybe graduate school for you means a certain program at a particular school. If you apply and are not admitted, ask the admissions committee or the department that rejected you for a review of your application. A frank evaluation will tell you a lot about how to improve your chances for next year.

Sample Worksheets

To help organize your search, use the Program Investigation Worksheet on the following pages. Photocopy this worksheet so that you can use one for each school you're exploring. After you've narrowed down your list, use the Application Worksheet that follows. Again, photocopy it so you can use one for each school.

Program Investigation Worksheet

Contact Data

School

Address

Phone/fax number

Contact in admissions office

Department

Address

Phone/fax number

Department chair

Department administrative contact

Professors in Department to Investigate/Contact

Name

Areas of interest

Phone/e-mail address

Name

Areas of interest

Phone/e-mail address

Name

Areas of interest

Phone/e-mail address

Departmental Financial Aid Available

Teaching assistantships

Research assistantships

Work-study

Fellowships

Grants/scholarships

KAPLAN

Notes from Your Campus Visit

Visit/interview notes

Politics/ambience of department:

Notes on professors you've considered working with:

Notes on research facilities:

Notes on practicum/internship opportunities:

Postgraduate employment info for program graduates:

Services available:

School Selection Worksheet

You may find it helpful to break down your list of schools into three tiers. The number of schools on the list depends on your individual circumstances.

Tier One: "Wishful Thinking" Schools

1.

2.

3.

4.

5.

Tier Two: "In Between" Schools

1.

2.

3.

4.

5.

Tier Three: "Safety" Schools

1.

2.

3.

4.

5.

CHAPTER 12

Evaluating Graduate Programs

Where do you start researching graduate programs? It's no small job: There are over 400 psychology programs, over 300 chemistry programs, and over 400 English programs, just to mention a few.

First Steps

The first step is to narrow down the options by figuring out what you want to specialize in, and to determine the best school location for you.

Specialization

This, of course, depends on your own interests, but you should also take into account what's happening in the job market. For example, if you're seeking a doctorate in chemistry, you should be well aware that jobs in both academia and industry are very tight right now. Your best bet might be specializing in areas of chemistry that are related to biomedicine and environmental issues, since both of these areas seem to be in a great position to grow.

Location

If you're planning on a career in academia, you'll probably want to choose a nationally known program, regardless of where it's located. If, on the other hand, your program involves a practical dimension (psychology, social work, education, or some interdisciplinary programs) you may want to concentrate your school search on the area in which you hope to live and work, at least initially. Your fieldwork will give you a terrific opportunity to make contacts in the community—contacts that may be the lead to your first job.

Your Adviser, Your Department

When you earn your graduate degree, you'll be joining a professional community, whether it's in academia, clinical practice, or business. Every professional community is its own little world, complete with well-known figures, schools of thought, and a network of contacts and acquaintances. Your adviser will be your entrée into this world, and his or her reputation will greatly influence yours. As you begin your career, you'll be identified as "one of Professor So-and-so's guys" (in some academic circles, even distinguished professors are still referred to as "Professor A, a student of Professor B" when Professor B has been dead for half a century). And it may very well be your adviser's connections that help you land your first job, in academia or outside.

The same is true of your department. Most graduate departments focus their research and teaching efforts on a few subfields, and particular schools of thought or approaches become identified with the department. For the rest of your career, you'll be known as "one of the Boulder people," or "a Berkeley guy."

It's crucial, then, that you find the right match between your interests and a department's, and even more crucial that you find an adviser with whom you can have a working relationship that is productive, respectful, and happy.

Program Requirements

This is really two separate issues. First, most graduate programs generally have suggested undergraduate majors or at least a list of coursework that will provide adequate background for work on the graduate degree. These requirements or suggestions are listed in the program catalogs. Second, each program will have requirements for graduation.

Background Requirements

This is the stumbling block in the application process for many people who've been out of school for five years or more and are interested in career changes. Before you get set on applying to a particular program at a particular time, be sure you understand the required background. If you don't have it, you may be able to fill it in, or at least demonstrate the ability to handle the work, by taking courses or by passing subject area tests. Or you may be admitted to the program provisionally. One graduate catalog puts it this way: "A student whose undergraduate background is considered to be inadequate in one or more areas, but who otherwise is qualified for graduate study, may be admitted in some instances. The student, however, will be required by the area and/or advisory committee to make up deficiencies by either registering for, or testing out of, the appropriate courses."

Graduation Requirements

The program catalog will also list the requirements for graduation. Most of these requirements will be filled through coursework, research, or clinical/field work. The one requirement that seems to hang many people up is the foreign language requirement. At the master's level, reading ability in another language, specified by the department according to the international scholarship in this area, is generally required for graduation. At the doctorate level, however, the requirements may be far more stringent, especially in fields in which there is a great deal of international scholarship. Or in history, where source materials appear in other, and ancient, languages. Failure to fulfill language requirements is responsible for many delays and even derailments of doctoral programs. Check out the language requirements for graduation from various programs and think about how you will meet them. You may choose to start working on them before you enter a program, or you may want to build extra time into your time/cost estimates if learning other languages is difficult or unpleasant for you.

Master's Thesis Option

Quite reasonably, your program will expect you to demonstrate your new expertise before it allows you to graduate. At the doctoral level, this is what the dissertation is for. You will hardly be able to avoid writing one if you pursue a doctorate. At the master's level, however, the thesis may be an option. If the thought of writing a 50- or 100-page thesis as a graduation requirement makes you cringe, find out whether programs in your field have another path to graduation. It is not at all unheard-of for the thesis requirement to drag out for a year or two after all coursework and fieldwork is complete. If you are earning your master's to be licensed or credentialed in a particular field, this kind of delay will obviously thwart your job search and your ability to earn more money.

Program Cost

Money is an enormous issue for nearly every graduate student, master's or doctorate. People who choose law school or business school, while confronted with hefty tuition bills, are also looking at a short program (two years or less to earn an M.B.A., three years to earn a J.D.) and the potential for a very lucrative career that will make paying off those bills a lot easier. A master's or doctorate, on the other hand, isn't likely to provide its owner with that kind of earning potential.

Generally speaking, the most expensive kind of graduate program (per semester) will be a terminal master's degree at a private school. Loans are available to master's-level students, but grants, scholarships, and other forms of "free" financial assistance are harder to find. Furthermore, most private schools apply the same tuition rate to in-state and out-of-state residents. In a terminal master's program at a private school, you're not likely to find ways to cut down the total cost of tuition. Savings will have to come from finding the cheapest living and housing expenses and from working your way through the program as quickly as possible.

At the doctoral level, tuition remission (you don't pay any) and grants or stipends (they pay you) are common. Percentages of doctoral students in a program receiving full tuition remission plus stipend/grant money can range anywhere from 0 percent (although students in these programs may be receiving either tuition remission or stipend/grant money) to 100 percent—every student in the program pays no tuition and receives some grant or stipend. In these programs the major financial burden is living expenses over the years of coursework, language requirements, qualifying and field exams, research, and the dissertation.

The world of financial aid gets a section all to itself in this book. Before you turn to that, though, you can lay the groundwork for a good financial plan during the school investigation and selection process. How tuition is charged and the location of the school can have a significant impact on your financial situation before you even begin to work out how you're going to pay for this degree.

Tuition Payments

Some graduate programs charge "per credit" or "per hour," meaning that your tuition bill is calculated by the number of credits you take each semester. Other programs charge per semester or per year with a minimum and maximum number of credits you can take per semester for that flat fee. Each type of program has financial advantages. With the "per credit" system, you can take the minimum number of credits each semester at the lowest possible cost, since you're paying only for the courses you actually take. This can save you money over the course of your degree program, particularly if you are a part-time student. On the other hand, the per-semester system can be cheaper if you can devote more than full time to the program. If you can squeeze in an extra course each semester (maybe with a summer course or two), you may be able to knock a whole semester off your tuition bill, and get to your job search that much quicker. A graduate school may use "per credit" in some of its programs and "per semester" in others. It may also charge different per-credit or per-semester rates for different programs.

School location

You'll remember from undergraduate school that state colleges and universities usually give in-state residents a tuition break. This can also be true at the graduate level, in both the per-credit and per-semester systems. Each school has its own state residency requirements; if you hope to get a state-resident break on your tuition from a particular program, it may take some planning ahead (including a move) to qualify for the lower tuition.

Location also has everything to do with the other part of your graduate school expenses: everyday living. University housing may be cheap, but it is likely to be available only for nine months of the year, forcing you to find other housing for the summer months. This will be particularly disruptive if you have a family. Cost of living (including typical rents) and the availability of work (for both you and your spouse or partner, if you have one) will have a great impact on both your total expenses and your ability to earn some money.

Quality of Life

Graduate school will be a way of life for the next two to ten years. If you have a spouse (partner) and/or children, it will be their way of life too. In selecting a school, consider the following factors. While some may not be relevant or important to you, others will affect the quality of your life over the years you spend in school.

Family Resources

- Is child care available on-campus, or otherwise conveniently located and affordable?

- Are there employment opportunities for spouses or partners?

- Is there a good school system?

- Is there on-campus housing? for you? for a family?

- If family housing is not available on-campus, is there decent and affordable housing near campus?

- Will there be activities and groups for your family to join, both on campus and off?

- What kind of medical coverage is available from each program?

Financial Issues

- What is the local cost of living?

- What will your moving costs be?

- How much will it cost to travel "home" for holidays and vacations?

- Are there employment opportunities, particularly summer jobs that will enable you to put aside some savings for the school year?

Fieldwork Issues

- Are the fieldwork sites in each program accessible on foot or by public transportation, or will you need a car?

- Are they in areas where you feel relatively safe and comfortable?

People

- If you are an international student, are there other students and/or a local community from your native country?

- If you are a member of a racial or ethnic minority group, gay or lesbian, very conservative or very liberal, or a devout practitioner of your religion, are you comfortable with the politics and values of your department and the surrounding community?

- If you or a member of your family has a disability, how accessible is the campus? How accessible is the city or town where your program is located?

Program Offerings

- What kind of services does your program provide? Are counseling, career services, job placement, child care, disability services, and international student advisement available to you and your family?

- Is the atmosphere of the department competitive or cooperative?

Free Time

- Do the weather, the cultural life, the people, and the local forms of recreation appeal to you?

- Is this a place where you can have some fun?

Part-Time and Evening Options

If there is a possibility that you will have to work while you are in school, particularly while you're in the course-work stage, check out the flexibility of any program that interests you. Is part-time study an option? This can make all the difference in the course-work years, where carrying two classes per semester instead of four can make balancing work and study possible. Part-time programs are slow, however, which can be discouraging, especially when licensure or salary increases are at stake.

Are there night/weekend classes? When is the library open? the lab? Talk to students who are currently in the program, especially those who work. Professors can be intolerant of working students' limited study time and work obligations (especially when that means missing class). If you are in a master's program for specific training or job advancement, this may be annoying but will cause no permanent damage to your career. If you plan to apply to a doctoral program, though, in which relationships with professors are more crucial to your progress and success, the burden of pleasing a boss and an adviser at the same time may be unmanageable. If there is any way that you can manage full-time, or nearly full-time, studies at the higher levels, do it. You can graduate quicker and start picking up the financial pieces that much sooner—and often with a more secure base for your job search in the form of good support from your adviser.

Students who are part time or work, or both, are sometimes not taken seriously in the academic community. One mother of two elementary school children, who was also working, remarked to one of her tutors that she was a part-time student. The tutor replied quite seriously, "Oh, you're doing it the easy way!" The perception that part-time students are taking it easy lingers, even though working students and students with families are common in graduate programs. Ask current students how part timers and working students are regarded in these programs.

Also, ask a few critical questions of part-time programs (including evening programs). Do the same faculty members teach at night/part time as in the day/full time? Are the admissions standards for both the same? If the part-time program has different admissions or faculty standards, investigate the program more carefully. It may not be up to the standards of the full-time version.

PART THREE

Admissions

CHAPTER 13

Meeting Admissions Requirements

Clinical psychology programs are the most competitive graduate programs; some top programs have acceptance rates as low as one percent. Yet the student quoted in our Getting In section intro, a real student at an Eastern university, was accepted to three of the five schools she applied to. Notice what she says about her success. She doesn't attribute it to her great GPA or GRE scores, even though they're a standard part of the application. Instead, she researched the admissions process in her field, found out that experience would make her a competitive candidate, and got the experience and great letters of recommendation that got her in.

This is the kind of approach to graduate admissions that most frequently pays off. It may sound simple, but finding out what the requirements are for admission—and then delivering exactly what is expected—is the most important aspect of the admissions process. Every school's expectations are different in one way or another: In fields like psychology, social work, and health, your research and practical experience will play a role in the admissions decision. If you're applying to film, writing, or other arts programs, you'll be asked to submit samples of your work. And if you're planning on an academic career, your research and publications will be very interesting to the admissions committee. The way you present yourself and your achievements should be tailored to the programs you're applying to.

Numbers Aren't Everything

Sure, GPA and GRE scores matter. But, so do a clear personal statement, positive letters of recommendation, and documented commitment to your field.

Tell It Like It Is

If Your GPA was pulled down by personal problems one semester or year, say so in a brief note. Admissions officers are human, too.

Some admissions requirements, however, are universal to almost all graduate schools. No matter where you apply, these four factors will always count:

- Undergraduate GPA (especially in your major)

- GRE scores

- Letters of recommendation

- Your personal statement

Let's take a look at at how each of these does—and doesn't—influence the admission committee's evaluation of your application.

Undergraduate GPA

Keep your GPA as high as you can. Graduate programs want some objective measure of an applicant's intellectual ability and self-discipline. Since everybody has one, the undergraduate GPA is one of the easiest ways for programs to distinguish between applicants. A low GPA will limit your opportunities: Most graduate programs expect a minimum GPA of 2.7 to 3.0, at least in your major.

A truly low GPA will almost certainly eliminate an applicant from competitive programs. If your GPA is borderline, however—hovering around the 3.0 mark—you may benefit from a more holistic reading of your transcript, where someone on the admissions committee reviews your transcript course by course. In this case, your performance in your major is examined with an eye towards noticeable trends (bad sophomore year, great junior year, one horrendous semester) that might put your overall GPA in a different light. For example, say that the holistic reading reveals that in your freshman year, when your maturity and discipline were not exactly at their peak, you bombed in a few courses outside your major. Yet your grades improved steadily for the next three years, and you maintained a 3.6 average in your major. This certainly says more about your abilities than your overall GPA does.

Of course, a low GPA isn't always a question of academic ability or discipline. Sometimes a GPA is pulled down by a semester or a year that was disrupted by personal (health, family, financial) problems. In any of these circumstances, include a short, businesslike note with your application. Doing this will help admissions committees consider your transcript to your advantage.

Major Effort

The admissions committee will give the most serious consideration to your GPA in your junior and senior years, on the theory that these are the years in which you have been concentrating on your major and have therefore done your best work.

The role your GPA and the rest of your undergraduate education play in the application process is also affected by when you decide to apply to graduate school. The GPA of applicants who are about to complete, or have recently completed, their undergraduate degree is given much more weight than the GPA of applicants who return to school after several years.

GRE and Other Standardized Test Scores

The Graduate Record Exam (GRE) General Test is typically required for entrance into North American graduate schools, and some programs require that you take one or more GRE Subject Tests as well, particularly in psychology and the sciences. In addition to, or in lieu of, the GRE, some programs require the Miller Analogies Test (MAT), a thinking-skills test of about 100 problems in analogy format. These standardized tests are a required part of the application process. Admissions committees value them because standardized scores provide another way of comparing applicants on some sort of objective basis.

The GRE

The GRE General Test tests your knowledge and skills in three "measure types": Verbal, Quantitative, and Analytical. The Verbal and Quantitative are a lot like the SAT you took for admission to undergraduate school (although not much like the ACT, if that's the test you took). The Verbal section tests your reading comprehension and vocabulary skills; the Quantitative section tests your high school math; the Analytical section tests your reasoning skills with games and short reading selections. The sections are always timed, so that answering the questions efficiently is part of the challenge of getting a high score.

The GRE is available in two formats, the pencil-and-paper and the on-computer versions. The pencil and paper is given several times a year, nationwide, on Saturday test dates. The computer version is available year-round by appointment. Which version is right for you will depend on how quickly you need your scores and whether you are comfortable taking a test on a computer.

Compared to the undergraduate GPA, there's a lot more diversity of opinion when it comes to the value of GRE scores in graduate admissions. Some programs consider the GRE very important, others don't. Some programs give all three scores equal consideration; others focus on two of the three scores. The best way to find out how each program regards standardized test scores is to ask. Read the catalog first, so you don't waste the admissions department's time with questions they've already answered for you. If you're lucky, your program doesn't require the GRE at all, although you're welcome to send scores if you have them.

> ### *Get It While It's Hot*
>
> If you can, take the GRE while you're an undergrad, or within a few years of graduation. Your knowledge will still be fresh, and chances are you'll do better than if you wait.

If you know that you will apply to graduate school within two years of undergraduate school, take the GRE soon. Studies show that performance on standardized tests declines with each year that you are out of school, so get the test out of the way while your knowledge is still fresh. Scores are good for a few years, so a test taken during or immediately after undergraduate school need not be used right away. Many graduate programs will accept scores up to five years old, although you should check that when you begin your application process.

Students returning to school after several years are often exasperated by the GRE requirement, especially if they've already proven themselves in a career. "Why do I have to pass another test?" is the most common question. It's true that standardized test performance declines with each year out of school, so the longer you've been out, the better the chances that your knowledge and your testing skills have gotten rusty. However, your GRE score is not set in stone the way your undergraduate GPA is. It's a test you take now; this number is under your control. If you've forgotten a lot of math or vocabulary, a little preparation can go a long way towards bringing your score up.

GRE and Financial Assistance

Some graduate programs award fellowships and assistantships partly on the basis of GRE scores. Since most programs have limited funds and therefore limited positions to offer, the awards process can be quite competitive. Not only should you take your scores seriously, you should also confirm the submission deadline with your department. The financial aid deadline is usually earlier than the application deadline.

Letters of Recommendation

Letters of recommendation can rank very high on the admission committee's list of evaluation criteria, generally in the top three along with GPA and GRE scores.

Most programs require three letters of recommendation. Some specify that exact number; others suggest a minimum number but allow some flexibility if you want to submit one or two more letters.

Your Personal Statement

The essays you write must be honest and clear. They must be as original and interesting as you can make them. And above all, they must show you at your best. Chapter 15 contains all of the information you'll need to write a good personal statement.

Deadlines

"If you have a problem with procrastination, you should try and straighten that out before graduate school. You can end up being in graduate school for ten or twelve years. Then if you want a job in academia they ask, 'Why did it take you twelve years? We expect you to write a book within your first two years.'"

—M.S.

Getting an application submitted on time involves orchestrating your undergraduate school (which will mail your transcript), ETS, your recommenders, and your own efforts. Start early. Some departments, especially very competitive ones, are quite strict about submission deadlines and will simply not allow extra time (except under very extraordinary circumstances). Even if you can get a little grace period, an incomplete application makes you look disorganized and undisciplined.

Check and doublecheck with each program for the admissions deadline. Some graduate schools admit new students only at the start of the fall semester; others allow people to start at two, three, or even four points during the year. Application deadlines shift accordingly. To further complicate things, financial aid deadlines are often earlier than the admissions deadline. If you plan to apply for financial aid, you'll have to submit the entire application package months earlier. And to complicate things even further, a number of programs will consider financial aid requests only for the start of the fall semester. If you want to begin in the spring, you're free to apply, but you won't be considered for financial aid until the admissions process for the fall semester begins.

With all of that in mind, here's a timetable for the application process that should get everything there in plenty of time.

Winter

You can't hibernate just yet. If you're a nontraditional applicant or plan to switch fields entirely, be sure to get catalogs and investigate program requirements. If you don't have the required background, check into:

- Applying as a provisional student

- Enrolling as a nondegree student

- Taking courses to make up the missing background

Spring

As the weather starts getting warm, start getting yourself into gear:

- Research programs in your field. Collect school catalogs, contact the professional/licensing organizations, speak to current students/graduates of interesting programs, consult reference books or software.

- Identify which standardized tests are required for admission, and take a diagnostic test to evaluate how close you are to score requirements.

- Choose a test date for the GRE and any Subject Test. It's best to take the tests on two separate dates. Consider the General Test in June (allowing an October/December retake, if necessary) and an October Subject Test date (allowing a December retake, if necessary).

- Investigate GRE preparation and schedule it to end the week before your test date.

Summer

Before you abandon all worries except for applying sun protection evenly, be sure to do the following:

- Begin a preliminary list of recommenders.

- Investigate programs.

- Begin filling out financial aid forms.

- Begin drafting personal statement(s).

- Contact programs and get new catalogs/applications.

Fall

Now's the time to start turning on the heat in the application process:

- Begin filling out applications.

- Choose recommenders and get all necessary info to them one month in advance.

- Finish paperwork for financial aid.

If you're applying for admission sometime other than fall, adjust the dates accordingly.

CHAPTER 14

Preparing Your Application

Putting it all together requires a good deal of planning and attention to detail. As a soon-to-be applicant for graduate school, the last thing you want to hear after a yearlong campaign of preparation is that you overlooked a crucial detail or failed to fulfill some requirement properly. This chapter will explain the whole process, so that by the end you'll know exactly what you'll need to do to meet and beat the admissions requirements.

Getting the Required GPA

Study hard now and you'll never have to bemoan the way your undergraduate GPA is preventing you from pursuing the career or the financial security of your dreams. A misspent four years really can make acceptance into top programs difficult. If your grades are excellent, fine. But if you have a few less-than-stellar grades on your transcript, see to it that your transcript shows a rising trend in your GPA. This shows that you've developing maturity and discipline, and will put your academic performance in a considerably better light.

Also important is your GPA in your major area, especially if your major area directly prepares you for graduate study (psychology, biology, English). It's one thing to have a few low grades early on, or in required courses outside your major area. But if you can't

Undecided?

If you're not quite sure what you want to do, can you submit applications to different programs at the same school? That depends on the school. Some schools forbid applying to more than one degree program within the school. Others allow you to designate an alternative program in case you are not accepted at your first choice. Other schools simply allow you to apply to as many of their programs as you like.

earn a high GPA in your major area, which is presumably where your interests and strengths lie, admissions committees will likely question your suitability for graduate study.

Covering the Necessary Coursework

Getting the numbers isn't the only important aspect of your coursework. You must also tailor your course selection—including but not limited to the coursework for your major—to provide the background required by the programs that interest you. Many graduate programs itemize majors and courses that they consider appropriate preparation for graduate study in that field. Find out what those courses are and take them. Be forewarned, though, that loading up on easy (100-level) courses isn't the way to cover these subjects. Admissions committees will note whether your As came from easy, nonmajor courses or whether you earned them in upper-level courses relevant to your undergraduate major and/or your graduate field. Writing a senior thesis and taking upper-level independent study counts for points to most admissions officers.

Getting the Recommendations

Graduate programs will require three letters of recommendation, possibly more. These letters are supposed to vouch for your ability to study at the graduate level. Professors in your major area are ideal recommenders, because they can speak about your talents and expertise in the areas that apply most directly to graduate school. In fact, a number of programs specify that at least some of the recommendations come from your professors. So if you've been spending your time at the back of the lecture hall doodling in your notebook margins and watching the clock, consider moving up to the front of the room and making some eye contact, or even participating in the discussion. The more the professor knows about you and your work, the more specific her or his letter will be, and the more seriously the admissions committee will take it.

Choosing Recommenders

Whom you ask to write your recommendations can impact how you as an applicant are perceived. Your best choice for recommenders are academics and employers:

- Undergraduate professors

- Other professors

- Professionals who have supervised you, particularly in volunteer/paid work related to your graduate field

- Employers

Though professors are your best bet, there are other people whose standing is less impressive but who can attest to your suitability for graduate school. These include:

- Your TA

- Colleagues

- Graduate students in your proposed field, or even in the program you're applying to

Getting the Best Recommendation

Most recommendation forms begin with a section asking whether you are willing to waive your right to see these recommendations, on the principle that your recommenders will write much more honestly about you if they know that you are not going to read the letter. It is wise to waive this right; it tells the schools that you are confident of your recommendations—and that inspires confidence in them. Your recommenders will either mail their letters directly to the schools or give them to you in sealed envelopes.

If you don't see the recommendations, how can you know they're good? By choosing your recommenders wisely in the first place. If you choose people who know you well and are enthusiastic about recommending you, the letters will be good.

No Name Dropping

A few years ago, a member of an admissions committee received a letter of recommendation from a prominent television personality. The letter said, "To the Admissions Committee: Mr. McKay asked me to write a letter of recommendation for his son, Dylan. I told him I would do so. I know Mr. McKay and he is a fine man. I have never met his son. Here is the letter. Sincerely . . . ." It was clear that the writer was uncomfortable with this assignment, and rather than create a lot of meaningless copy about a person he did not know, he did as he said he would and wrote the letter, but let the committee know that his offering was not to be taken seriously.

The Envelope, Please

Most programs that ask you to include your recommendations with your application also ask that you guarantee the security of your letters by having the recommender sign his or her name across the sealed flap of the envelope.

To draw up a preliminary list of recommenders, keep the following tips in mind.

Pay attention to the program's guidelines for number and type of recommendations.

Some programs specify the exact number of recommendations and the ideal recommenders (for example, undergraduate professors). As you make final choices from your preliminary list, keep any requirements or recommendations in mind. If there is no way that you can meet the requirements or recommendations, contact the admissions office and ask for suggestions on how to handle the matter.

Certainly submit no fewer than the minimum number; if you want to submit more, one or two above the minimum is sufficient. The admissions committee has plenty to read without having six or seven recommendation letters in your file. In fact, it's a good idea to speak to the admissions office before you deviate from the application guidelines. There's no point in annoying the admissions committee if extra recommendations are not welcome.

Choose recommenders who know you well.

Yes, it's good if your recommenders are famous or well known in your field—if they know you well enough to say something meaningful. Truly impressive recommendations come from someone who clearly knows you personally, has seen you do good work, and can compare you (favorably) to other graduate program applicants. The senator for whom you were a summer campaign gofer, or Professor so-and-so, who is an authority in your field but has only briefly glanced at your term paper, are simply not impressive to the admissions committee. After an application season that involves reading three letters each from three hundred program applicants, they certainly can tell the difference between someone who knows you and someone who doesn't. Your list should contain only those who know you well enough to comment in detail on your potential as a graduate student. Of course it's great if a distinguished professor fits this description; by all means, ask for a recommendation. But if it's an either-or situation, go with the person who knows your work.

Consider the recommender's attitudes.

This is really two issues. First, don't even think about asking someone who dislikes you for a recommendation. Professors have been known to write devastatingly negative letters about students they dislike, and a bad letter can definitely keep you out of the program of your choice. Don't be afraid to ask if he or she feels they can write a favorable letter. Second, consider whether the professor is likely to write the letter. Most professors are used to these requests and will be honest with you about whether they have the time. Others will say yes and then fail to write the letter. If a professor strikes you as unpredictable, she or he is probably not a good bet.

Consider the recommender's writing style.

Admissions committees love stories and quotable sound bites, so avoid asking a very terse stylist for a recommendation. Looking at the comments a professor has written on one of your papers can give a clue as to his or her style.

Consider the recommender's qualifications.

Someone who is familiar with your chosen field will produce a more credible letter than someone who doesn't really understand what you plan to do.

Asking for Letters

Once you have a preliminary list and your applications in hand, compare applications to list and draw up a final short list of recommenders. Have a backup or two in mind in case one of your first choices says no, or in case disaster strikes at the last minute.

Ask nicely, and be willing to take no for an answer. If you're asking professors, they are almost certainly familiar with the recommendation-letters process; if you're asking an employer, for instance, you may have to give a little more background. How long is the letter? What issues should it discuss? How many programs are you applying to, and will there have to be variations on the letter for different programs? Let the person know that you think highly of his or her opinion and you'd be happy and honored if the person would consider writing you a letter of recommendation. Also let your recommender know how much work is involved and what you will provide to make the job easier. Remember that your recommenders are doing you a favor, and no matter how much they like you, it's extra work for them. Assure them that you will make the process as painless as possible—and then be sure to do just that.

If someone says no, no matter how much you wanted that person as a recommender, accept the no and look elsewhere. "No" may indicate that this person does not consider you "graduate school material" and could not honestly write a positive recommendation. Or it may simply mean that the person doesn't want to take the trouble to write the letter. It's tempting to rationalize that if you can just persuade this person to write the letter, all will be well. It usually isn't. The result can be a downright negative letter, or it can be a sloppy, last-minute job, or it can be no letter at all, leaving you stranded days before your application deadline. The last two will hurt your admissions chances just as much as the first. You and your application are much better off without the risk.

Making It Easier

Make an appointment to get reacquainted with your recommender. Bring copies of your transcript, your résumé, personal statement, and any other "leave-behinds" that may help your recommender write the letter of your dreams.

Helping Your Recommenders

Once your recommenders have agreed to help you out, here's what you can do to help them out.

Schedule an appointment.

Two months before the application is due, arrange an appointment to discuss your background and your future goals. This is particularly important if your recommenders haven't seen you and your work for a while, if they are unfamiliar with the recommendation process, or if they are unfamiliar with the programs you plan to enter. It's also something that not many people think to do. Most recommenders will be willing to schedule an appointment with you; they'll be happy to have the opportunity to get some more information about you.

You should bring with you copies of appropriate documentation, such as your transcript, papers you've written, your résumé or curriculum vitae, your personal statement, and/or a sheet of bullet points that you plan to feature in your application and essay. These "leave-behinds" will go a long way toward making sure that your recommenders say relevant things about your good points and your background. Give your writers a good idea of why you want to go to graduate school and your reasons for interest in particular programs. Play up your good points, of course, but be reasonably humble. If you have a specific image that you are trying to stress in other parts of the application, let your writers in on it because they may want to focus on some of the points you're trying to stress. It's often a good idea to explain to recommendation writers why you chose them, because it will give them an idea of the perspective from which you would like them to write.

Keep your appointment relatively brief; you're already taking up enough of the person's time. If you discuss your personal statement with the recommender, stick to the main points and don't expect to get a style or grammar review. The purpose of your appointment is to give your recommenders appropriate material about which to write. Above all, don't tell your recommenders what to write. Don't even give them the impression that you are doing so! Recommenders tend to resent attempts at manipulation, and the consequence may be a refusal to write your letter after all.

Gather any forms required by the program.

Some programs insist that the letter be written on the actual form, while others will accept a letter on school or company letterhead—which usually has to be attached to the form anyway. And be sure that you sign the forms before you turn them over, since you will not see them again once the letter of recommendation is finished.

Supply stamped, addressed envelopes.

Some recommendations may be mailed directly from the recommender to the school; others are to be submitted, in a sealed envelope, along with the rest of your application. Whether the letters are to be sent directly to the school or to you, be sure to provide your recommenders all envelopes necessary.

Give clear instructions.

Don't expect the recommender to sort it all out. Indicate in writing or on a chart exactly what the requirements are for each letter in each program. Some forms ask recommenders to rate your strengths and weaknesses on a chart, or fill out a questionnaire, as well as write an original evaluation of you. Be sure to point out any such forms. Note any requirements such as, "Attached letter must be submitted on organizational letterhead with your signature and title." Above all, list due dates, especially if they are very different.

Provide your phone number and address.

Let the recommender know that you're available at her convenience to answer any questions that might make her task easier.

Follow up your request.

Realistically, no matter how far in advance you submit your materials, most recommenders won't get around to writing your letters right away. Many procrastinate until the deadline is about a week away, and appreciate when the applicant reminds them of the upcoming deadline to avoid jeopardizing the application.

So a few weeks before the deadline, call to ask whether the recommender has any further questions. If she is already working on your letters, she may indeed have questions that you can answer. If the recommender hasn't gotten started yet, this is a gentle and politic way to light a fire under her. It also can be an early-warning signal to you. If a recommender seems to be stalling, you might start working out a backup plan. Just in case.

A week before the deadline, call both your programs and your recommenders. Check with your programs to see whether your letters have arrived. If they have not, get on the phone again and check with the recommenders. If there seems to be a problem—and sometimes there is—you will still have a few days to pull off your backup plan.

Finally, when you get your acceptance letters and choose a program, send your recommenders a thank-you note with the happy news. Writing recommendations is tedious, and purely a favor to

> ## A Gentle Reminder
>
> Call your recommenders a few weeks before the deadline to ask if they have any questions you can answer. It's a gentle way of reminding them that the deadline's approaching.

you; most recommenders feel rewarded to learn that they've contributed to your success by writing the letters.

Taking the GRE

Test Preparation

A first-rate test-prep program can boost your GRE score significantly. Nearly all students can benefit from preparation. Before you ponder how you can best prepare for the GRE, take the following steps.

Know the GRE requirements of the programs that interest you.

Be aware of the score requirement language used by program catalogs or other guides to graduate programs. Be particularly careful with "minimum" score language. This usually indicates that the listed score is the lowest the program will consider, and that most applicants who are accepted have significantly higher scores. Ask the admissions office or current students about the GRE scores of those accepted to the program. You may have to shoot for a higher number than the one listed in the catalog.

Also find out whether any of the three scores is emphasized or minimized by the programs. It always looks good on your application to have three high scores, but in the real world study time and money is limited, and if you have to prioritize your preparation, focus on the scores that count most for admission. Also see chapters 2–10 for some general guidelines on score emphasis in the specific programs we featured.

Take a diagnostic test.

ETS sells "used" exams as practice material, and they come with score conversion charts that allow you to compute a score. You can also get free diagnostic tests from test-prep companies like Kaplan. Take advantage—take a practice test under timed conditions and compute your score. That way, you can see how you stack up against your program requirements.

Don't use an actual GRE administration for diagnostic purposes. First, test administrations are expensive, and the above alternatives are a much cheaper way to evaluate where you stand. Second, you can't get GRE scores "just to see." If you take the GRE and let the score stand, it becomes part of your permanent record, reported every time you submit score reports to schools for the next five years. If you take the test and cancel the score, the record is clean—but you don't get to see the score either, thus defeating the whole purpose of your test run.

Investigate test-prep alternatives.

At a minimum, read through the informational material, practice questions, and explanations provided free by ETS. Be sure you understand the timing, directions, and purpose of each test section, and how the "raw score" is computed.

If you feel that you need more comprehensive prep, there are books, review courses, and computer software that not only give you practice questions but review the math and vocabulary tested in the Verbal and Quantitative sections. Particularly for non-traditional applicants, review can make the difference between mediocre scores and scores that are well above the minimum program standards. The key is taking some sort of diagnostic GRE test to find out which areas of your GRE score need work.

Subject Tests

Unlike the General Test, which is meant to assess skills that you have developed over a long period of time and (except for some high school math) are not related to a particular subject area, Subject Tests assess your familiarity with a particular field of knowledge. They enable admissions officers to compare you with applicants from different undergraduate programs, and to determine whether you have the foundational knowledge you'll need to work in your field at the graduate level.

Except for the Revised Music Test, Subject Tests consist exclusively of multiple-choice questions that are designed to assess your knowledge of a subject as it's covered in the typical undergraduate curriculum. Some of them also contain subtests, groups of questions within the questions. Subtest scores are reported along with the overall score.

GRE Subject Tests

Biochemistry, Cell, and Molecular Biology

Biology

Chemistry

Computer Science

Economics

Revised Education

Engineering

Geology

History

Literature in English

Mathematics

Revised Music

Physics

Political Science

Psychology

Sociology

When to Take the Tests

Standardized test scores generally arrive at schools about six weeks after the test date. To be on the safe side, then, you'll want to take the GRE at least two months before your earliest deadline. Take it even earlier, if you can. The June test is ideal, because it allows you a little slack; in case you want or need to retake the test, you can do so in October and still meet most financial aid deadlines easily.

On most test dates, the General Test is administered in the morning and the Subject Tests in the afternoon. Although you can register to take the General and Subject Tests on the same day, we don't recommend it. By afternoon you'll probably find your energy and concentration waning, which could easily result in a lower score on the Subject Test.

The Application Process

Some Dos *and* Don'ts

Following these tips will help keep you organized throughout the application process, and will guide you towards presenting yourself in the most favorable way.

DO photocopy all applications.

These forms are not always well designed; when you try to type in the requested information, you may discover that there isn't enough room, or that the information will fit only if bizarrely configured. Find this out on a photocopy and spare yourself the trouble of having to get a new application.

DO have a good filing system—and use it.

File everything pertaining to a program, and keep notes on phone calls, interviews with faculty and students, research, and other sources of information. You will be gathering a lot of information, possibly on many programs; don't expect to keep track of it all in a big pile on your desk.

DO call the school if there is a question or problem you can't answer.

But remember to read the catalog first so that you do not waste someone's time. Identify yourself when you call; it's good for the administrative staff to know who you are. If they recognize your name, the components of your application are likely to get more attention and be filed more carefully—unless, that is, you have been rude or demanding. Then you may find that your transcript has mysteriously disappeared!

DO follow all rules.

Demonstrate that you have the discipline for graduate work by observing such requirements as the page limit on your Statement of Purpose, any guidelines for letters of recommendation, and, of course, deadlines.

DO have your final-draft application proofread by someone with a good eye for detail.

Admissions officers in every type of graduate program say that most application mistakes are procedural—that is, rules ignored or overlooked, messy corrections, illegible handwriting, misspellings, and outrageously ungrammatical sentences. Just about every admissions officer has seen a personal statement that ends with a passionate explanation of why the writer wants to attend a particular program—only it's been sent to the wrong school! Errors like these simply give the committee an excuse to reject you.

DO use a word processor for your statement; beware of using one to fill out the application proper.

A word processor is invaluable for the statement; it's easy to make changes, so you're more likely to do the editing you need. If you can use a laser printer, the statement looks more attractive. To understand why this is an issue, put yourself in the place of the committee members who will read several hundred essays each application season. Do not annoy them by making your essay hard to read or unpleasant to look at. Colored ink or illegible handwriting won't be welcomed.

On the other hand, unless you're very good at feeding application-type forms into printers, and aligning and fiddling and so on, it's better to use a typewriter than a word processor to fill out the application form. Even if you manage to line everything up properly, the printer can shred or mangle the edges of the form, giving it a beat-up look that suggests you carried it around in your backpack for several weeks before mailing it. Needless to say, a fresh, crisp application makes a better impression.

DO put your name and Social Security number on any additional pages, including your essay.

If they are accidentally separated from the rest of the application, they will be easier to return to your folder.

DO keep a photocopy of the final application.

They do get lost, and if you discover days before the deadline that yours has not arrived, you can quickly replace it using your photocopy. We know of one student who wrote the required twelve essays for his Harvard application, mailed off the whole package, and found out one week before deadline that it had never arrived. Because he had kept photocopies of everything, he was able to replace the application in time, and then sit down and have a good laugh about it afterwards. (He was accepted.)

DO call several days to one week prior to deadline to be sure that your application is complete.

(This, of course, presupposes that you have not waited until the last minute to submit your application.) It's particularly important to know whether there is a problem with your letters of recommendation or your transcript, since you can't directly provide either one, and in case of an emergency you will need a few days to contact a new recommender or have your undergraduate school mail another transcript.

DO be very professional in all aspects of your application.

Read all catalogs, be courteous when you contact the school, keep your application form flawless, and submit all pieces well before the deadline.

CHAPTER 15

The Personal Statement

What's the purpose of the personal statement?

There are two, really: to show the admissions committee how you think, and to show them how you write. If you can write cleanly and grammatically, explain your thoughts logically, and—above all—portray yourself as an individual who will be an interesting asset to the program, you will have created a successful personal statement.

The personal statement (it goes by other names as well: Statement of Purpose, Candidate's Admission Statement, and so on) is included on the application precisely to let you speak for yourself. Others have already spoken for you—the professors who assigned your undergraduate grades, your recommenders—and your GRE score is a number only, not to be used as the sole criterion for granting or denying admission. The personal statement is where you can explain why you're applying to graduate school, what interests you about this program, and what your future goals are. It terrifies most applicants, yet it is the part of the application over which the applicant has the most control.

It can also make or break your application. While nothing will make up for serious academic or testing deficiencies, and a bad recommendation will almost certainly result in rejection, there are other times when a terrific statement can tip the balance in your favor. For example, most applicants have at least one weak spot in their applications, either the undergraduate GPA or the GRE scores. Admissions committees have been known to over-

> ### *Personal Best*
>
> The personal statement is your chance to speak for yourself. It can help committees see those intangible qualities that make you a strong candidate.

Toot Your Horn

Don't be afraid to state directly why you consider a program to be right for you. Back it up with evidence.

look the weak spot because the applicant presents herself so compellingly in her personal statement, with such a clear sense of how she fits into her chosen field and how her chosen field fits into her life, that they want her in the program. The same can be true in the final stages of the committee's deliberations, when the decision between one qualified applicant and another may be made on the basis of the "intangible" qualities that come across in the personal statement. Even if you have the best qualifications and the highest numbers, do not neglect your personal statement.

What Committees Ask

Some personal statement topics are open-ended, worded something like this: "Tell us anything about yourself that you think we need to know." This sort of thing drives many graduate applicants crazy, because it doesn't say very much about "what the committee wants to hear"!

Whether the topic is specific or open, there are two main goals of the personal statement: to create a portrait that is persuasive, and to create a portrait that is personal. You want the readers to put your essay down and think, Wow! that was really interesting and memorable, and, Wow! this person really knows why she's going into this program and has real contributions to make to the field.

Real Schools: Statement Topics

Here are some recent personal-statement topics we found in graduate school catalogs:

Brown University

"Please give your reasons for deciding to do graduate work in the field you have chosen. Include a statement concerning your past work (study and research) in your chosen field, your plans for study at Brown, including issues and problems you want to address, and your professional goals."

Bank Street College of Education

"Select and describe those experiences and relationships in your background which seem to you to have been significant for your development and as a person going into the field of education. What connections can you make between those experiences and your ideas about children and youth, parents, your own dominant patterns of actions, your plans for graduate study, and your future career? You may include more recent experiences which you consider especially significant for the development of new insights into yourself."

The American Film Institute

"Submit a narrative letter (original and two copies, typed and double-spaced, 5-page maximum) which details your background and philosophy. Please describe your desires and goals and explain your motivation to enter the program at the Center for Advanced Film and Television Studies. The Center encourages you to explain your individual abilities, capacities, and uniqueness."

Carnegie Mellon Engineering

"Type or print a one- or two-page concise statement that includes the following information:

1. A brief statement of your primary educational and research interests

2. An outline of your research experience and a list of any publications

3. A description of your background in engineering and allied fields that is particularly relevant to your objectives—include any relevant industrial or work experience and any academic honors."

How to Make It Good

You can actually start working on your personal statement long before you get your applications. Remember the two goals of the statement: to be persuasive and to be personal.

Make It Persuasive

Persuasive is about two things: how right you are for the program, and how right the program is for you. Your statement should demonstrate the pattern in your life that has led to your decision to apply to this program. This does not mean that you must write a comprehensive biography. In fact, your decision to apply to a graduate program may have come later in life and may have little to do with even your undergraduate major. You will submit a résumé or CV, as well as an academic transcript, and those are the appropriate places for your life story. Your aim in the statement is to focus in on the part of your life, or the one consistent theme in your life, that has led you to apply to this program.

Part of demonstrating why you are right for the program involves demonstrating that you understand what the program is and where it will lead you. There are a lot of ways to do this. Some people directly explain why they consider the particular program at a particular school right for them. Others let this show in less explicit ways: by describing relevant working or volunteer experience, by talking about classes they have already taken, and so on.

> ### Knowin' Where You're Goin'
>
> Part of demonstrating why you're right for the program involves demonstrating that you understand what the program is and where it will lead you.

Sob Stories

Feel free to acknowledge personal challenges you've faced. But focus on facts and on the future. Don't make it a tearjerker.

Either way, the statement should clearly show that your decision to enter this program is not naive or uninformed.

Make It Personal

Personal involves honesty and distinctiveness. Many statements of purpose are dull and tend to evade the real issues. It's not that applicants are intentionally dishonest; it's that fear and embarrassment stifle the personality right out of the essay.

Persuasive and personal aren't mutually exclusive, but in your essay there should be a balance between them, depending on the program you hope to enter. In some programs, such as psychology and the sciences, you will need to focus more on being persuasive, that is, highlighting your clinical experience and theoretical or practical interests. In art and literature, there is probably more room for a bit of creativity: You can get away with an essay that does not focus on your professional qualifications but simply gives the admissions committee a window into your mind. In many social work programs, your personal perspectives, including your childhood experiences and your social and cultural background, are all fair game for the personal statement.

Getting Started

Three or four months before you fill out your application, you should start compiling information. As you work, reflect on the following:

Personal History

Are you heading for graduate school straight from undergraduate school? If so, what has happened during your undergraduate years to make you so certain that you already know what you want to do with your life? Many undergraduates haven't made that decision yet. Part of what makes you unusual, then, may be the circumstances and beliefs that have made you ready for such a decision this early on. Are you a nontraditional student, five, ten, or even twenty years past undergraduate school? Then an interesting part of your story will be what in your adult life has led you to return to school.

Personal Life

You're just gathering raw material, so don't edit your thinking. It's all fair game. Were there any unusual or difficult circumstances in your childhood? in your undergraduate years? Does your ethnic or cultural perspective give you a different take on the world? Did you travel or move frequently? Do you have any famous relatives, especially in your chosen field? Was there an adult in your life who was especially influential? Don't worry yet whether you can tie any of this directly to your career choice. Just get it down on paper.

Academic Life

Particularly if you are going into a doctoral program in preparation for advanced research or professorship, think over who and what has influenced you. Which ideas, fields of research, or problems especially intrigue you? Among the professors you have studied with and in the reading you have done, who has influenced you the most? Why?

Work Life

This includes jobs, volunteer work, extracurricular activities, and so on. "Real-world" work experience is often the major influence behind a nontraditional student's decision to go on to graduate school. Some people discover that without graduate training there are limitations on professional growth and development. The "moment of truth" in this type of situation can make a very compelling statement. Some people discover that they loathe their work and through personal interests, volunteer work, or something outside of work, discover a new field. The story of this evolution is another fertile area for statements.

Another slant on the work/activities theme is demonstrating familiarity with, and competence in, the field you want to enter. Going at the statement from this angle can be important for traditional students, because an admissions committee can think, "What does she know about this field at the age of 21?" It can also be important for nontraditional students who are switching fields. It shows that the decision is informed, and that you've already showed some aptitude for the work.

Real Students: Between Degrees

We spoke with many nontraditional students who took time to pursue other interests between their undergraduate and graduate programs. Here are some of their stories:

History undergrad, education and history grad

Worked as a chef, writer, and editor for sixteen years

Undergrad/grad in history

Worked in advertising agency, as editor of encyclopedias, as a mother for eight years

> ### *Busy, Busy*
>
> While you may want to impress schools with your broad range of interests and activities, stick to listing only those pertaining to your field of study. Don't appear too scattered—try to focus!

Undergrad/master's in Spanish/comparative literature, Ph.D., comparative lit

Worked as interpreter/translator, tutor, poet for two years

Undergrad in Spanish, New Testament grad

Worked as teacher, education writer, mother for eleven years

Undergrad in English and history, Ph.D. in American studies

Worked in a bank for eight months—"I realized from this experience that I absolutely could not work in the corporate world even though they were begging me to stay."

Undergrad in electrical engineering, grad in bioengineering

Designed military electronics for three years—"After three years in the defense sector as an engineer, I became very disenchanted with the idea of applying my talents to designing military electronics and was bored with the day-in, day-out routine of a bachelor's-level engineer."

Writing a Draft

After doing your preliminary "research," pick your story and write a personal statement draft. Don't try to edit at this point; just write. Don't pay strict attention to length guidelines, either. If you end up rambling on for 15 pages, you are probably trying to do too much and will have to cut down later, but it's better at this point to have too much to say than too little. Your goal is to get everything down on paper.

Next, put your draft away for at least two weeks. Don't even look at it. Time lends an interesting perspective to these essays; you may look at yours and decide you're off to a good start, or you may hate it. If you need to, repeat the write-and-put-away process.

At this point, it's more constructive to focus on what the essay shouldn't be than what it should be. You're trying to get on the right track, so it's time for broad changes, getting rid of what doesn't work and focusing on what does. Here are some essay approaches that usually don't work out.

Funny

Very few people can do funny. A joke or a wry remark is fine, but for the most part play it straight.

Maudlin

Admissions committees are rather conservative about reading extensive discussions of personal problems, particularly if the problems are ongoing. It's fine, and even advisable, to acknowledge the role personal difficulties have played in your decisions about graduate school. For example, illness or financial difficulty may have delayed your plans or affected your undergraduate grades; personal problems may have influenced your career choices. But keep the emotion to a minimum, and focus on the facts and the future. And don't ask for special consideration.

Iconoclastic

If you're applying to art programs, you'll probably be able to get away with some creativity on your application. If not, stick to the rules. There is a persistent rumor that unusual, even outrageous, responses to the personal statement will get the admissions committee's attention. They will, but it's almost always negative attention.

Exhaustive life history

Don't try to be comprehensive or strictly chronological. For example, "I first realized I wanted to go into forestry when I was four years old and my grandfather helped me plant a tree. As I grew, so did my interest in trees and forests. When I was in high school, I planted many trees. In college, my interest was reinforced by my botany teacher." You don't have to prove that you were born to your field of interest. In fact, your story may be more intriguing if it shows how you were not born to a field but came to it through your life experiences. Try to avoid beginning the essay with: "As a child, I . . ." or "Such-and-such has always been my passion . . . ."

The résumé

Since you are free to attach a résumé or CV to nearly all graduate school applications, there's no need to waste your essay space by recounting your work history. If your statement is about how your work experiences have led you to apply to graduate school, keep the focus on the why and the how, not on the what of your work and your job history. If there are awards, honors, or special achievements you would like the admissions committee to notice, point them out briefly, or mention them in a separate attachment.

Next Steps

When you are satisfied that you are on the right track, do some editing. Get your draft down to, or near, the right length. Then get some feedback from a couple of people who know you well. Is the essay coherent? Does it reflect your story as they understand it? Most of all, does the essay make them say, "Yeah, that's you, all right"?

At this point you should begin to look at the essay more closely. Now it's time to focus on what the essay is.

Stress unique material.

Use the essay to talk about something that doesn't come up anywhere else on your application. You want to give the admissions committee something new to think about, something that can't be gathered from your transcript or CV.

Concentrate on one theme.

"What led me to apply to this program," "The kind of practice I want to go into," "The person who has most influenced my thinking," and so on.

Show, don't tell.

Instead of saying, "I am extremely well organized," show it by explaining that you held down a demanding job at the same time you were a full-time student earning top grades. The admissions committee has no reason to believe any general, unsubstantiated statement you make about yourself unless you back it up with facts and evidence. That's what makes an essay persuasive.

Tell why, not what.

Keep description to a minimum. Use your essay space instead to explain why an event was significant to you and what you learned from it. Provide enough background so that your reader can follow what's happening, but no more. This is especially important when you are talking about your job or other professional accomplishments. Many essays spend too much time listing accomplishments and events, or recounting the "plot" of a significant episode, and not enough time describing the influence these events had on the writer's decision to attend graduate school.

Have someone whose opinion and writing skills you trust read your final draft, make suggestions, and above all, help you proofread.

Extracurricular activities

When you were applying to college, you probably either listed a lot of extracurricular activities (if you had them) or worried about that awful blank space on the application (if you didn't). Should you be concerned about this on your graduate application? First, you'll notice that graduate applications generally do not ask for extracurricular activities as such. They will ask instead for awards, papers, publications, professional association memberships, and employment or volunteer work directly related to your field. Generally speaking, all that interests the admissions committee is the depth of your involvement in your field. Play up these activities on your application; don't load up on unrelated information. At best it will be considered irrelevant, and at worst, in some departments it may make you look scattered, unfocused, and not sufficiently dedicated to your proposed future career.

The Most Common Mistakes Applicants Make When Writing a Personal Statement

We've asked admissions officers from New York University and George Washington University to identify the five most common mistakes they've seen in applicants' personal statements. Here is what they
report:

Admissions Official #1

1. Sloppiness

Avoid spelling, punctuation, formatting, and grammatical errors by carefully proofreading your work.
Leave adequate time to edit your writing.

2. Writing one general statement for all schools

Learn about each school's curriculum, the research areas of the faculty, and facilities. Be specific as to
why each particular school interests you and how you will contribute to the program. Clearly state your
reasons for pursuing graduate study there. Read each school's application instructions and be sure to follow the guidelines for their essays.

3. Boring content

Have a positive tone, vary the length and structure of your sentences, and use precise language. Avoid
numerical lists, clichés, and chronological histories.

4. Sounding like everyone else

In your preliminary self-assessment, identify your strengths and decide what sets you apart from other
applicants. Communicate that uniqueness in your personal statement. What motivates you? What are
your aspirations? What academic challenges most excite you? What are your plans for the future?

5. Being shy

Write with confidence about your intellectual development. What events or ideas most influenced you?
How have you changed intellectually as a result? What key decisions have you made, and why?

Admissions Official #2

1. Writing what you think someone wants to read

Don't do this if what you write doesn't truly reflect who you are. Enrolling in a program that isn't truly suited for you will only make you uncomfortable later and decrease your chances of success. It will also inhibit the establishment of valuable connections for the future.

2. Dwelling on crises

When explaining a personal crisis, there is a fine line between too much and too little. The explanation of crises and misfortune are essential if they affected personal and academic development and perspective. A superficial mention that doesn't provide the reader with insight is useless, and too much disaster and destruction also reflects negatively. For example, I once read an essay that described how the death of a roommate affected the student's ability to concentrate. The circumstances were horrific and they were described in bloody detail. There are better ways to accomplish the same purpose.

3. Failing to check spelling and grammar carefully

It should go without saying, but many people just don't do it.

4. Appearing unrealistic

When discussing goals and plans, make sure that they and the related timetables are feasible. You don't have to know it all, but naiveté is not a valued commodity at the graduate level.

5. Spinning irrelevant yarns

Make absolutely certain that whatever you decide to reveal about yourself or your life addresses the question asked.

Sample Essays

The following pages contain actual statements written by applicants to graduate schools. The applicants' names and the schools to which they applied have been masked, but the words are genuine. Each essay is followed by personalized critiques from the two admissions officials cited on the previous pages.

Essay A

"Maybe sisterhood does still exist," my professor said as she pulled me aside between classes. She was referring to a conversation we had the previous afternoon about various issues affecting our campus. I believe that these types of conversations between students, faculty, and staff are one of the many benefits I derived from my experiences at a small college. Such contact between profes-

sors and other students helped to broaden my youthful view of the world and also served to spark my interest in pursuing women's studies, both personally and academically. In a field such as women's studies, where scholarship and personal experience often merge, I believe that women professors can serve as valuable role models for young students. In my own life, I credit the mentoring I received from my professors with instilling in me the desire to pursue further study in women's history and an eventual career of teaching at the university level.

While an undergraduate, I was fortunate to have the opportunity to work with women's historians and build a strong background in both U.S. women's history and women's studies courses. During my senior year, I continued my concentration in women's studies with the writing of my senior thesis on the activities of women volunteers during World War II, a portion of which I have included as my writing sample. In conducting research at the archives of the Minnesota Historical Society, I attempted to assess the impact of the World War II era on women's lives. Traditionally, historians have pointed to increased work force participation and the glorification of working women in government propaganda to argue that World War II marked a shift in gender roles, a shift that would set the stage for the emergence of the modern women's movement two decades later. However, while women did assume male roles during the war years, labor statistics and public images of employed women failed to reveal how these women perceived their changing position in society. In order to evaluate these statistical changes, I believed it necessary to employ sources created by the women, such as pamphlets, minutes, and letters. I felt that by limiting the focus of my research group to a select group of middle-to-upper class women in Minnesota, I would be able to develop a clearer picture of their lives during World War II, while also drawing conclusions that speak to the larger historical debate about continuity versus change in the World War II experience.

My research revealed that although Minnesota women entered the public sphere to make a contribution to the war effort, their activities did not function to fundamentally challenge traditional gender roles. Just as Rosie the Riveter worked in the factories while the male workers served in the armed forces, women achieved their wartime contributions within the context of a national emergency which allowed them to expand into the public sphere only "for the duration." Although, statistically speaking, millions of women assumed previously male roles, their private beliefs were not changing to match these public activities. A close examination of the rhetoric employed by Minnesota women's organizations reveals that they placed great value on continuing their roles as wives and mothers. In fact, women who sold war bonds tended to limit social change because they emphasized their femininity as they assumed male responsibility. In emphasizing these traditional roles, the women did not challenge ideas about gender; rather, they reinforced them. In the same manner that Rosie the Riveter remained glamorous beneath her overalls, Minnesota women remained feminine behind their war bond sales booths.

My academic interest in women's studies increased my awareness of political concerns facing women and prompted me to become active outside of the classroom. As the enclosed curriculum vita indicates, I was involved in the women's community both as a leader in campus organizations and as a counselor for survivors of sexual harassment and assault. I spent a large portion of my senior year acting as co-chair of the committee which arranged transportation to the National March for Women's Lives in Washington D.C. Individually, my main responsibility was to monitor *the $8,000 budget, costs, and the payments made by each person. Although this experience was often stressful and hectic, it was also well worth the effort. Working collectively with a group of people was a rewarding experience that taught me the importance of keeping careful records and group cooperation. I devoted considerable time to activities of this type because I believe that it is important to be active outside of the classroom and to make a contribution to my community.*

The graduate program in women's history at Cornell University will provide me with an opportunity to participate in a community in which I can develop both as a scholar and as a future university professor. Related to my work on women during World War II, I intend to continue my research in women's history by examining the connection of women's organizing to consciousness. I am interested in investigating groups of women who volunteered in organizations to discover how they perceived themselves and their roles in society. Another area in which I intend to research while at Cornell is the process of change over time with regard to women's organizations and gender roles.

Critiques of Essay A

Admissions Official #1

This applicant does an excellent job at creating a strong first impression by immediately setting a tone and providing a sense of self. She draws the reader in by using a true story to show how she has developed intellectually, and imparts an excitement for education and a strong sense of purpose about her future plans.

Using a narrative to describe how her interest in women's studies evolved over time, the applicant demonstrates confidence in her subject. She interrelates a description of her research with a sense of how she analytically approached the research problem and expands the concept to show how her education changed her personally and affected decisions she has made.

She also shows another side of herself by linking her academic interests to her extracurricular activities. Multiple interests show a confidence and enthusiasm for learning and an ability to succeed in different situations.

It's clear that this applicant knows her goals: She clearly articulates her specific research interests and professional plans. But she leaves her options open by describing several related areas of interest, making it likely that several faculty will be excited to work with her. Her concluding paragraph ties her essay together and leaves a strong impression of what she hopes to achieve with her education.

This is a clear and concise statement. The writing is crisp—events are described concretely and in precise language without clichés. Not only does it hold the reader's interest, but it also makes the reader want to meet her and engage her in an intellectual debate.

Admissions Official #2

This author accomplished a lot, successfully weaving in facts and information while keeping a conversational tone. The words, the construction, and design didn't tell me a story; they invited me in as a conversational partner. In the process, she provided insights into her value system, field, and skill sets. She values interchange and inquiry. She demonstrates that history is alive and conveys the special spirit of women's studies. I know what she wants to do and why. She integrates the essay with other parts of her application, i.e., writing sample and curriculum vitae. This enables her to reinforce ideas and demonstrate organizational skills and an ability to create a total package. The way she addresses the chosen issues invites me to share her enthusiasm. Her discussion of nonacademic activities demonstrated management skills, a commitment to the world at large, and a sense of responsibility as a member of a community. Women's studies isn't an isolated topic for her; it sheds light on how she lives her life. I can sense energy and commitment.

The author certainly didn't play it safe. Integrating research rationale and findings into a personal essay is difficult, but in this case it was appropriate. She did it reasonably well and I learned something in the process: How a specific set of women's roles during that period link with history. I also noticed that she knows how to narrow a subject, integrate it, and then to apply her findings to a bigger picture. These are important skills.

Each applicant has a different personality and a unique set of skills. An honestly written essay like this allows me to envision how she would fit in, and what roles she would play. I can envision the type of faculty member she can become. If these were things that my institution valued, and if her academic record and recommendations were satisfactory, I would recommend strongly that she be admitted.

Essay B

I was born in Seoul, Korea on September 16, 1972. I am the oldest son, having three sisters. My father is 52 years old and is an auditor for Sam-Won Environment Company. My mother, 51, is a housewife. In my childhood, I was brought up with the utmost care and affection by my parents.

When I took the entrance exam for the university, a very severe problem in the environment, specially river and air pollution, was occurring in my country. At this time, I really wanted to help solve the problem, so I chose to study Environmental Science at Yonsei University.

Majoring in Environmental Science for 4 years at undergraduate school, I worked very hard to have a comprehensive understanding of the fundamentals of environmental studies. I received two prizes for high academic achievement and two scholarships in my sophomore year. I also joined the military immediately after completion of three semesters and served in the Air Force for 18 months. I learned self-control, cooperation, and patience from being in the military. After completion of military service and before I came back to school to continue my studies, I traveled to several countries including the United States. From this travel, I gained a strong motivation to study in America because I feel this country's research is highly developed in my field of study and can offer unlimited possibilities to achieve my goal.

I am especially interested in the areas of ground water pollution and solid waste pollution. There are two reasons for this. The first reason is that in Korea, the lake and ground water was polluted by industrialization, and no one can drink any water in the lakes or wells. Until 20 years ago, our country was famous around the world for clean water, but now we must buy spring water for drinking. Second, our country is very small but heavily populated. All the people produce much waste. Because of this fact, it is hard for us to find the method to eliminate wastes. That is to say, we don't have space to dump them or the techniques to solve the problem. These two reasons stimulated me to study, and I really want to know more about these areas. This is the reason why I am applying to your school.

The ultimate goal in my study is to obtain a Master's degree and Doctorate in Environmental Engineering. To achieve that, I would like to undertake my graduate study in your university for three reasons. First of all, Environmental Engineering and its applications are underdeveloped in Korea. But the United States has a tradition of being the best country in this field. Moreover, your school, out of many graduate schools in America, is very famous for and has a good reputation in this area. Secondly, I found the curriculum of your university to be suitable and fascinating for me. Thirdly, if I get admission to your school, I am sure that I can get the best quality of education and opportunity to broaden my knowledge in this field. This is the best way to achieve my dream.

Upon completion of my master's degree in environmental engineering, I would like to pursue doctoral degree immediately. After completing my doctoral degree, I hope to devote myself to research in this field and receive more professional experience.

I am glad to apply for admission to your school and hope my plan will be accomplished. Thank you for your kind consideration.

Critiques of Essay B

Admissions Official #1

One of the most important steps before writing a personal statement is to decide on a central theme. The applicant should begin with a strong introductory statement: What motivates you? What are your goals and aspirations and how will this particular program help you achieve them? This writer begins with a chronological personal history, an approach that should be avoided unless it is a central theme that will be shown to have a unique and significant influence on your educational plans.

The applicant shows how his past experiences contributed to his educational goals, explaining how his interest in environmental science developed from a concern for problems facing his country. Tying his educational plans to his personal experiences helps to individualize him. However, the tone of the writing is distant. The statement would be strengthened by citing specific incidents he observed directly or by describing interesting problems he read about in the literature. Examples of how he hopes to solve such problems in the future should also be provided.

Unfortunately, this applicant does not present a vision of what he will study while in school nor does he state what he hopes to achieve after graduation. His goals should be clearly articulated. Does he hope to teach, conduct research, write, perform? Graduate students are expected to have a strong sense of why they are pursuing advanced studies and what they plan to do with their degree.

When writing a personal statement, it's important to be specific in explaining why a particular program interests you and how you will contribute to the program. This applicant only vaguely states why the curriculum is suitable for him, and never differentiates between study at this university in particular and study at any other school in the United States.

The applicant also tends to repeat his résumé. He should focus on his achievements, research interests, and educational objectives. Personal information such as years of education, prizes, military experience, and travel is better reported in a résumé.

This essay could also have been strangthened by a strong, positive statement. The concluding paragraph should tie your thoughts together and provide a strong impression of what you hope to achieve.

Admissions Official #2

Some of the phrasing is awkward, but this is not a bad essay for an author whose primary language isn't English. Cultural differences may also affect content.

This essay is somewhat reserved and requires me to make inferences that may or may not be accurate. The author lost an opportunity to make a complete and comprehensive case. I would feel more comfortable if there were more explanation and less need for inference. I have facts but I don't know what they mean to him. What did "care and affection" do for him? As the only son, and eldest child, did he feel pressure to succeed, and thus did this affect what he did? A complete personal history is not necessary, but there should be some explanation of how these personal facts affected the author.

The next few paragraphs were more successful . . . with one exception. I learned that the author traveled and from that he jumped to his motivation to study in America. What did travel to the United States do for him? There was a leap but I am missing the connection. It is inappropriate to make a statement unless it can be tied to what you are attempting to state. For example, the author could have stated that travel to access other perspectives and to discover different viewpoints is beneficial. That statement could be the basis of a reason to study abroad, too. While the essay was lacking in that respect, I did learn what motivated the author to choose environmental science and that he feels a need to study and ultimately contribute to his country, improve the quality of life, and make a difference. These facts provided me with insights and enabled me to make clear inferences because there is a rationale and a track record of effort.

The author does provide a quick résumé of achievements and work (academic awards and military commitment) and shares what he learned, and by doing so he identifies the skills and abilities he will bring to a new community. I understand that he is disciplined, works hard, and can be a member of a team. His description of environmental change in Korea has passion and communicated frustration; this was good. It added flavor and personality to this essay. If a class is constructed of more than academic numbers, these are important aspects to consider.

The final sections of the essay raise another set of issues. Some statements are, or could be interpreted as, platitudes. Don't use valuable time and space telling an institution that it is famous and has an excellent reputation. If the institution is renowned in an area, describe the particular achievements that appeal to you and why. Saying that the curriculum is "suitable and fascinating" isn't enough: Why is it suitable and fascinating?

In conclusion, see the statement about research and experience. Don't throw in a tag statement; ensure that each statement makes sense and counts towards something.

Essay C

I apply to the Catholic University of America with the intention of completing my Ph.D. in Philosophy in order to pursue a life of university teaching and scholarship. I am currently a graduate student in the Ph.D. program in philosophy at the University of Miami, Florida (UM). Reflection on my scholarly interests suggests that my goals may be better achieved by coming to study at the Catholic University. I have three reasons for leaving my current program: the lack of resources for work in classics, especially ancient philosophy; the lack of both fellow students and professors who share my interest in ancient philosophy; and consequently the lack of an environment in which for me to write a dissertation on my primary scholarly interest, Aristotle.

My interest in ancient philosophy began only during my last semester as an undergraduate while writing my honors thesis, "Socrates and the later Wittgenstein: A Critical Comparison of Their Respective Philosophical Methods." My thesis argued for the affinity of the later Wittgenstein's philosophy as therapy and Socrates' elenchos, both in contradistinction with and as superior to Platonic essentialism. After writing and thinking about my thesis I became much less interested in Wittgenstein and more interested first in Socrates and then in Plato and Aristotle. I began to see the philosophies of Plato and Aristotle as developments rather than distortions of key Socratic theses and so realized my earlier misunderstandings. By the time my interest had shifted from contemporary to ancient philosophy, I had already applied to and been accepted at UM, a school with no classics department and a department with strongly contemporary interests in logic, epistemology, and philosophy of science. While I have profited much from my time at UM, my continued interest in Aristotle has been a continuing frustration. While many of my professors here are sympathetic to my interests, they recognize that UM suffers from the three inadequacies I just mentioned and support my attempts to study elsewhere.

Should I be accepted into your School of Philosophy, I would have two concurrent goals, the first propaedutic for the second. First, I desire to do intense language work in Greece. While a college freshman I suffered from 'Latin ennui'—I was studying a subject about which I had no interest at the time and so did poorly. I have lived to regret my freshman indifference. By necessity, I since have improved my Latin and have been tutored and have been tutored in Greek. While my skill in both languages is now at a level I can read Aristotle in the original and use reference works like Ast's Lexicon Platonicum, I lack the fluency and exactness required to make scholarly translations.

Second, I desire to do more study of Plato and Aristotle. I have no grand plans for my dissertation. I intend only to defend a careful and modest thesis on Aristotle of relevance to contemporary philosophical debates. While I am still uncertain as to the focal issue for my dissertation, I have particular interest in questions about the relation of the study of the psuche to metaphysics. Aristotle's treatment of questions about the relation between the mind and the objects of knowledge and desire are positions still worth articulating and defending in contemporary philosophical debates about intentionality, consciousness, ethics, and philosophy of action. I have spent much of my time at UM focused on contemporary discussions of these and related issues. I desire now to inquire into the problems associated with these debates in the somewhat different context they occur within the philosophy of Aristotle. As I have been deeply influenced by the Thomistic commentaries on Aristotle, I would welcome the opportunity to study Aquinas as well. Catholic University would an excellent place to pursue these scholarly enquires. Thank you for your consideration of my application. I look forward to your response.

Critiques of Essay C

Admissions Official #1

This applicant does a fair job of describing how his philosophical thinking developed over time through his studies and research. This demonstrates his intellectual development. His arguments would have been stronger if he had more fully contrasted the thinking of the scholars he mentions and detailed the philosophical concepts he found most intriguing. How have their theories challenged him intellectually? Also, greater confidence in his thinking would be demonstrated by avoiding self-deprecating statements.

This negativity carries over into his descriptions of the less-than-satisfactory aspects of his educational experience. The department may assume he will find similar problems with their school, and may be concerned he won't fit comfortably with students and faculty. He would do better by focusing on the positive aspects of his prior experiences and by placing his reasons for change within the context of his personal and intellectual growth and development.

Express clear educational objectives and creative thinking. The applicant does express clear educational objectives and creative thinking in the way he describes the areas of philosophy in which he plans to study. It is okay that he doesn't yet have a topic for the dissertation; one will develop after continued study and thought. However, he is too modest in his research plans—if he can't express excitement about the potential for future research, neither will the admissions committee. Faculty look for motivated students with strong aspirations and creative thoughts.

Perhaps the most important thing the applicant should have done was to proofread his work. Review, review, review! There should be no errors in spelling, formatting, punctuation, and grammar. This statement has several errors, and the faculty will therefore question the applicant's seriousness, attention to detail, and writing ability.

Admissions Official #2

For a student, sharing an interest with an advisor in a chosen topic of study is frequently a key to admission and, once the student is admitted, makes a graduate program more satisfying. This applicant learned that lesson the hard way, and faced the challenge of explaining—in a tactful, positive light—why a change of school would be appropriate and why the "new" program would be a successful fit. In my opinion, the student did so successfully.

It's important to speculate what sort of unasked questions the reviewers might have about your record, and to answer those questions if possible. The questions addressed here were easily anticipated because of the student's situation and the nature of a doctoral program: Why change programs? Where will you fit? Should I trust that you and we are a good match? What will you contribute to the field and community?

The situations expressed in this essay appear to be genuine and understandable: Poor performance due to immaturity; the perennial and ever-refined search for a doable dissertation topic. Even a reviewer who hasn't experienced these things firsthand can empathize.

The conclusion of this essay is especially intriguing because it highlights how the author's previous scholarship pursuits will enable him or her to contribute in a new academic community. That's what a doctoral program is all about: scholarly inquiry, new research, or additional illumination of previous thought.

It is essential that the essay be well-written and not contain careless errors. See the next-to-last paragraph, where there was either repetition of a clause or the omission of some essential word(s).

The applicant indicates that faculty in his or her current Ph.D. program recognize that there are inadequacies in the program. If this is true, the application materials should contain corroborating evidence. Are there letters of recommendation from these faculty that confirm what the applicant states? In this case, the faculty must vouch for the limitations of the current program and why it can't meet the applicant's newly articulated needs. The application materials and credentials should support the essay, not refute it. Honesty is essential.

CHAPTER 16

After You Apply

Should You Interview?

In some programs, an interview with the department is conducted at the applicant's discretion: If you want one, you're welcome to ask. In other programs, only the most promising applicants get invited to interviews; the department issues invitations after a preliminary cut at the applications.

Some programs, especially in the sciences, can afford to pay your transportation to the school for a visit, and others, usually humanities and social science departments, will regretfully tell you that the trip is at your own expense. This is completely a function of how financially secure the department is; don't take it personally.

If a program cannot pay your way for a visit, should you spend the money yourself? Yes. Whatever you can afford, make the visit. Some people on limited budgets wait until the acceptances have come in and then visit only the top contenders, to cut down on the expense. But make every effort to visit at least your top two choices. It's not simply a matter of the department interviewing you, although that will certainly be happening. It's also a matter of you interviewing the department, checking out the location, and getting a sense of the school's "flavor."

First, it's much harder to tell via mail or telephone how you feel about the professors and the other students in a given program. Even if you have gotten good, useful information from them, there is still the question, Do I feel comfortable with these people? Will I fit in well with this group? That's something you may not really know until you're face to face with the group, eating dinner, listening to small talk as well as professional talk. Second, if you're considering an unfamiliar part of the country, you might want to take a look at it before you move. If you're entering a social work, education, or psychology program, for instance, can someone from that program show you where the field sites are? How long does it take to get there? Do you need a car, or can you take public transportation? Are the sites in safe areas, or will you be traveling through or into less secure parts of town? Is transportation a problem in the winter months? Take a look at the local newspaper; check out what's going on around town, what apartments rent for, what houses sell for, what things cost in the supermarket. Is this a place where you want to live and can afford to live? These are all tough questions to answer without a visit.

Whenever you make a visit to a department, go prepared with your list of questions to ask everyone about everything. If you are interviewing prior to the admissions decision, be sure you've read the catalog carefully and are not asking questions that were already answered for you there. Use the time you have with professors and students to find out what the catalog can't tell you.

The Admissions Decision: Theirs and Yours

So what happens when the application review process actually starts?

First, that depends in part on who has the authority to make admissions decisions. At some schools, that authority lies in the Graduate School itself, that is, in the central administration. At others, it lies with the individual departments. Either way, faculty in the department will be involved in evaluating your application.

Things work differently at each school, but roughly, the process goes something like this. A group does an initial review of the applications, making a first cut at separating possible acceptances from clear rejections. At this early stage, there are a number of reasons an application can be disqualified:

- It is incomplete.

- The grades are simply way too low for the program's standards.

- The applicant displays a serious lack of preparation for the program.

- The recommendations are clearly negative.

Next, the remaining applications are reviewed in more detail. In some programs, the applications are divided among the committee members and each group settles on its favorite candidates. The committee then reconvenes, the favorite candidates are presented to the group, and the committee makes its final choices. In other programs, each committee member reviews each application before decisions are made. Some departments circulate applications for review as they become complete and then convene to make the final decision.

During the later stages, the selection process gets more and more detailed and subjective. If you're applying to an arts or literature program, in which your creative work is the primary criterion, obviously things will come down to the subjective judgment of the committee. Even in academic programs, however, it's not always possible for the committee to admit every applicant with good numbers and recommendations and outstanding relevant experience. Here's an extreme case: In 1995, Stanford's psychology department received 340 applications for five openings in their clinical psych program. Obviously, there wasn't room for every worthy contender.

It is at this final stage of the proceedings that your contacts with the department—professors you've spoken with, a visit, or interview—can weigh heavily in your favor. If you've impressed a professor and he really wants to work with you, you'll have an advocate on the committee. This can be invaluable if you're competing with other excellent applicants for precious few spots. This is also a time when your personal statement can be very influential. Especially if there are weaknesses in your application, a personal statement can tip the balance in your favor by highlighting the outstanding contributions you hope to make to your field.

Ultimately, the committee will arrive at a final decision, with a first tier of applicants who will definitely be offered spots in the program, and a second tier of applicants who will be offered admission if people in the first tier turn down the offer.

> ### Peer Review
>
> Some graduate programs have one or two student members in the committee. They are sworn to secrecy, so you needn't worry that your colleagues in the program will have access to all sorts of personal data about you.

When You'll Be Notified

Since most people apply for fall admission, submitting their applications sometime in the previous winter, notification usually comes sometime in March. If you're applying at another time of the year, ask the department when they think they will notify applicants of their decision.

Rolling Admissions

Some programs periodically review applications from early in the submission period right up to the final deadline. After these periodic reviews, a certain number of applicants are notified immediately that they have been accepted. If you're seriously interested in a program that has rolling admissions, get your application in early. If you wait until the final deadline, it's entirely possible that all available slots will be filled and no matter how great you are, there just won't be any room left.

The Final Cut

At the final stage of the admissions proceedings, all applicants are strong contenders with top credentials. Three things make the difference at this point:

 • Your uniqueness (including gender/ethnicity)

 • Prior contacts with the department and faculty

• The match between your interests and theirs

Official Notification

Formal notification of acceptance can come only from a letter of acceptance. If a professor with whom you have been communicating is encouraging about your application, by all means be happy. But do not take your admission for granted until you have the letter from the department or the school in your hand. If the department has the final authority to admit, you'll hear from them; if the graduate school itself reserves the right to admit, your letter will come from them. The program catalog usually tells you how and when the school makes its formal notifications of acceptance.

The Waiting Game

If you haven't heard anything, is it okay to call your school? Yes, within reason. It's very unlikely that anything has gone tragically wrong with your application, so there probably isn't anything you can do to move the process along. If you've applied to art, literature, history, or other programs in which your creative work is a very important part of the admissions process, expect the review to be slow. It takes time to give it all fair consideration. One phone call inquiring about the expected decision time is probably fine; more than two and you'll be pestering either the administrative staff or the professors themselves, neither of which is a good idea.

A lot of graduate school applicants find that their acceptances, rejections, and financial aid information arrive piecemeal. It's very hard to decide which offer to accept when you don't know whether your top program has decided to give you decent financial aid, or whether the two schools you haven't heard from yet are going to accept or reject you.

If You Get Accepted

Some people, fearing that they'll lose a coveted spot, say yes to the best offer they get early on and then turn down the offer later when the program they really wanted, or a better financial offer, comes along. Schools expect a certain amount of jumping around and actually work it into their admissions planning. Before you accept an offer, however, you should be aware of the Council of Graduate Schools' (CGS) resolution concerning financial aid offers. It says that no student is obligated to respond to financial aid offers before April 15. If a student accepts, say, a teaching assistantship before April 15 and then changes her mind, she may simply withdraw her acceptance. After April 15, however, an acceptance is a commitment, and if this same student changed her mind, she would have to get a written release from the first program to switch to a different program.

The schools are not supposed to make offers after April 15 unless students can present written releases from any prior offers they may have accepted. This resolution, which over 300 U.S. schools support, gives you a chance to consider all offers before you commit yourself to a program, and you should not feel pressured to accept any offer before April 15; but you should make every effort to finalize your decision by that date.

Of course in practice such an agreement doesn't solve everything. All graduate departments realize that not every single applicant who is accepted will decide to attend that program. That's why they keep a second "accept" list, usually known as the waiting list, and each time one of the initial acceptances declines, the next person on the waiting list is notified that a spot has opened up and they are now accepted. So there is still jockeying around after April 15, but the CGS resolution encourages it to happen in a very aboveboard way and with the chaos kept to a minimum.

Getting Back on the Horse

Five ways to show the admissions committee how badly you want to go:

- Take nondegree courses in the department, if available

- Find a relevant job

- Do volunteer work in the field

- Write a new statement of purpose

- Get an additional recommendation

If You Don't Get Accepted

Try to speak to someone in the department about your application. Some departments are quite willing to let you know what caused the rejection, and it's often something you can fix, like insufficient academic background or procedural mistakes on the application. Even if it's more subjective, like a boring personal statement or a bad recommendation, you can make changes in your application. Don't just reapply next year; find out what went wrong and deal with it.

Special Considerations

CHAPTER 17

The Re-Entry Student's Guide to Success

By Adele Scheele

The national average age for graduate students in the 2000s will be 35! So if you are 30 or 47 or 55 or more, congratulations! You are finally in the right place at the right time! That is, if you make it work that way.

Success in grad school isn't what it used to be . . . and that's good. Coming back to school is an experiment in hope. It's also a risky investment, an expensive program in which you entrust this time in your life to school for both a new identity and a ticket to the outside professional world. Yet you come with the expectation that it will be done for you. You expect to be made acceptable, valuable, and, finally, highly employable. You hope that answers will be revealed through academic study which will, in turn, lead to future guaranteed success.

I've counseled and consulted with countless people who had faith in this magic—many of whom were disappointed when the expected alchemy never took place. They discovered, years later, that it doesn't just happen. *You* make it happen. Here are six strategies for success:

1. Change Your Knee-Jerk Conditioning

Reverse the conditioning to wait for good things to happen, which you learned from early schooling. You probably learned that you would pass if you did the work assigned by your teachers. And that's exactly what happened. You'd find out whether a certain test covered all or part of chapter 5, whether the assigned paper was 10 or 12 pages long, whether extra credit meant two or

Can All that Riverboating Experience Be Wrong?

"Don't let schooling interfere with your education."

Mark Twain

Hail to the Veterans

Real-world work experience is often the major influence behind a re-entry student's decisions to go on to graduate school.

three books by the same author. Remember? You unconsciously learned to find out explicitly what was expected of you, and then, once you delivered it, you learned to wait for a response.

And a response you always got, in the form of a grade. When all your grades were averaged, you were passed and promoted automatically from first grade to second, first year of college to second, first year of graduate school to second. The context of schooling remained the same. Caught in the "good-student trap," you were actually learning system dependency! The lessons in system dependency boil down to this hard-and-fast rule: If you do your work well enough, you will be taken care of. Nothing could be further from the truth.

In my book, *The "Good" Student Trap,* I define the "good" in the title as "waiting passively for good grades, and for not much else." You are faced with this conditioning now, when you are coming back to school. No matter how old or experienced you are now, if you don't watch it, you will regress to this old mode. You are the same passive student at 34 as you were at 14, continuing the same student-teacher dichotomy that you automatically transferred to the employer-employee relationship. Now's the time to change by becoming an achiever and responding to graduate school differently.

2. Demonstrate Your Interests and Talents to Your Professors

How do you begin this change? Instead of only waiting for your professors to grade, direct, praise, and then promote you to the next level, become curious about the subject at hand. Link it to what already interests you or the area of possible interest by talking to your professors. You may never have done this before with teachers without being called a teacher's pet or "apple polisher," but pay no attention to these labels. All achievers learn to connect with professors as well as top management, so start practicing now. Think of professors as special advisers, consultants, even mentors. During their office hours, talk to them about their work and then yours. If this seems unnatural, think of them as benevolent bosses whose worlds and connections can be opened to you. Tip: They are not your enemy, as they might have seemed when you were in grade school.

Don't be nervous—easy to say, harder to do—about being the same age, or even older, than your professors. It happens in life all the time. In the same way that you outgrew the segregated mindset of eighth graders not talking to lowly seventh graders, you now have to get over the barrier of the old student-teacher split. Now it's essential to use your professors as a link from their areas of expertise.

As a returning student, you may make one of two basic errors—sometimes overplaying but more often underplaying your role. While you might feel you should be more collegial, you still have to seek advice and guidance. But in your terror of failing, don't make the same mistake of falling back to a completely subservient student role. It is all too easy to slip back from your real age to become an anxious 18-year-olds again. That's a costly mistake.

Yet, at the same time, you can't overstate your position. If you recognize a professor's error in a field you have direct experience with, don't engage in being "right" at the expense of a professor losing face or waging war with you—another essential life megaskill. Let it go, or learn to be tactful in bringing the issue up. How do you really learn? By trial and error, how else? Learning to network with your professors is one step toward building one of the key megaskills you'll need throughout your life.

Take the risk of forming relationships with some of your professors, even if it feels uncomfortable at first. Discomfort is a characteristic feeling of all new and worthwhile pursuits. Be fair to yourself; you are not stupid or you wouldn't have earned your undergraduate degree. Wanting to learn more is the reason you are here, so start by recognizing your own fears. One of the traits that separates achievers from nonachievers is that achievers try for more even when they are afraid, whereas nonachievers paralyze themselves with their fear. The truth is we're all afraid: success lies in whether we act or not. Courage is defined as acting even though you are afraid.

3. Use Papers and Projects to Catapult You into the Career You Want

Take this assignment: Double your agenda. Whenever you're assigned to write a paper or prepare a project, apply the assignment to another field or area that you hope your graduate degree will lead you to. Then it will.

Don't just take the "quick-and-dirty" road to assignments: Spend some time figuring out how to use each assignment to your own advantage. That way, you'll receive class credit and a leg up into what you really crave. So, match your own curiosity and interest to the list of topics or else create your own and present a case for it. Take the time to think about the best outcomes you can achieve for yourself by the course's end, or the semester's end, or graduate school's end.

The most common best way is to formulate academic goals based on your own agenda. If you can identify one goal, you can get an extra boost from what could have been only an obligatory classroom assignment into mining the gold you seek. If you are a business student and yearn to make the transition from insurance to investment banking, use one of your assignments to study and survey investment banking. Go into the field, interview bankers, write a great paper (show a draft to your professor; then rewrite it to make it better), offer to show it to the investment banking firm, maybe submit it to a banking journal. You'll get so much more out of it this way than by merely complying and writing on the first topic on the list.

Another approach is open exploration. If you don't know what you want to do, ask your professors what interests them and join in. Find ways to help, expand on one of their ideas, or just shoot the breeze for a while . . . you may discover a topic you'd never have found on your own. This very act can also be a springboard into a mentor-protégé relationship.

Instead of just being a "good" student content with an A, you'll take advantage of the opportunities that graduate study can give you by allowing for scientific, intellectual, and psychological explorations. If you can then connect these explorations to others whose careers you admire, you'll make this investment pay off.

Give up worrying too much: studies show that while re-entry students worry more, they are actually more successful than other students. And, not so surprisingly, re-entry students find that younger students turn to them for study tips, advice, and presentation skills.

4. The Hidden Curriculum: Discovering Yourself Through Activities

While they used to be called extracurricular activities, they are now thought of as "co-" curricular because they teach students so much about themselves through direct experience.

And no, you are not too old to engage in these clubs and events. You can always join the radio, newspaper, drama society, student government, or professional clubs. These activities are the perfect place to practice the skills that it takes to audition, perform, take coaching from your sponsor, learn to improve and buoy up a team, and maybe find yourself a career.

Satisfied and successful people learn to form their careers around activities they are vitally interested in. Many of their callings are first seen in the activities they choose on their own—quite different from majors they originally considered worthwhile. So experiment: After all, you can't be fired. You'll learn the great life skills of how to build personal courage, develop self-presentation skills, further the risks of connection, develop organizational savvy and the human dynamics behind "office politics," and learn to establish real professionalism. Leadership in activities proves that you can do more than follow directions and becomes another kind of track record to demonstrate your initiative, drive, ability to work with people, and solve problems—all skills requisite for corporations or nonprofits, entrepreneurial or free-agent work.

5. Real World Ventures: Internships, Work, and Volunteering

Wonderful chances to explore a profession or career or test out what you've been yearning for exist within work-related activities, paid or not, for academic credit or not. Internships provide great practical experience. They allow an outside chance, not provided in real life, to grow and develop intellectually and personally, and to experience an organization firsthand.

Check the lists of internships at your university's career center and within your major's department. Internships are also listed online through services like Jobtrak.

When you decide on a few that interest you and schedule an interview, remember that you still count. Apply your own past experience and decision to return to school enthusiastically. Don't hang back from competing for an internship. Getting it—even if it doesn't pay—and succeeding in it can position you for a real job offer, whether part-time during school or full-time after graduation. Or it can lead you to related fields and competitors, providing valuable experience. In the worst case, it can reveal work you find you don't want, after all, saving you time later.

If you are already working and want to advance in your business following your graduate studies, you might think of relating papers and projects to solve problems at work, to add to a task force's direction or to generate business. Make yourself visible on the job through initiating new or enlarging existent projects and through relationships with your bosses, coworkers, and clients. If you want to change direction after graduation, use your workplace coupled with assignments to catapult you.

If you want to enlarge your network as well as your heart, get involved in volunteer activities and get yourself on a committee. Take time to meet other members and speakers, ask their opinions and advice, and thank them when you report back. Organizations such as The American Heart Association, National Cancer Institute, Habitat for America, and The United Way as well as professional associations—all bring you into contact with a rich and diverse group of citizens from employees to employers. Through working together or worthwhile projects, you'll come to know and be known by others who will be important to you throughout your career.

6. Use the Career Center

Don't wait until the month before graduation to find and use the career center to help you find an appropriate career resources. Sign up for workshops and professional campus conferences and lectures on career trends, self-assessments, internships, and jobs. Take advantage of any interview coaching, including having yourself videotaped. Go to job fairs and talk to recruiters with an open mind for positions you want and others you stumble on and wouldn't have thought of. And before you choose graduate school, look up information as well as alumni who might advise you on programs, fellowships, opportunities.

SPECIAL CONSIDERATIONS

Take advantage of career counselors whose very mission is to help you find your career. They have extensive training in assessing career choices and connections in the business, arts, and service communities both on and off the campus. Besides, they are terrific sources of support and can be powerful allies if you cultivate them.

Finally, behave toward career counselors as you learn to behave to professors, administrators, and the world-at-large: Take the initiative. Make appointments. You'll undoubtedly benefit from getting to know them and letting them get to know you.

KAPLAN

CHAPTER 18

African American Students

By Silas Purnell

If you're seeking admission to graduate school, you need to be aware of both the pitfalls and the opportunities that await you. African American students not only face the same problems white students encounter in their quest for higher education, but also face a whole other set of circumstances cast upon them simply because they are of African American descent. You do not live in a racially neutral society; racism is a fact of everyday life. But this does not mean that you should give up your dream of admission to graduate school. Rather, it simply means that you must alter your approach.

Remember that graduate admissions is like poker—the best hand doesn't always win.

A Word about Affirmative Action

Recent developments in affirmative action have been the topic of many news reports in the past year, and you're probably familiar with instances like California's Proposition 209 and Texas's Hopwood case, in which significant decreases in African American and Latino enrollment were reported after these states' affirmative action policies were rescinded or modified. As an ideal, affirmative action is a laudable goal but in most cases, it is more talk than action because there are very few graduate schools that have effective affirmative action programs in place. On many campuses, affirmative action is a buzzword and not a priority, so you must be careful not to be misled by a school's claims. When you visit a campus, ask the affirmative action officer if there are hard statistics to support that school's commitment. You may or may not arrive at the truth by cross-checking multiple sources of information. But regardless of the survival or demise of affirmative action, you can be sure of one thing: There will always be schools interested in admitting African American students. To find the one that best meets your needs, you must be creative in your admissions strategies—and first and foremost of these is the way you seek and find the facts about that school.

Gathering Information

The keys to successful admission to graduate school are information, initiative, preparation, contacts, and action. The most important of the aforementioned criteria is *information,* because good information is the precursor to good results. It is very difficult to obtain African American–oriented information on higher education in general, and information on graduate education is particularly elusive. In your search for a graduate school, you should seek two types of information on graduate school—general and specific. General information can be found in most current publications on graduate school. Specific information, however—information that speaks to the issues that affect African American students—is harder to find. Publications that contain specific information are almost nonexistent, with the exception of a periodical called *Black Issues in Higher Education.* That's why the best source of specific information is not books but people.

People Who Can Help

Many students rely too heavily on formal print sources such as brochures and catalogs, and on information provided directly by the graduate schools or departments. This can be useful, but when it comes to gathering information about a particular department, faculty, funding, course content, and program quality, advice from someone with firsthand experience is often far more valuable. You need this type of informal counseling because no catalog will tell you which departments, faculty, and staff will be more helpful to minority students than others.

Often, African American students currently enrolled in a particular program, or who have already completed their degree, are the most informed about the requirements and competitiveness of a graduate program or institution. Most colleges and universities have graduate student associations, and some even have associations for minority students. These are good places to look for people who could share insight on a school's policies towards minority admissions.

You should also make it a priority to meet with someone on the admissions committee, for several reasons. First, the verbal skills of most students of color are a great deal more impressive than their writing skills. Second, a face-to-face meeting gives the admissions committee member an opportunity to associate a face with the student's folder. Third, meeting an admissions committee member allows students the opportunity to get a feel for the type of students that admissions committees are looking for. Finally, potential graduate students can ask questions about the weight placed on the various admissions criteria.

Other groups and occasions to investigate are graduate conferences, seminars, and minority graduate meetings. The U.S. Department of Education sponsors Trio Programs, which are educational outreach programs designed to motivate and support students from disadvantaged backgrounds. Trio currently includes five distinct outreach programs targeted to help students progress through the academic pipeline from middle school to postbaccalaureate programs. The programs focus on developing college survival skills and career awareness through a variety of activities, and they employ numerous minority directors and support personnel who have earned graduate degrees themselves. These employees have been through graduate programs and can speak from experience when it comes to the academic climate at their former schools. These people are a rich source of information, and many will gladly volunteer information and counseling to prospective graduate students. In many cases, they can also tell you about the hiring policies at the institutions where they are employed.

Focusing Your Efforts

After the information has been gathered, you should consider it from an African American point of reference. Ask yourself, "How does this information apply to me?" When examining books, catalogs, brochures, and first-person advice, search as hard as possible to obtain data regarding the recruitment, retention, and the graduation rate of African American students on that particular campus. All questions asked to staff, faculty, and administrators should be asked from an African American perspective. For example, a question regarding the graduation rates of a school would not be as informative as a question regarding the graduation rates of African Americans at that same school. The latter question is a great deal more informative and meaningful to you.

In your personal statement or on-campus interview, never be reluctant to discuss the issue of race if it comes up. There is nothing wrong with requesting information about the racial history of a graduate program that you are interested in. You should question whether the program discriminates against African Americans. You should also ask:

- What is the program doing now, and what are the program's goals and vision for the future?

- How many African Americans have been admitted to the program?

- What were their qualifications?

- How well were they funded, and from what sources?

- How many actually graduated, and how long did it take them?

These are all pertinent questions because race is a legitimate issue that should be discussed openly. Of course, you should not be confrontational in your approach, nor should you have an apologetic attitude where race is concerned. Rather, you should be honest and open about your racial concerns and ask for as much information as possible. Any graduate program that resists or resents racial inquiries may be the wrong program for black students.

Financial Aid Resources

Numerous individuals and organizations focus on graduate opportunities and financial aid for minority students. Some well-known examples include the McKnight Foundation, the Gem Program, the University of Illinois Urban Health Program, the Chicago Health and Medical Careers Program (CAHMCP) at the Illinois Institute of Technology, and the Washington University Chancellor's Graduate Fellowship Program for African Americans. Students interested in locating programs like this should check out publications like *The Black Collegian, Blacks in Higher Education, The Journal of Blacks in Higher Education,* and other minority-oriented publications.

Selecting a School

A major problem for African American students is their choice of schools. Many often balk at reconciling their aspirations to fit their preparation: Too many students believe that schools like Harvard, Stanford, Northwestern, and the University of Chicago are actively seeking them regardless of their grade point averages and test scores. Avoid this trap by making sure you get the education you are paying for.

The most important thing that black applicants should bear in mind when choosing a graduate school is to focus on the particular department they are interested in. In many instances, students waste an exorbitant amount of time talking about the reputation of the university and completely ignore the quality of the department—they are not one and the same. You need to know the reputation of the department as it applies to minority students. What are the positive or negative aspects of a department's history? Does it provide a good environment for minority students? How do current students evaluate the department's track record in recruitment, acceptance, funding, housing, advising, counseling, and graduation of minority students? Many good universities have one or more underperforming departments. Therefore, the real question may not be how many minority students the program admits, but how many of those students graduate. You should also pay attention to the presence or absence of minority faculty in the department.

HBCUs

In your eagerness to find a good graduate school, don't overlook the Historically Black Colleges and Universities (HBCUs). For many students, these schools can provide a good education that is free from the stresses of racism. Some students find that life on a predominantly black campus is more enjoyable and supportive than that of a traditionally white institution. Others seek out the academic opportunity to study and interact with black faculty, who are well aware of the needs of black students and who can provide them with information, advice, counseling, and mentoring. Inquire into the drawbacks of HBCUs as well, if you are considering them; a common problem, for example, is the paucity of financial aid.

HBCUs offer a wide choice of majors and professional schools, and at least 31 have graduate degree programs. Howard University, for instance, has an enviable record for graduating a sizable number of Ph.D.'s and M.D.'s. They also graduate students with master's degrees in a wide variety of other fields. Some other universities with major graduate programs are Morehouse College, Southern University at Baton Rouge, Clark Atlanta University, Texas Southern University, Prairie View A&M University, Hampton University, and many others. Black students attending these universities are welcomed with open arms.

Facing Reality Realistically, Not Negatively

In general, with the exception of the HBCUs, graduate school has traditionally been the domain of white students, with African Americans few and far between. Research shows that over half of the graduate programs in a number of states have no African American students, so you need to know that a graduate program operating without African American students is the rule rather than the exception. If you were to examine the roster of almost any graduate program, foreign students usually outnumber the African American students. The absence of African Americans is especially apparent in challenging subjects such as hard sciences, health sciences, computer science, engineering, and mathematics. Consequently, you must exercise diligence in choosing a user friendly graduate program.

That doesn't mean that you should approach the admissions process with a negative or defeatist attitude. Rather, it merely indicates that you should be aware of the negative factors that may influence admission to graduate programs. After all is said and done, some schools actually recruit African American graduate students and can provide you with a challenging opportunity.

Good contacts can be very helpful in helping you obtain admission to a school that has a good environment rather than a hostile one. Many people throughout the country have insight, influence, or power concerning graduate school. They may be located on campus or in the local community, but these are the people to look for.

Some Final Words of Advice

There is a dire need for African Americans in the work force with graduate degrees that are marketable. African Americans with good quantitative skills will be rewarded for completing degrees in the health sciences, computer science, engineering, mathematics, and business. All of the fields mentioned above are especially rewarding at the doctorate level. In addition, there are numerous opportunities for African American males interested in pursuing teacher education. You should be cautioned, however, to be objective when making choices about graduate school and be sure to make choices with the market in mind.

To be admitted to graduate school, you must take the initiative to explore all avenues. You must begin with the idea that you will gain entry to a graduate program, but you must also realize that there are programs with all types of entrance requirements and costs. The requirements may vary from average academic performance to superior performance. You must determine where you fit, then shoot for the best program possible. Have no fear of rejection, because chances are if one school rejects you, another will select you. Never assume a begging attitude: Let the people at the program know that you are negotiating, not begging. Emphasize your strengths and be extremely positive. Finally, explain to them that you are bringing something positive to the program that will be beneficial to all concerned.

Good luck in your search.

CHAPTER 19

Yes You Can!
For Students with Disabilities

By Chris Rosa

"Remain at home and stay rooted in your network of support."

"Go away to the program that is your first choice and embrace new experiences."

These were the conflicting voices that echoed in my head during the fall semester of my senior year of college, as I struggled mightily with the decision of where I should go to graduate school.

During my college career, I came to love sociology and its distinctive approach to the study of human behavior; I looked forward to further cultivating my sociological imagination by enrolling in a doctoral program in sociology. I was a good student with great GRE scores, a rich extracurricular background, and strong faculty references. My candidate profile offered me a range of graduate school options. However, these options were not only shaped by the factors that impinge upon the decisions of most prospective graduate students, they were also shaped by my status as a wheelchair user with muscular dystrophy. In choosing a graduate program, my ability to meet my disability-related needs while attending a program would emerge as consideration that was equally important to the academic quality of that program and its affordability.

My first choice was a premiere West Coast program with world-renowned faculty that had published extensively in disability studies, the area I wished to explore in graduate school. However, choosing this elite program and moving from my home in New York City to benefit from its vast academic opportunities and resources would mean turning my back on equally important resources that served as foundation of my independent life. I had spent the last ten years of my life working out the complicated logistics of attendant care and personal assistance; accessible housing and transportation; finding doctors

Call AHEAD

The Association for Higher Education and Disability (AHEAD) provides key information on issues concerning students with disabilities. AHEAD members can access a job bank, or post résumés through the organization. Contact:

AHEAD
P.O. Box 21192
Columbus, OH 43221-0192
Voice/TTY: (614) 488-4972

that I trusted with the medical complications that resulted from my disability; cultivating a vast network of advocates that I could call on for assistance when things went awry. The thought of rebuilding from scratch this elaborate basis for an independent life in a setting where I did not know anyone was extremely daunting.

Ultimately, I resolved this dilemma in favor of "staying at home." I was very fortunate to find an excellent doctoral program close to home, with a strong commitment to equal access for students with disabilities, which enabled me to pursue my dream of a doctorate in sociology while at the same time remaining able to rely on the network that had taken years to cultivate to continue my independent life.

Prospective graduate students with disabilities are confronted with similar choices when attempting to choose the right graduate programs. Many of these individuals will resolve this dilemma in favor of going away; others will decisions similar to mine; still others will factor in other disability issues when attempting to choose the right program. This chapter will attempt to guide you through the constellation of unique factors that impact upon your choice of graduate programs when you are a person with a disability.

Are You Ready?

The decision to go to graduate school involves a major commitment of time, money, energy, and the development of a professional sense of self. It is an enormous commitment for any individual, but especially for individuals with disabilities. In choosing a graduate program, people with disabilities not only commit the same personal resources that all students devote to the graduate school endeavor, they must also realign all of the access resources they rely on for independence and success in other parts of their lives in order to support their efforts in graduate school. This reallocation of independent living resources to support graduate study often significantly diminishes people with disabilities' quality of life in other life domains. If one is truly ready for graduate study and chooses the right program, these sacrifices are surely worth it. However, in order to avoid regrettable decisions, candidates with disabilities must understand what it takes to be ready academically, logistically, physically, and emotionally for the rigors of graduate school; they must then be willing look at themselves self-critically and ask, "Am I ready for this?"

The Right Stuff

Like all candidates for graduate study, students with disabilities must ensure that their candidate profiles meet the criteria for admission to the programs to which they apply and that their profiles are sufficiently attractive to earn the serious consideration from admission committees. In constructing candidate profiles, people with disabilities should consider disability issues that will affect their presentation of self as candidates.

It's Academic: Undergraduate Performance

Candidates' performance in undergraduate courses will be a significant factor in whether or not they are admitted to their programs of choice. If your undergraduate performance was affected by a disability issue (i.e., an undergraduate institution's failure to adequately meet your needs for reasonable accommodation, a learning disability that went undiagnosed throughout most of a college career), you might be able to use other aspects of your candidate profile—your personal statement, letters of reference, admissions committee interviews, etcetera) to "explain away" a lower grade-point average. While such explanations may improve your chances for admission, they often do so at the cost of disclosing your identity as a candidate as a disability.

To Tell or Not to Tell: Candidate Profiles and the Issue of Disability Disclosure

While your personal statement, letters of reference, GRE scores, and interviews with admissions committees offer candidates with disabilities the opportunity to demonstrate their richness and strengths as applicants, for those concerned about the disclosure of their disabilities, these dimensions of the candidate profile are fraught with opportunities for others to learn about your status as a candidate with a disability. For those concerned about disability disclosure, these aspects of your candidate profile must be carefully managed. The following are some tips to successfully manage disability disclosure in the admissions process:

- The decision of whether or not to disclose a disability in a personal statement is a very difficult, very personal one. This decision pits people's pride in their disability identity against their concerns that lingering cultural biases against people with disabilities will cause candidates who have disclosed their disabilities to be perceived as somehow less

> ### *Think Accommodations*
>
> For information on reasonable accommodations, contact HEATH, a U.S.-funded clearinghouse about postsecondary education for individuals with disabilities. Free information is available in print, disc, and audiocassette formats.
>
> HEATH Resource Center
> 1 Dupont Circle, Suite 800
> Washington, DC 20036-1193
> Voice: (800) 544-3284
> TTY: (202) 939-9320
> Fax: (202) 833-4760
> E-mail: HEATH@ace.nche.edu

attractive by admissions committees. If you are at all concerned about disability disclosure, unless it is central to your personal statement's thesis or to your ability to "explain away" a subpar undergraduate performance, follow this general rule: when in doubt, leave it out!

- Speak to those providing you with letters of reference who are aware of your disability and let them know how you feel about disability disclosure so that they do not unwittingly disclose information that you're uncomfortable with in their reference letters.

- If you have a disability and are at all concerned with the implications of disability disclosure, do not volunteer any information about your disability during interviews with admissions personnel or program representatives. While the asking the question, "Do you have a disability?" is illegal in most admissions contexts, if asked such an inappropriate questioning during an interview, asserting your Americans with Disabilities Act right to confidentiality will probably not help your admissions chances. If asked about your disability, you may consider simply and honestly informing the interviewer that you have a disability that, with the necessary reasonable accommodations, in no way limits your ability to be successful in graduate school.

Resources on the Web

- **The Society for Disability Studies (SDS)** is a nonprofit, multidisciplinary and international organization composed of social scientists, scholars in the humanities, disability rights advocates, providers, and agency personnel concerned with people with disabilities. http://www.uic.edu/orgs/sds/

- **Disability Information for Students and Professionals:** A Web site with news updates, requests for information, and resources for students in the field of disability and for professionals with disabilities. http://www.abilityinfo.co

The "Maris Effect"

In 1961, the New York Yankees' Roger Maris hit home runs at a torrid pace that enabled him to eclipse Babe Ruth's single season record for round-trippers, a record that the experts swore would never be broken. In breaking Ruth's record of 60 home runs, Maris was the subject of much controversy and criticism among contemporaries who thought his accomplishment was less valid because he hit his 61 homers during a 162 game schedule, while Ruth reached 60 home runs during a 154 game schedule. As a result of this controversy, Baseball Commissioner Ford Frick placed an asterisk next to his home run total of 61, which forever stigmatized and diminished Maris' record-setting total.

When candidates with disabilities take the GRE under accommodative conditions, they run the risk of experiencing the "Maris Effect." Even though reasonable exam accommodations do not provide testers with disabilities with a distinct advantage over standard exam takers—includes a statement in exam reports indicating that accommodative exams were taken under nonstandard conditions. This distinction may cause even the highest scores to be considered less valid and may serve as a "red flag," altering programs to candidates' status as applicants with disabilities. Those who are concerned about the issue of disability disclosure should beware of the "Maris Effect" and weigh the potential costs of disclosing their disabilities through this process against the benefits of accommodative testing when considering taking the GRE under nonstandard conditions.

Reasonable accommodations are available to test takers with documented disabilities for the GRE General and Subject tests, in both the paper-based or computer-based exam formats. Among the accommodations available to individuals with appropriate disability documentation are exams in accessible formats, readers and amanuenses, access to assistive technologies, and extended exam time.

An official request for exam accommodations must include a completed Eligibility Questionnaire and certification document, both of which are available in the center of the GRE Bulletin. In the absence of a certification document, test takers must provide documentation of your accommodation needs, on official letterhead, from a licensed or certified professional and documentation of your testing accommodations history from your college or institution on its official letterhead.

When a candidate with a disability takes the exam under nonstandard conditions, a statement is included with reports of scores indicating "the special nature" of the score results. This statement may alert admissions committees to your status as a candidate with a disability. For those individuals concerned about the issue of disability disclosure, it is important to weigh the potential costs of disclosing their disabilities through this process against the potential benefits of taking the GRE in the most accessible setting. There are two possible alternatives to disclosing your disability through the "nonstandard examination process." One option would be to test under standard conditions with minor modifications to the exam setting: If ETS determines that you can test in the standard setting with minor reasonable adjustments (i.e., a wheelchair-accessible setting, exam materials in an alternate format, etcetera) by taking your exam under these conditions, your scores will reported in the standard way, with no "red flags" to reveal your disability status. The other option would be to contact the graduate school or fellowship sponsors to which you are applying and ask if they are willing to waive the GRE requirements and evaluate your application based upon other criteria.

For additional information on accommodations for computer based tests, contact: Graduate Record Examinations, Educational Testing Service, Services for Test Takers with Disabilities, Mail Stop 05-Q, Princeton, NJ 08541-0001; (609) 771-7670; TTY (609) 452-9342; fax (609) 520-1092.

For additional information on accommodations for paper-based tests, contact: Graduate Record Examinations, Education Testing Service, P.O. Box 6000, Princeton, NJ 08541-6000; (609) 771-7670; TTY: (609) 734-9362; fax (609) 520-1092.

Choosing the Right Program

Once you have taken the necessary steps to ensure that you are prepared for graduate school and have sufficiently honed your candidate profile, you are now ready of make a list of factors to consider when narrowing your choice of graduate programs. Beside the factors covered in this book that pertain to all prospective graduate school candidates, the following are some issues of particular relevance to candidates with disabilities:

Home or Away?

Limiting your choices of graduate programs to those available locally offers students with disabilities the opportunity to draw upon the support of a familiar network of resources in their efforts to meet the very rigorous demands of graduate study. However by limiting their choices in this manner, they often exclude themselves from programs in other regions that would represent a better fit for them academically and professionally.

Sunbelt or Snowbelt?

There are distinctive regional benefits for people with disabilities to attending graduate school in different locales. For example, many graduate students have found that when they have moved to the northeast and midwest, they often enjoy a comparatively higher rate of disability benefits than those available in many southern and western states. They also often find that graduate programs located in northeastern and midwestern cities tend to offer them proximity more accessible mass transit than those in many southern and western cities. However, graduate schools located in the northeast and midwest are also frequently situated in cold and snowy climates and on hilly terrain that tends to undermine access for individuals with physical disabilities. Schools in the south and west are more likely to have newer, more accessible facilities, are situated in places that are warm, flat, and dry, and are more likely to be near off-campus accessible housing units than those in the northeast and midwest.

Full Time or Part Time?

Some graduate programs offer students the option of attending full or part time. Given the rigorous demands of most full-time graduate programs, students with disabilities may find that attending part-time may offer them greater opportunity to perform to their potential. For example, students with learning disabilities or those who are blind or have visual impairments may find it easier to keep up with the enormous among of reading that graduate study demands by attending part time. The major drawbacks to part-time study are the fact that in the long run, part-time study costs more (both in terms of tuition costs and lost earnings from time out of the workforce), vocational rehabilitation agencies will often not subsidize the tuition of graduate students with disabilities who attend part time, and part-time students lose the sense of social solidarity that is fostered by attending graduate school with your fellow students.

Cultural Consciousness

According to Sharon Lerner, Assistant to the Vice President for Student Affairs at the Graduate School and University Center at the City University of New York, adjusting to graduate school involves the acquisition of a new identity and an acculturation to a new way of life. "Participating in a graduate program is not so much about being a student; it's about embarking upon your professional life.... In graduate school, your school is your work. Your identity as an economist or psychologist becomes paramount—even more salient, in many respects, than your identity as a person with a disability." She further points out that your graduate-student identity is acquired in a unique institutional context; while different programs' curricula may look about the same, each institution will have its own distinctive culture. These cultures will affect how welcoming and accessible these programs are to individuals with disabilities. So when you're investigating different programs, speak to faculty, students, administrators, and student services professionals to get a feel for the culture of the institution and for how comfortable it is for people with disabilities.

Assessing Accessibility

Once you've narrowed the field and have a short list of graduate programs you're interested in, you'll have to make some tough choices. But before doing that, there's more work to be done. Here are the main factors to consider in judging how accessible the graduate programs on your short list are to people with disabilities.

Ramps, Raised Dots, and TTYs: Physical Access

The architectural and technological accessibility of a campus should play a significant role in your evaluation of graduate programs. The following questions will help you to evaluate the physical accessibility of a school.

1. What is the campus terrain like? Is it hilly or flat?

2. What is the campus infrastructure like? Are walkways and roadways well paved or littered with cracks and potholes?

3. Are the buildings that house all aspects of the graduate student experience accessible to students with mobility-related disabilities? If not, what is the institution's policy regarding moving classes and other graduate student activities to accessible sites to accommodate students with disabilities?

4. The institution's library will play a central role in your graduate education. How accessible are its facilities and services to students with disabilities?

5. Are the assistive technologies that you need available, and are the academic computing facilities accessible to students with disabilities?

6. Many graduate programs have practicum components in schools, community settings, hospitals, and other institutions. Are these institutions' facilities accessible to people with disabilities?

7. Similarly, many graduate programs require that students serve as teaching or research assistants as part of their financial aid packages. Are the facilities that house these activities accessible to people with disabilities?

Get with the Program: Programmatic Access

For all students with disabilities, but particularly for students with learning, sensory, and psychiatric disabilities, the programmatic accessibility of graduate institutions will significantly impact your choice of schools. When assessing the programmatic access of graduate schools and programs, keep the following questions in mind:

1. Most graduate programs demand large volumes of assigned and unassigned reading. What are the institution's policies regarding the provision of reading and other course materials in accessible formats?

2. What are the institution's policies on the provision of reader, notetaker, and sign language interpreter services?

3. What are the graduate program's policies on incomplete grades and leaves of absence?

4   What are the institution's policies on accommodative testing?

5. Where does the institution keep confidential student disability documentation? It should not store such records in your graduate program student files. This file is a quasiprofessional file to which faculty may have access; it is not appropriate for disability documentation to be kept in this file.

Office of Services for Students with Disabilities

Effective services and accommodations for graduate students with disabilities is usually an indicator that an institution has a high quality Office of Services for Students with Disabilities (OSSD). Effective OSSD's will work closely with you and your graduate program faculty and administration to ensure that your accommodation needs are met. A good indicator of the quality of OSSD's is whether or not the institution has established an actual office that coordinates the provision of reasonable accommodations and support services to students with disabilities, as opposed to assigning this responsibility to a person or office that has multiple responsibilities. The commitment of significant resources to accommodate students with disabilities through an OSSD is often indicative of an institution's larger commitment to equal access and opportunity for individuals with disabilities in all aspects of graduate student life.

There's Nothing Like Being There

In order to assess how accessible a graduate program is and how welcoming the program's culture is to individuals with disabilities, there is no substitute for visiting the program's campus, checking out its facilities, speaking with faculty, the coordinator for services for students with disabilities, and students with disabilities enrolled in the program.

The Early Bird Gets the Accommodations

Once you're sure about the program you'd like to attend, it's a good idea to commit to your program of choice as early as possible so that the necessary reasonable accommodations, auxiliary services, and assistive technology can be set up for you in a timely fashion.

CHAPTER 20

Especially for International Students

Graduate education in the United States offers a level of excellence and a diversity unparalleled anywhere in the world. American universities and colleges are major contributors to all fields of research, and the research being conducted in U.S. graduate schools is generally considered to be of the highest caliber and on the cutting edge of nearly every field of study. Faculty members will often rely on graduate students to assist them in conducting experiments and performing other vital research responsibilities. In addition, graduate students assist their departments by teaching courses, offering tutoring to undergraduate students, and grading examinations.

Because of the emphasis on excellence in graduate education, admission to these programs is very competitive. Not only are applicants competing for admission, but in many graduate schools they are also competing for fellowships, scholarships, and assistantships as well.

As an international student, there are several important steps you can take to maximize your chances of gaining admission to a U.S. graduate school. To start, it is helpful to understand the culture of graduate education in the United States.

Understanding Graduate Education in the United States

Graduate education (generally referred to as graduate school or grad school) has become an important component in building a successful career. Prior to the 1980s, a bachelor's degree (undergraduate education) was sufficient to secure a job with a good salary and benefits in nearly any field. However, with the advance of technology and research over the last two decades, and as businesses continue to downsize their work forces, education beyond the undergraduate level has become highly desirable. Therefore, many people are applying to graduate schools.

Global Grads

Percent of doctorates awarded to international students at U.S. colleges and universities:

Engineering 55.7

Economics 53.5

Mathematics 53.4

Computer Science 50.8

Physics, Astronomy 43.1

Chemistry 42.1

Biological Sciences 36.0

Health 26.5

Political science/
International relations 23.1

Anthropology/Sociology . .22.8

History 13.1

American/English
Language/Literature 10.4

Educations 9.9

Source: National Research Council

Graduate education is considerably different from undergraduate education. The first major difference is that graduate school is much more competitive. Many undergraduate schools admit many hundreds or even thousands of students every year. Graduate schools, on the other hand, admit much smaller numbers of the most qualified students. Some highly competitive graduate and professional programs in the United States, such as law, medicine, and clinical psychology, might admit no more than 10 applicants per year out of several hundred.

Another unique feature of graduate school is the narrow focus of the curriculum. The undergraduate education is multidisciplinary; in addition to the major subject, the curriculum is composed of courses in the sciences, humanities, and social sciences. Graduate education focuses on one subject or a series of closely related subjects. Because of this concentrated focus, it is expected that applicants to a specific graduate program will have a strong background in the field and a demonstrated record of achievement.

Admission to graduate school is usually offered by a single department or program, as opposed to a central admissions committee. Graduate students become closely affiliated with the faculty and administrators in their department. Students are assigned an academic adviser, usually a faculty member who shares a research interest. Graduate students meet regularly with their adviser to discuss progress in courses and research, and to resolve any problems that may arise.

The main focus in graduate school is original research. Part of the curriculum is devoted to courses and lectures, while much of the academic work will involve researching topics related to your primary field of study or assisting faculty members with their research.

Graduate school usually culminates in a major examination or written thesis. Some graduate programs will require a final oral examination covering topics from your primary area of research. Other departments will require a written thesis. Doctoral candidates are required to write a major work of original research (the dissertation) and then orally defend the findings of that research.

Choosing the Right Graduate Program

Because of the wide diversity of graduate schools in the United States, choosing the best program for you requires considerable thought and a good deal of research. In order to narrow your focus and make the most educated choices, you should consider the following questions.

What Are Your Career Goals?

The answer to this question can help determine the level of graduate education you should seek. It is important to understand how a graduate degree from a U.S. university will create employment opportunities in your home country. If you are seeking employment in a financial field (stock broker, accountant, marketing firm), a Master of Business Administration (M.B.A.) might be the most appropriate graduate degree for you. If, on the other hand, you would like to continue doing research in your chosen field, then a doctoral degree (Ph.D., Ed.D.) might be most appropriate.

What Type of Graduate School is Best for You?

The best graduate school for you is the one that fits most or all of your academic and personal needs. The graduate schools with the most outstanding reputations may not always offer the best programs for your needs. Some small graduate schools in the United States offer outstanding academic programs. You should investigate the graduate schools with the faculty that are conducting the most recent research in your area of interest.

Where Students Come From

Students from many countries studied in the United States last year. Here are the top 10:

Japan	.47,073
China	.46,958
Republic of Korea	.42,890
India	.33,818
Taiwan	.30,855
Canada	.22,051
Thailand	.15,090
Malaysia	.14,597
Indonesia	.13,282
Hong Kong	.9,665

Source: *Open Doors 1997/98: Report on International Educational Exchange,* published by the Institute of International Education

---

Graduate education in the United States is offered through a variety of educational institutions. For example, state universities (University of Michigan, University of California, etcetera) are large, state-funded institutions that offer a wide variety of undergraduate graduate and professional programs. Tuition is usually higher for out-of-state students (including international students). Private universities (Harvard, New York University, Stanford) are similar to state universities, except that their main source of funding is derived from tuition. Therefore, they tend to be more expensive than state universities. Some private universities have a religious affiliation (Georgetown University, Brigham Young University, Southern Methodist University).

You should also consider the location of the graduate school (rural or urban, warm or cold climate), the facilities (library holdings, sports facilities, housing opportunities), the diversity of the student body, and the size of the international student population.

What Graduate Degree Should You Obtain?

Graduate education is divided into several stages, each culminating with the awarding of a degree. The master's degree is awarded after one to three years of study, depending on the field of study. These programs usually require a final oral or written comprehensive examination or a written thesis or project. There are many types of master's degrees. A few of the more popular degrees include: Master of Science (M.S.), Master of Arts (M.A.), Master of Education (M.Ed.), Master of Business Administration (M.B.A.), Master of Social Work (M.S.W.), and Master of Fine Arts (M.F.A.).

Popular Majors

Below are the most popular majors chosen by international students.

Major	%
Business and management	20.9%
Engineering	14.9%
Math and computer sciences	8.5%
Social sciences	8.1%
Physical and life sciences	7.7%
Fine and applied art	6.5%
Health professions	4.1%
Humanities	3.4%
Education	2.7%
Agriculture	1.8%
Others	9.7%

Source: *Open Doors 1997/98: Report on International Educational Exchange,* published by the Institute of International Education

The doctoral degree requires a minimum of three years of study beyond the master's degree. Doctoral programs require original research and a final written work, known as the dissertation, which must be defended orally. The Doctor of Philosophy (Ph.D.) and the Doctor of Education (Ed.D.) are two of the most popular doctoral degrees offered in U.S. graduate schools.

What Do You Want to Study?

For the most part, undergraduate education encompasses all of the main academic disciplines (humanities, sciences, and social sciences). Graduate education, however, is more narrowly focused. Most course work in a graduate program is related to your chosen field of study. Therefore, you should apply to graduate programs in which you have a strong academic background. Carefully review the course requirements for the graduate program you are interested in and determine if you have all of the necessary qualifications to pursue a graduate degree in that program. In addition, because you will become closely affiliated with your department, you should select a program that has at least one or two faculty members who share your research interests.

Do You Have the Equivalent of a U.S. Bachelor's Degree?

If you obtained your undergraduate degree at an institution outside the United States, it must be considered equivalent to a U.S. bachelor's degree if you want to apply to graduate school. If you are unsure, you can have your academic credentials evaluated by an evaluation agency in the United States that will review your credentials and give you an official evaluation, indicating the equivalence of your degree in terms of the United States education system. Graduate schools in the United States set their own standards for what they consider to be the equivalent of a U.S. bachelor's degree.

How Well Do You Speak, Read, Write, and Understand English?

If English is not your native language, you will need to demonstrate sufficient command of the English language, not only to secure admission to a graduate school in the United States, but to secure a student visa as well. Lectures, reading assignments, and written or oral examinations are extremely complex in graduate school, and it is important to your success as a graduate student that your English language skills are very good.

The Most Popular Schools for International Students

New York University	4,964
Boston University	4,603
Columbia University	4,080
University of Southern California	4,034
Ohio State University	3,878
University of Wisconsin—Madison	3,820
University of Texas—Austin	3,666
University of Michigan—Ann Arbor	3,368
Harvard University	3,249
Purdue University	3,266
University of Illinois—Urbana-Champaign	3,107

Source: *Open Doors 1997/98: Report on International Educational Exchange*, published by the Institute of International Education

States with the Most International Students

California	.65,292
New York	.51,264
Texas	.29,542
Massachusetts	.27,121
Illinois	.20,703
Florida	.21,096
Pennsylvania	.18,094
Michigan	.17,878
Ohio	.17,522
Washington	.11,195

Source: *Open Doors 1997/98: Report on International Educational Exchange,* published by the Institute of International Education

How Will You Pay for Your Graduate Education?

Tuition and housing costs vary widely among graduate schools in the United States, but one thing is certain—graduate school is expensive. In order to secure a student visa to study in the United States, you must show that you have sufficient funds to pay for your full graduate degree program. How will you pay for your graduate education? Can you and/or your family pay all associated costs? Have you been offered financial aid from your school or department? Are there agencies in your home country that will fund your education in the United States? You should investigate all possible options for funding your graduate studies.

Obtaining Application Materials

Each graduate school has its own application and requires that the application be received by a specified deadline. In order to allow plenty of time to collect and thoroughly review the application information, you should request application materials 12–18 months in advance of the application deadline for each graduate school you are interested in attending.

There are a variety of methods you can use to obtain application materials. The quickest and easiest way is through the World Wide Web. Almost every university and college in the United States has a Web site containing useful information. Many schools offer the option of downloading an application from their Web site, saving many weeks of mailing time.

If you are not able to utilize the World Wide Web, call the department in which you are interested in studying and the graduate admissions office and request that an application and other information to be sent to you. Requesting application materials by letter and/or e-mail usually results in the longest response time.

Another method for obtaining information on U.S. graduate schools is by visiting a U.S. educational advising center in your country. These centers are usually operated by the United States Information Agency (USIA), the Fulbright Commissions, or other agencies, and may carry application materials for U.S. colleges and universities.

Completing the Application

The first step in completing the application is to read all directions carefully. If you do not understand a part of the application, immediately call the graduate admissions office and ask for clarification. Errors in completing the application or missing information will delay a decision on your application, potentially jeopardizing your chance of admission. When you are reviewing the application directions, look for the following important information:

- What is the application deadline for the program you are interested in studying? Some graduate schools will have a flexible deadline, others will have a very strict deadline. Some departments within one graduate school will have different deadlines. Also, there may be an earlier deadline if you are submitting credentials from a foreign school, or if you are applying for an assistantship or scholarship.

- Does the program you are applying to allow for admission in any semester? Many graduate programs admit students only in the fall term. You should familiarize yourself with the admission policies of every department and school to which you are applying.

- How does the graduate school want you to submit your application materials? Some graduate schools prefer that all materials (transcripts, letters of recommendation, etcetera) be submitted in one large envelope. Others will allow you to submit materials separately. If you are required to submit all materials in one envelope, and something is missing, include a note of explanation. Make sure that your name, address, and date of birth appear on every form and credential.

If possible, you should type the application so that the admissions office and the department you are applying to will not have difficulty reading your information. If you cannot type the application, you should print as neatly as possible.

Most graduate schools will require that you submit the following materials with the application for admission:

Academic Transcripts

In order to attend graduate school in the United States, you must present official documentation indicating that you have completed the equivalent of a U.S. bachelor's degree. With each application you submit, you must include original, official transcripts (mark sheets, grade reports, etcetera) of your academic work after high school. Some graduate schools may require you to obtain a certified evaluation of your credentials, verifying that you have completed (or are completing) the equivalent of a U.S. bachelor's degree. Other graduate schools will do their own evaluation of your credentials. If your academic credentials are in a language other than English, you must include both the original language transcripts and a certified English translation.

Letters of Recommendation

Most graduate schools require letters of recommendation. Ideally, these should come from faculty members who know you well and who can favorably comment on your previous academic performance and your ability to successfully complete graduate school in the United States. Most graduate school applications provide recommendation forms that may be given to your recommenders. If they do not, letters should be written on official letterhead, and your name and date of birth should be at the top of each page. It is important that you follow up with your recommenders to make sure that they complete and send your recommendation.

Test Scores

Most graduate schools require you to submit official scores from one or more standardized examinations. These include the Graduate Record Examination (GRE), the Graduate Management Admissions Test (GMAT), the Test of English as a Foreign Language (TOEFL) and other examinations. These examinations are conducted by private organizations and are not affiliated with colleges or universities. Carefully read the graduate school's application or catalog to determine which examinations are required. You should register for any required examination well in advance of the application deadline. Official results are usually sent directly to the graduate schools you designate four to six weeks after the examination date. If you have a copy of your test results, you should include a photocopy with your application, but you will still need to request that official copies of your results be sent to every graduate school that requires them.

Statement of Purpose

The statement of purpose is an essay that you must write that expresses your educational objectives. You should include a concise description of your previous academic work, any current research or other scholarly work you are engaged in, and your career plans. The admissions committee that reviews your application will want to know why pursuing graduate education is so important to you and why you have chosen to apply to that particular graduate program. At this point, it is appropriate to mention any specific faculty member whose research you have followed and with whom you would like to study. The statement should be typed and no more than two pages in length.

Supplemental Information

Some departments may require you to complete additional forms that detail your academic and/or professional experience and background in the field you have chosen. These forms are usually part of the application packet. Read the instructions carefully to determine if the department you are applying to requires any additional information beyond the standard application for admission.

Application Fee

You will be required to submit a nonrefundable fee for the processing of your application. This fee should be in the form of a check or money order payable in U.S. dollars. Failure to submit the application fee may delay the processing of your application and will jeopardize your chances for admission.

Additional Materials to Include With Your Application

Depending on the school and department to which you are applying, other items that may be required as part of your application include:

An updated résumé.
You should include this even if it is not required.

Writing sample.
Some departments will want to see a sample of your scholarly writing. This can include a journal or newspaper article that you wrote, poems and works of fiction or a screenplay (if applying to writing programs), or a portion of your thesis or other significant paper.

Official notices of funding.
If you are receiving funding from your government or other agency to study in the United States, you should include a copy of the terms of your funding (stipend amount, duration of award, etcetera) with your application.

Audio or video tape.
Some programs, particularly in the performing arts, may require you to submit an audio or video tape of your performance.

A picture of yourself.
Some graduate schools may require you to attach a passport-size photo of yourself to the application.

If there are any required items that you cannot submit with your application at the time of mailing, you should include an explanation and make every effort to send the missing pieces of your application to the graduate admissions office as soon as possible.

Because of the fluctuation in service among global postal systems, you should consider sending your application via courier service. The better known courier services (FedEx, UPS, Airborne Express) offer a variety of secure ways to ship your application in less than one week.

Correspondence About Your Application

You may receive a letter from the graduate admissions office confirming the receipt of your application. If you have not received any word six weeks after sending the application, you should call the admissions office to confirm receipt of your application.

About 8–12 weeks after the application deadline, you will receive a decision letter from the schools to which you applied. If you are admitted to a graduate program, you will be asked to respond to the offer of admission by a certain date. Most graduate schools will then ask for a deposit to secure your place.

An important document that you will receive is the application for a student visa. More specific information on obtaining the student visa appears below. Other information that will be sent to you may include housing information, orientation information and information on student activities and clubs.

If you have been selected to receive a fellowship, scholarship, or assistantship, this information may be included in your acceptance letter or in a separate letter.

It is important for you to understand that if you accept an offer of admission, especially if it contains an assistantship or fellowship, you have made a commitment to the department who admitted you and they will expect you to attend. If you are unable to attend in the semester to which you were admitted, you should ask the department if they would be willing to defer your admission to a future semester.

Obtaining a Student Visa

The Immigration and Naturalization Service (INS), an agency of the U.S. Department of Justice, is responsible for issuing visas to temporary visitors, including students. If you are admitted to graduate school in the United States, you will receive from each school a document known as the Application for Certificate of Eligibility (AFCOE). This form is used to apply for the I-20 form. If you are participating in a recognized education exchange program, or are entering the United States to conduct specialized research or teaching, the agency sponsoring your visit will issue you a form known as IAP-66. The graduate school you have chosen to attend will not mail you the I-20 until you have returned the completed AFCOE with official documentation showing that you have sufficient financial support for the entire duration of your academic program. This is known as the Affidavit of Support.

Once you have received the I-20 or IAP-66, you must take it, along with your passport, the Affidavit of Support, and letter of admission from the graduate school you will be attending, to the United States embassy or consulate with jurisdiction of your permanent place of residence. If the visa officer approves all of your documentation, you will be issued an F-1 visa (for the I-20) or a J-1 visa (for the IAP-66).

It is your responsibility to know the rules and regulations governing foreign students in the United States. One of the first things you should do when you arrive at graduate school is visit the office that handles international student affairs. They will need to know that you have arrived and will make copies of your visa. If you have any questions about your visa, travel regulations or employment restrictions, make an appointment to meet with an international student counselor.

PART FIVE

Financing Your Degree

CHAPTER 21

Planning Your Investment

Most graduate students fall into one of these broad categories:

- Part-time master's student working at least part-time, if not full-time

- Full-time master's student using part financial aid and part self-pay

- Full-time doctoral student using part financial aid and part self-pay (usually in humanities or social science)

- Full-time doctoral student with substantial university financing (most in science, some in other disciplines

One thing all these people have in common is that they are working during a significant part of their graduate programs. For most graduate students, the choice is not, "Should I work?" but "How much and where should I work?"

The bottom line is that even "full" financial aid, such as a fellowship or assistantship with tuition remission and a stipend, is not enough to cover most students' expenses. A student who is single and living in an area with a reasonable cost of living can sometimes get by, but throw in a partner and/or children, life in an urban area, or a lengthy dissertation process, and you are likely to need additional income. If you do not receive full aid, or do not receive aid at all, you will certainly need alternative ways to pay for your education.

Loans are an option, but most graduate students prefer to keep loan debt to a minimum for two reasons. First, if you already have undergraduate debt, financing your graduate education with loans just digs the hole deeper. Second, because most master's and doctoral students cannot expect to make a great deal of money in their chose fields, paying off large loans is too burdensome. For this reason many graduate students consider working during their programs.

Working While You Study

Most grad students make a distinction between "inside" and "outside" work. "Inside" work is assistant-ships, internships, practica, and all other work directly associated with the program. "Outside" work is unrelated work undertaken for one reason only: the money. Ask graduate students whether it's possible to work "outside" and still get through the program at a decent pace and you'll get every answer from "Forget it" to "I did it; you can, too." The one thing they all agree on is that it is tough; however, it has some significant advantages. The trick in deciding whether to work "outside" during your program is to balance the immediate financial advantages with the potential disruption to your progress. Here's what working graduate students recommend.

Work no more than half time.

Many graduate students find that work is manageable, even a welcome change from study and research, as long as it doesn't take up more than about 25 hours per week.

Find an employer who's willing to be flexible and understanding.

Constant pressure to put your job first will not help you progress through your program.

Prioritize.

Most working graduate students will tell you that a social life and such homely comforts as a well-stocked refrigerator, clean floors, and a full night's sleep won't be a big part of your life during your degree years, unless you have an incredibly supportive partner.

Try to connect your job to your program.

Social work programs, for instance, are sometimes willing to allow students to work full time in social service settings, counting the hours spent there towards the practicum requirement.

Affording Your Doctorate

Even with full aid, doctoral students often find themselves with a big black financial hole between them and their dissertations. Funding is generally available through the coursework and exam years, but very few programs provide the same level of support, or in fact any support, for the one to two years it nor-mally takes to complete research on, and write, the dissertation. Of course, since you no longer have to attend classes or prepare for exams on schedule, you're free to work, but financial need often outweighs all other considerations and the dissertation never gets written.

Thinking Ahead

Planning ahead for the dissertation stage of your degree can literally make the difference between earning your doctorate, and doing it in a reasonable amount of time, and never finishing the degree. When you estimate the total cost of your degree, include at least one year, if not two, of completely unsupported work on your dissertation. Then try to get support anyway.

First-Year Blues

In some graduate fields—history, for instance—the first year of doctoral programs is generally an unsupported year as well. One of two outstanding students may get some fellowship support for this year, but most students are on their own financially. Check with the departments that interest you to find out whether first-year students are eligible for aid.

Attending Conferences

A final financial problem doctoral students encounter regularly is not having the spare cash to allow them to participate in annual conferences and meetings of their field. Simply attending these conferences gives you a chance to "see and be seen" by the very people who will consider your job applications in a few years; if you can manage to present a paper or otherwise participate in the goings-on, that's even better. It's definitely to your advantage to participate in as many of these professional gatherings as possible, particularly the academically oriented ones; because job competition is so fierce, whatever you can do to get yourself noticed early on will help. Unfortunately, conferences and professional gatherings are often prohibitively expensive. Airfare, hotels, and registration fees often put this kind of travel far out of the reach of the average doctoral student.

Other doctoral students know the cheapest possible ways to attend conferences, and graduate departments often have some discretionary funds that help defray the cost of such travel; some financial aid offices allow you to borrow money to cover some of these costs. Even so, some of the expense will still fall to you. Try to budget at least $500–1,000 per year for travel.

Financial Tips

You can get a jump on your financial planning by getting a sense of graduate school costs, as well as your overall financial status.

Calculate your costs.

Start the financing process by getting a handle on your current living expenses. First, doing so may help you find some places where you can cut expenses now and save as much as possible before you begin your program. Second, if you are applying to programs in other cities, you'll want to compare your current expenses in your present location with projected expenses in these other locations.

Minimize your debt.

One of the most important things you can do prior to starting a grad program is pay down your consumer debt. Obviously every dollar you pay in high credit-card interest rates is one fewer dollar you save for graduate school. Significant consumer debt can even limit your ability to borrow from private sources to pay for your education. And financial aid officers rarely consider credit card and car payments when calculating your student living expense budget.

Stay in your job.

Plan to stay at your job as long as possible before enrolling in a graduate program. It's very appealing to thing of taking a long vacation or traveling in the month or two before you start school. But you need to be saving as much money as possible towards your educational expenses, not depleting your bank account. If you voluntarily leave your job early, many financial aid officers will still calculate personal resources based on earnings up to the start of school. If you do leave your job, contact your school's financial aid officer.

Avoid new expenses.

Similarly, try not to incur major expenses or make major purchases in the final months before you begin your program. You won't look more needy to the financial aid office if you deplete your bank account; the financial aid officer is usually reviewing your prior year's income tax return and expects that any funds you saved that year are still available. And if you do have an unavoidable and justifiable major expense after submitting your financial aid applications, don't hesitate to contact the financial aid office and ask if they will review your application based on the new information. They may be able to help.

Ask your family for help.

Even though you may be in your twenties, thirties, or forties, you may want to investigate the possibility of family funding. If you are uncomfortable with borrowing from family members (or any other benefactor), draw up a repayment agreement with clearly stated payments. You will have to report your parents' contribution on a financial aid form, but it probably won't affect any funding you are receiving.

Liquidate your assets.

If you've invested your savings in stocks, bonds, or other financial instruments, make sure that you can liquidate these assets in time to pay your tuition. You may want to reorder your investments in order to make them more liquid, even if that means reducing your profit margin. You need to plan for your cash flow requirements by making sure your funds are available well before the semester begins.

Plan for moving.

Finally, don't forget about moving expenses. They can be significant, especially if you have to give a substantial deposit on a new apartment or need a car to get around in your new location. Investigate your various moving options well in advance to get the best price. Also, do not assume that your moving expenses are deductible from your taxes. Talk to a tax person to find out how the IRS currently regards graduate education moving expenses.

Use the following worksheet to plan your expenses. Some may be costs that you already plan for every month, such as medical insurance or child support. You'll be able to calculate others by reading catalogs or calling financial aid offices. If you're considering a number of schools, copy this worksheet so you have one for each school you're applying to.

Student Budget Worksheet

Fixed Living Expenses	Annual	Monthly
Rent or Mortgage Payment		
Utilities (gas, electric, phone)		
Insurance (homeowners/renters, fire, health, but not auto)		
Child Care/Child Support		
TOTAL FIXED LIVING EXPENSES		
Flexible Living Expenses		
Food and household goods		
Books and supplies		
Personal (including laundry, cleaning, toiletries, and entertainment)		
Transportation (car expenses including gas/oil, repairs, parking, license, insurance; or fare for public transportation)		
Medical and Dental Expenses		
TOTAL FLEXIBLE LIVING EXPENSES		
TOTAL FIXED AND FLEXIBLE EXPENSES		
TUITION AND FEES		
TOTAL COST OF ATTENDANCE:		

Tax Credits

Last year, the federal government has realized that higher education has value to society and has passed several laws to help families offset part of the costs on their federal tax returns.

Hope Scholarship

While the Hope Scholarship is the best known, graduate students do not qualify for this tax credit.

Lifetime Learning Credit

Student taxpayers may be eligible to claim a nonrefundable Lifetime Learning Credit against their federal taxes. The Lifetime Learning Credit may be claimed for the qualified tuition and related expenses of the students in the taxpayer's family (i.e., the taxpayer, the taxpayer's spouse, or an eligible dependent) who are enrolled in eligible educational institutions. Through 2002, the amount that may be claimed as a credit is equal to 20 percent of the taxpayer's first $5,000 of out-of-pocket qualified tuition and related expenses for all the students in the family (including student loans). After 2002, the credit amount is equal to 20 percent of the taxpayer's first $10,000 of out-of-pocket qualified tuition and related expenses. Thus, the maximum credit a taxpayer may claim for a taxable year is $1,000 through 2002 and $2,000 thereafter.

Students may claim the credit for as little as one course. Although there is a yearly maximum credit for the Lifetime Learning Credit, there is no limit on the number of years that this credit can be claimed.

CHAPTER 22

Getting Federal Financial Aid

Unlike law, business, or medical students, who generally look forward to generous incomes after graduation and can therefore take on a sizeable loan debt to finance their educations, most graduate students need to keep their debt to a minimum. Paying off a $50,000 loan with interest is far more feasible on a surgeon's salary than on a social worker's, particularly if you already have an undergraduate debt to contend with.

Yet many student are daunted by the prospect of applying for financial aid. There are too many forms, too many different deadlines, too much competition. Since the application process seems so overwhelming, many people either don't bother at all or leave it till the last minute, missing deadlines and discovering that funds are no longer available. This outcome simply reinforces the idea that even if they had taken the time to read the material and apply, they "wouldn't have gotten anything good." Often that's just not true, and no prospective graduate student should pass up the chance to finance as much of her degree as possible through "free money"—money you don't have to pay back—before borrowing or spending her own money. A number of studies have documented a clear correlation between financial circumstances and time to completion of degree. People with fewer financial worries complete more degrees, faster.

Financial Aid Basics

Graduate financial aid falls into three basic categories: gift aid, assistantships, and loans.

Gifts

Scholarships, fellowships, and grants are all forms of "gift" aid, which you don't have to work for and don't have to repay. Naturally, it's the most sought-after kind of funding, and therefore the most difficult to receive. Also, with budget tightening in so many university departments, free money is less available now than in the past; and even in the most prosperous times, full financing through gift aid is rare. Obviously, though, whatever gift aid you can obtain makes your life that much easier. Gift aid can be awarded on the basis of need, merit, or both, depending on the source of aid.

Assistantships

A major source of funding at the doctoral level is assistantships: research (RA) and teaching (TA). Usually an assistantship provides a stipend for the nine-month school year, and tuition remission for the same time period. Some assistantships provide either the stipend or the tuition remission, but not both. In exchange for the support, you either teach introductory-level classes or assist professors in their research. In some programs, assistantships are awarded to every student; in others they are awarded competitively, based on academic performance. This is generally a function of how well funded the department is; things get competitive when there simply isn't enough money to support every student in the program. Some programs deal with funding problems by awarding smaller assistantships to more students—for example, granting either tuition remission or a stipend but not both, and reducing the number of hours students are expected to research or teach. Others prefer to give full, or nearly full, support to the very best students in the department on the principle that good financial support will seriously increase the chances that these students will complete the program and do so as quickly as possible.

Loans

Most graduate students try to minimize the loan component of their financing, but sometimes that simply isn't possible. Graduate students in the sciences tend to have the least need for loans, given the sizable amount of federal grant money funneled into science programs; humanities, social science, and education programs are less well funded, and students in these fields, particularly education, tend to spend more of their own money and borrow more money to get through their programs.

Real Students: Paying Your Way

We asked graduate students, "How are you paying for your degree?" and we received a variety of real-life responses.

Ph.D., Comparative Literature. "A multiyear tuition fellowship, language tutoring, and a research assistantship."

M.A., History. "Eighty percent tuition remission from my company, plus a loan for additional expenses."

Ph.D., Biomedical Engineering. "Savings, a student loan, and my research assistantship."

M.A., Education. "Two jobs, scholarship, work-study—and I live with my parents to save money."

Ph.D., Clinical Psychology. "Tuition remission, teaching stipend, small loans, and summer jobs counseling."

M.S.W. "My husband and I are paying for this out of our own savings, which is proving to be a financial strain."

Who Gets Aid and Who Doesn't

Financial aid packages vary tremendously from program to program. In some fields, support is nearly guaranteed, while in others, you'll probably have to fend for yourself.

Social Work

Because so many students are at the master's level, TA and RA jobs are scarce (unless you are on the academic rather than the practical track). Most programs recommend a mixture of the following types of financing: competitive school- or program-based fellowships and scholarships, paid practica, loans, and work-study. Most program catalogs outline various aid sources, including private and public scholarships and grants.

Education

At the master's degree level, TA and RA jobs are rare. Many master's degree students are in service teachers who simply pay for the degree themselves. For those seeking financial assistance, most schools of education recommend a combination of loans, school aid, and federal/local grants and scholarships. Even at the doctoral level, most education student are self-supporting: 79.8 percent use personal funds, 13.9 percent receive university aid. Here are some other statistics:

				Personal	Spouse/
Education Doctoral Support Sources					
	TAs	**RAs**	**Fellows**	**Funds**	**Partner's Funds**
Men	23.6%	19.1%	6.8%	87.5%	35.8%
Women	25.3%	19.7%	6.7%	87.0%	41.8%

Psychology

Some programs guarantee support at the doctoral level, others award it on a competitive basis. TA and RA jobs are available and reasonably plentiful; most get tuition remission as well as a stipend. Samples: $2,000 annually for minimal RA hours; $10,000 annually for more extensive RA hours.

History

In many programs, fellowships are awarded to a limited number of first-year students, but TA jobs are not available until the second year. RA jobs are scarce. There is also a strong competition for the TA and RA jobs, based on first-year performance. Some programs give higher awards to applicants who already have a master's degree. Samples: $8,271 annually for a TA, nine-month assignment; $11,000 annually for a TA, nine-month assignment. Summer funding is also available in some programs.

Sociology

There are some entry-level fellowships available in some programs, on a competitive basis. TA and RA jobs are both available. Some programs pay hourly, or in less than full-year assignments. Applicants are urged to look for other sources of aid, especially social science grants and scholarships. Samples: $11.91/hr. for RA work; $9,950 annually for RA. At the doctoral level, more students use personal funds than receive university funding: 41.6 percent receive university money, while 47.8 percent use personal funds. Here's a further breakdown:

				Personal	Spouse/
	TAs	**RAs**	**Fellows**	**Funds**	**Partner's Funds**
Men	62.0%	47.4%	23.3%	68.9%	29.7%
Women	57.6%	48.8%	20.8%	73.1%	38.6%

Social Science Doctoral Support Sources

English

In many programs, fellowships are awarded to a limited number of first-year students, but TA jobs are not available until the second year, and the competition is fierce, based on first-year performance. Sample: $8,200 for a nine-month TA, plus tuition remission; summer support is also available.

Humanities

More than half (50.5 percent) of humanities doctoral students receive university funding, while 43.3 percent use personal funds. By gender, this breaks down as follows:

Humanities Doctoral Support Sources

	TAs	RAs	Fellows	Personal Funds	Spouse/ Partner's Funds
Men	76.8%	20.9%	33.5%	75.1%	34.9%
Women	77.8%	21.6%	34.7%	71.7%	38.2%

Teaching and research assistantships are not guaranteed in most programs. Fellowships are available on a very competitive basis. The majority of students earn stipends as teaching or research assistants. Samples: $8,800 for a nine-month RA; $13,200 for a 12-month RA. Some programs award more to more experienced teachers/researchers.

Physical Sciences

In the physical sciences (including math and computer science), 77 percent of students receive university money. Only 12.1 percent use personal funds.

Physical Science Doctoral Support Sources

	TAs	RAs	Fellows	Personal Funds	Spouse/ Partner's Funds
Men	72.2%	76.9%	15.7%	33.7%	17.9%
Women	78.3%	76.2%	15.9%	34.1%	24.2%

Life Sciences

More than half of students (56.8 percent) get university aid, while 21.4 percent rely on personal funds.

Life Science Doctoral Support Sources

	TAs	RAs	Fellows	Personal Funds	Spouse/ Partner's Funds
Men	38.7%	67.9%	15.2%	41.9%	25.1%
Women	41.3%	62.7%	16.1%	47.2%	28.1%

Engineering

At the master's level, financial aid is spotty. At the doctoral level, there are some competitive fellowships and TA/RA opportunities. Stipends can be nine-month, 12-month, or monthly. Fellowships and TA/RA positions are not guaranteed. Samples: $5,000 annual fellowship; $11,160 for a nine-month TA or RA. The majority (69.3 percent) of engineering students receive university money, while 14.7 percent rely on personal funds.

	TAs	RAs	Fellows	Personal Funds	Spouse/ Partner's Funds
Engineering Doctoral Support Sources					
Men	44.0%	78.7%	11.4%	36.0%	15.7%
Women	51.6%	78.8%	18.4%	33.4%	23.4%

Health

Because so many students are at the master's level, TA and RA jobs are scarce (unless you are on the academic rather than the practical track). Most programs recommend a mixture of the following types of financing: competitive school- or program-based scholarships, traineeships, loans, and work-study. Federal traineeships in health services shortage areas, programs from the Public Health service, and programs like HCOP are also available to grad students. Most program catalogs outline various aid sources; there are many private and public scholarship and grant opportunities.

Science

Most top programs guarantee full support for all students, usually tuition remission plus a stipend. A majority of students earn stipends as research assistants; some work as teaching assistants. Stipends are based on either a nine-month or a 12-month assignment. Fellowships are available on a very competitive basis. Samples: $9,800 plus tuition remission for a nine-month RA; $17,000 plus tuition remission for a 12-month RA; many are around $14,000.

Master's Programs

Assistantships in master's programs are not common. Many master's students just pay for their own degrees, often by working while they go to school. Also common is the patchwork approach, whereby a combination of part-time work, loans, and gift aid pays the bills. Don't assume, however, that it isn't worth your trouble to pursue aid in a master's program. Some well-funded master's programs do offer substantial gift aid, and even those that cannot afford to do so will try to direct you to other sources.

Women and minorities in particular have good chances of finding both school-based and outside sources of aid.

Doctoral Programs

The first and last years of doctoral programs are the hardest to finance. Most assistantships are not available during the first year of your program, partly because the department wants to give you a chance to settle in before putting you to work and partly because to see if you're going to be a washout before they turn you loose on a classroom full of undergraduates. Once you have proven yourself, however, you will be eligible to apply for teaching and research assistantships. Some programs offer first-year doctoral students a one-year fellowship to finance the settling-in period, with the understanding that by a certain point each student will have found a research or teaching position and will work in return for support for the next few years.

Unfortunately, once you have completed your coursework and passed your exams, the money tends to dry up. Support for the dissertation phase of doctoral programs is skimpy to nonexistent, and this lack of funding has been responsible for many a failure to complete the dissertation. Here's a typical experience: "I financed my education through loans and work—I took on a job working for the college as an advisor to undergrads. The job began on a part-time level and then moved on to full-time. As I became more involved in my job, I had less and less time for school. But essentially, since I was strapped for cash, I had no choice but to remain more committed to my job."

Backed into a financial corner, this student still hasn't written his dissertation. Thus, when you plan your doctorate financing, you should begin planning ahead for the dissertation years, especially if you are in the humanities or social sciences. It may make the difference between making your investment pay off and throwing away five or six years of work.

You may be eligible to borrow money while working on your dissertation, so check with your school's financial aid office. Also, you may be able to defer payment on past student loans while working on your dissertation. Check with your lender.

Full Time vs. Part Time

Financial aid, both need-based and merit-based, is generally far more available to full-time than to part-time students. At the master's level this is less true; at the doctoral level, substantial aid for part-time students is rare. However, part-time students, whether master's or doctoral, have an important source of aid not available to full-time students: their employers. Education and social work students in particular can sometimes get employer reimbursement for all or part of their degree programs; if that's not an option, the programs themselves often allow students to count their work experience towards course credit or field placement requirements. While this does not directly pay for the program, it may allow you to complete your program earlier, which can save a great deal of money.

To qualify for some forms of aid—especially student loans—you must be enrolled at least half-time. Contact your school to find out how many credits qualify you for half-time status.

Start Searching for Money

Below is just a sample of the foundations, grants, databases, and other sources of financing you can find out there.

Using various free scholarship search databases on the web, you should be able to identify additional scholarship sources that you can pursue. This kind of research can result in one or more small grants that can help offset the cost of your graduate degree. The most comprehensive scholarship search is fastWEB. FastWEB is the Internet's first, largest, and fastest free scholarship search service. You can even submit a preliminary application to some of the scholarships listed on fastWEB directly via the Web through fastWEB's E-Scholarships Program.

Some other free scholarship databases that you may want to investigate are:

- Peterson's COLLEGEQUEST, which presents 800,000 awards from about 2,000 sources in 69 academic subject areas.

- Sallie Mae's Online Scholarship Service offers free access to the College Aid Sources for Higher Education (CASHE) database. The database lists private sector awards from more than 3,600 sponsors.

- The College Board's FUND FINDER scholarship database, also known as ExPAN Scholarship Search, lists scholarships and other types of financial aid programs from 3,300 national, state, public and private sources.

- CollegeNET MACH25 is a free Web version of the Wintergreen/Orchard House Scholarship Finder database. The database lists awards from 1,570 sponsors.

- SRN Express is a free web version of the Scholarship Resource Network (SRN) database. The SRN database focuses on private-sector, non-need-based aid, and includes information about awards from more than 1,500 organizations.

All these scholarship databases can be accessed on the Web through www.finaid.org under Scholarships.

Books

Bauer, David G. *The Complete Grants Sourcebook for Higher Education.* 3rd ed. Oryx Press, 1995.

Directory of Biomedical and Health Care Grants, 1995. 9th ed. Oryx Press, 1995.

Directory of Grants in the Humanities: 1995–96. 9th ed. Oryx Press, 1995.

The Foundation Center. *Foundation Grants to Individuals.* 9th ed. 1995.

Gale Research Inc. *Scholarships, Fellowships, and Loans 1996.* Volume 11, no. 96. Gale Research Inc.: Detroit, 1995.

Maloney, Wendy A. *Grants, Fellowships, and Prizes of Interest to Historians: 1994–95.* Washington, DC.: American Historical Association, 1994.

National Endowment for the Arts. *Literature: Application Guidelines Fiscal Year 1995.* Washington DC: National Endowment for the Arts, 1995.

Schlachter, Gail Ann, and R. David Weber. *Financial Aid for the Disabled and their Families: 1994–96.* San Carlos, CA.: Reference Service Press, 1994.

Williams, Lisa, ed. *The Grants Register 1995–1997.* New York, St. Martin's Press, 1994.

Publications by Mail

A Selected List of Fellowship and Other Support Opportunities for Advanced Education for U.S. Citizens and Foreign Nationals

The Publications Office
National Science Foundation
1800 G Street NW
Washington, DC 20550

Graduate Assistantship Directory

Association for Computing Machinery
Sharon Smith
ACM GAD
1515 Broadway
New York, NY 10036

International Funding Directory
NAFSA
1307 New York Avenue NW, Suite 800
Washington, DC 20005
(202) 737-3699

Student Guide
Published annually by the Department of Education.
(800) 4FED-AID

10 Ways to Pay for Part-Time Study
NUCEA
One Dupont Circle NW, Suite 615
Washington, DC 20036-1168
(202) 659-3130

Resources for Women

Resources for Women in Science. A database that provides specific information on more than 400 awards, 174 grants and awards; 205 fellowships and scholarships; 21 research assistantships, summer science programs, and internships; and a handful of visiting professors and loans.

Minnesota Women's Center
212 Nicholson Hall
216 Pillsbury Drive SE
Minneapolis, MN 55414

American Association of University Women Fellowships (AAUW). Information on dissertation funding, postdoctoral positions, and fellowships for women.

AAUW Educational Foundation
P.O. Box 4030
Iowa City, IA 52243-4030
(319) 337-1716

Minority Resources

National Consortium for Graduate Degrees for Minorities in Engineering and Science, Inc. You must be an engineering or natural science major and belong to one of the following groups to qualify: American Indian, African American, Mexican American, Puerto Rican, or other Hispanic Americans. Call (219) 287-1097.

Sample of Grants and Fellowships

Fulbright Program. For graduate students and faculty. U.S. citizens must be planning on research and study in Canada: Canadian citizens must be planning on research and study in the United States.

> The Canada-U.S. Fulbright Program
> 350 Albert Street, Suite 2015
> Ottawa, ON, Canada K1R 1A4
> (613) 237-5366

Spencer Foundation. A one-time award for doctoral candidates at U.S. graduate schools (U.S. citizenship not required, however). The dissertation must be related to education.

> The Spencer Foundation
> Spencer Dissertation Fellowships
> 900 North Michigan Avenue, Suite 2800
> Chicago, IL 60611-1542
> (312) 337-7000, ext. 616

AERA Minority Dissertation Fellowships. For members of groups traditionally underrepresented in higher education in the United States. You must be committed to working on your dissertation full time, and be interested in a career in higher education or educational research.

> AERA, Minority Fellowships
> 1230 17th Street, NW
> Washington, DC 20036-3078
> (202) 223-9485

Research Grants for Women's Studies. Form the Special Collections Library at Duke University. Anyone with a scholarly interest in women's studies research is eligible to apply for these grants.

> Ginny Daley
> Women's Studies Archivist at the Special Collections Library
> Duke University
> Box 90185
> Durham, NC 27708-0185
> (919) 660-5828

National Research Council. Fellowships for students in the sciences, social sciences, mathematics, and engineering.

> Fellowship Office
> National Research Council
> 2101 Constitution Avenue NW
> Washington, DC 20418

Mellon Fellowships. Fellowships for grad students in the humanities.

> Mellon Fellowships
> Woodrow Wilson National Fellowship Foundation
> P.O. Box 288
> Princeton, NJ 08542

CHAPTER 23

Scholarships and Other Sources of Aid

Financial aid application procedures can vary more from school to school than the procedures for admissions. This chapter will outline the general application requirements and discuss some of the documentation required.

The first step is to get the admissions material and read it thoroughly. Usually, general financial aid information appears in the admissions application, including the financial aid deadline(s). These deadlines drive the rest of the process for you. The admissions application deadline may be earlier or later than the financial aid application deadline. In addition, sometimes there is more than one financial aid deadline, In the case of multiple financial aid deadlines, the first one is usually for students interested in scholarship and fellowship assistance. A later deadline may be set for those students who are only interested in campus-based aid and federal loans.

Key Materials

The Free Application for Federal Student Aid (FAFSA) form is always required to request any type of federal financial aid. This form is used for "need analysis," the calculation of what you should be able to contribute towards the cost of your education. The detailed financial information you provide on the FAFSA form is then run through a federal formula to arrive at a contribution figure. The calculations are explained in detail in this chapter.

If you were in school the year before you plan to attend grad school, and you applied for financial aid, chances are that you'll receive a Renewal Application in the mail. This form is basically a FAFSA preprinted with the information that you provided the year before. All you need to do is update the information. If you're filing a Renewal Application, read and update the information carefully before you sign and submit the form.

For example, if you're in college, be sure to change your year. List the schools to which you're applying for the graduate program. The information will be electronically transmitted to them.

Both of these forms (the FAFSA and the Renewal Application) allow you to send your financial information to a maximum of six institutions. If you're applying to more than six schools, you need to list your top six choices. If you subsequently want to add a school to this list, you'll have to drop one from your list. Make your life easier—try to limit your financial aid application to just your six top choices.

Other required forms may include (but are not limited to):

- Separate school financial aid application

- Private "need analysis" form (such as the Profiles form from the College Scholarship Service or the NeedAccess disk)

- Your prior year's IRS 1040 form

- Financial aid transcripts (FATs) from any postsecondary school that you attended. (This requirement has been replaced at many schools by the National Student Loan Database System (NSLDS); check with your school to ask whether they still require you to file a FAT.)

Since many deadlines are as early as January 15, you probably won't be able to complete your federal tax form before the deadline. Most schools recommend that you estimate the numbers and then correct them once you get your taxes filed. But other schools may want you to wait until you have all the actual numbers. A school's individual policy about estimating tax figures versus waiting for the real figures may be stated in the financial aid application materials. Otherwise, check with the school's financial aid office.

Even though you should be careful on your financial aid application forms, don't work yourself into a panic about them. Mistakes happen, and financial aid officers don't expect you to be perfect. It's usually better to estimate a number than to miss a deadline while you're trying to verify it. You can always submit the actual figure to the financial aid officer when you get it. He or she will make the appropriate correction for you and recalculate your need analysis contribution.

How to File FATs and Other Forms

In the Fall of 1996, the FAT requirement changed. Schools are now able to access FAT information on the National Student Loan Database System (NSLDS). Because of this access, most schools have eliminated the requirement for prospective students to supply FATs. Still, some schools are not yet comfortable using the NSLDS information and are still requesting students to supply FATs. Contact each school you are interested in to find out what its current policy is. Don't necessarily believe what you read in the admissions material since more and more schools are dropping the FAT requirement as they get comfortable with NSLDS. The catalog information may be out-of-date even though it was printed for this year. As of January 1, 1998, all schools were required to have electronic access to NSLDS in their offices. Now that they all have access, they may have changed their requirement.

If FATs are still required, the school financial aid application material will contain a single copy of the FAT form. You'll need to make a copy for every school withing the United States that you have attended since high school, even if you didn't apply for or receive any financial aid.

Complete the top section of the FAT and then send the form to the financial aid offices at all your previous schools. They'll send the form directly to the graduate business schools where you're applying. If you're applying to a lot of schools, you'll get a lot of practice filling out these forms. Since completing FATs is no longer commonplace at many schools, give your previous schools a reasonable amount of time to send your forms out. After about a month, check with the financial aid offices at the schools you're applying to. Make sure that they received all your FATs.

Not all forms get sent to a school's financial aid office. Check out this chart for information on where to submit each form.

Where Do They Go?	
Form	**Where to Submit**
FAFSA	Federal processor (address on the envelope enclosed with the form)
School Financial Aid Application	School Financial Aid Office
CSS Financial Aid Profile Form	College Scholarship Service, Princeton, NJ
NeedAccess Disk	Access Group—Delaware
Signed Federal Tax Form	School's financial aid office
Financial Aid Transcript requests (if required)	Financial Aid Office of undergraduate or grad schools attended (even if you didn't get a degree)

Forms: Round Two

Once you've submitted all the required forms, you'll have to wait about a month before anything else happens regarding your financial aid. You might hear from admissions offices during this time.

Meanwhile, the federal processor, a number-crunching center for the government currently based in Iowa, is crunching away on the information you provided on your FAFSA. They run your numbers through a formula called Federal Methodology which is revamped every six years (although the numbers are changed yearly). Their calculations result in a Student Aid Report (SAR). You'll get a copy of it in the mail. Your SAR contains both the financial information that you provided on your FAFSA plus the results of the federal need-analysis calculation. The schools that you listed on the FAFSA will receive the data electronically, but may need you to sign an additional form to activate the financial aid process (especially if the school does not have its own financial aid application). The actual need analysis calculation parallels the process of estimating your family contribution which we discuss later in this chapter.

University Funding

Universities themselves are large sources of financial aid to graduate students. Assistantships and some fellowships are awarded by either the graduate school itself or the individual departments, while other fellowships, scholarships, and grants are funded by the federal government or private agencies and administered by the graduate school for its students.

Some schools simply ask you to indicate on the regular application form whether you are interested in being considered for university funding; others have separate, sometimes elaborate, application forms. Some departments require letters of recommendation and other documentation in support of the application for these funds.

Most assistantship positions and grant or fellowship money are awarded competitively, and one major criterion is often GRE scores. A top history program, for instance, specifies that only applicants with GRE scores above 1,400 will be considered for its fellowships. The application date for these positions is often earlier than the regular application date, all of which means that if you are going to apply to programs for assistantship positions or fellowship/grant money, you should plan to take the GRE no later than early October to be absolutely sure that your scores will be submitted well before the deadline.

Gift Aid

As noted in chapter 22, even the most generous "full" aid package won't put you far above the poverty level, and many departments can't afford anything near full aid for more than a few students. If you're at the master's level, fellowships and assistantships are not likely to come your way at all. However, there's still gift aid out there, in the form of grants and fellowships administered directly by government agencies and private sources. The National Science Foundation, for instance, funds a large number of scholarship in the sciences and social sciences.

Many graduate students, especially those who expect to get some kind of funding from their departments, don't take the trouble to apply for external funding. It's worth the trouble, however, as there is a fair amount of money out there, especially for women and minorities.

Organizing your search

There are two basic resources for starting your search: guides and databases provided by schools, funding agencies, commercial publishers, and the graduate schools themselves. Some of the students we interviewed for this book told us that while guides and databases gave them a good sense of what is out there and how to apply for funds, the most lucrative and successful leads came through the graduate departments themselves and personal contacts in their fields. Others, particularly in the sciences, have had a lot of success applying for grants from traditional sources like the National Science Foundation. Use the resources in chapter 22 to familiarize yourself with the world of grants and funding, but also check out every possibility in the departments you apply to, and don't forget to let professors know of your interest so they can pass on any leads they may have.

Remember, if you need money to attend school, this process is just as important as the process of getting admitted.

Aid Application Results

Once the financial aid office has all the forms and data that they need, they'll wait for the admissions decision before they review your application. During this waiting period, it's a good idea to check with the schools to make sure that everything is complete and ready for processing once the admissions decision has been made.

When the financial aid office finds out that you've been admitted, they'll review your application and make an offer of financial aid. This offer is called a financial aid package or award package. The financial aid package can include scholarships and grants, Federal Work-Study, Federal Perkins Loans, Federal Stafford or Federal Direct Loans, and suggested private loan sources.

Comparing your schools' financial aid packages will influence your decision as to where you'll attend school, and your choice might not be the school that offered you the largest scholarship. You need to weigh the merits of the financial aid package against the desirability of the school itself and your match with it. You may decide that finances will not be a part of your decision when you choose which school to attend. Probably, though, the financial aid offer will have an impact on your decision.

You need to look at more than just the amount of scholarship money included in the financial aid package:

- What is your contribution expected to be?

- How much will you be expected to borrow?

- What kinds of loans are offered, and are they loans with attractive rates?

- Will you have to work while you are attending school?

- Is the package guaranteed over your entire academic career? If not, what factors may cause it to change in the future?

Your complete aid package should be analyzed before you make your admissions decision. In order to make an informed decision regarding the value of the financial aid package, it is important for you to understand all the awards being offered. Chapters 21 and 23—"Getting Federal Financial Aid" and "Borrowing the Money"—explain the various programs in detail.

Calculating Your Need

The calculation of how much a student (and family) can contribute toward graduate business education always seems the most incomprehensible part of the financial aid process. It's actually quite straightforward once you know the guidelines and rules.

Basic Guidelines

The first concept to understand is financial need. Think of it as a simple matter of subtraction:

> Cost of Attendance – Family Contribution = Financial Need

As we discussed previously, the total cost of attendance is determined by the school and consists of the tuition and fees, room and board, books and supplies, transportation, and personal expenses. The family contribution is determined through the use of a federal formula called Federal Methodology (FM). The FAFSA form that you file gives enough information to the federal processor to run your figures through this formula and produce a family contribution. The federal processor is a selected firm under government contract that uses the methodology approved by Congress to calculate your contribution.

Don't let the words family contribution concern you. As a graduate student, you are automatically considered independent of your parents, even if you live with them. However, if you're married, your spouse or partner is considered part of your family and his or her income and assets will be assessed in the calculation of your family contribution. On the other hand, if you have children, your family contribution will be reduced.

For federal aid eligibility (Federal Stafford, Federal Perkins, and Federal Work-Study), the income and assets of your parents will not be assessed. The school does have the right to assess a Parental Contribution when calculating your eligibility for its own scholarship and loan funds. Very few graduate schools currently require that you provide parental information, but this practice could change in the future as the demand for financial aid becomes greater. If you receive direct assistance from any source including your family, it should be included in the analysis of your resources.

What are some of the components reviewed in assessing family contribution? They include several factors, as follows:

- Total family income from the previous calendar year (base-year income)

- Net value of any assets (value minus debt)

- Taxes paid (federal, state, and local)

- Asset protection for retirement

- Number of family members

- Number of family members in college at least half time

- Costs associated with both spouses working

- Income protection allowance (IPA) for basic living expenses

Before going on to the actual calculation, you need to understand the components listed above and why they are considered.

Base Year Income

The formula in Federal Methodology requires the use of the prior calendar year income to determine your contribution. This means that if you enroll in the fall of 2001, you'll be asked to provide your 2000 income. For the majority of the population, the best predictor of current year income is prior year income.

Income Protection Allowance (IPA)

This allowance provides for basic living expenses not included in the standard student expense budget. This allowance will vary according to the number of family members and the number in college at least half time. For a single student with no dependents, the IPA is $3,000; a married student with no dependents other than a spouse is allowed $6,000; for students with dependent children, the amount varies depending on the number of family members.

Asset Protection Allowance

The formula includes an allowance for protection of assets, depending on your age. This means that a portion of your assets will not be considered in the calculation because they're protected for your retirement. The older you are, the more of your assets are protected.

Employment Allowance

The concept of an employment allowance grows from the realization that it costs to have both members of a married couple work outside the home. The formula allows 35 percent of the lower income, up to $2,700, to be deducted as an allowance against total income.

Federal Methodology (FM)

The formula used in need analysis to determine eligibility for most federal financial aid programs has been written into law by the U.S. Congress.

Congress reviews this formula every several years and recommends changes to it. The federal formula was established to set objective standards that would be uniformly applied to all applicants.

Broadly, FM tries to take the income that is received by the members of the student's household, subtract the taxes paid and the cost of maintaining the members of the family other than the student, add in a portion of the assets, and then take a percentage of the result to produce an expected family contribution. Although this formula may not take into account all the vagaries of an individual student's situation, it produces generally comparable data on all students applying for financial aid. The financial aid officer at the school then has the option of adjusting data elements to make the contribution realistic for each student.

Estimating Your Family Contribution

We can't explain all the ins and outs of the FM in this book. Volumes of federal guidelines affecting federal methodology are produced each year. The instructions for using FM that financial aid officers receive would take up a few chapters. Instead, we've done some research on the World Wide Web and found several sources that allow you to do an estimate of you family contribution right online. The two best that we have found are:

http:// www.finaid.org—select "Calculators," then select "Financial Aid Estimation" under "Needs Analysis."

http:// www.kaplan.com—select the EFC Calculator for graduate students

These two sites each have family contribution calculators that will do the job for you. You don't need to manually do all the calculations and have access to all the charts because it's all automatic. What you do need is your most recent tax form and some idea of the value of your assets. All you have to do is enter the financial information that they ask for, and your family contribution will be calculated. You can even print out the results for reference. These results represent what the federal government considers to be the money you have available for your education. We can't guarantee that the figure you arrive at using the worksheet will exactly match the figure used in the financial aid office at your grad school, but it should give you a reasonable estimate. Use this estimated figure in your financial planning.

CHAPTER 24

Borrowing the Money

It's a fact worth repeating: Student loans are an important source of support for graduate students. Grad schools expect the majority of students with financial need to borrow at least part of their educational costs; you should research the loan possibilities early in the aid application process. This chapter provides you with the information you'll need to decide which loan programs fit for your particular situation.

It can take up to eight to 12 weeks from the date you applied to receive any loan proceeds, so planning is essential. Also, since the rules and regulations for borrowing through each of these programs differ, you should read each section carefully.

The Kaplan/American Express Student Loan Program

The Kaplan/American Express Student Loan Program provides students and their parents with information and step-by-step assistance in how to meet the high cost of graduate school. Through an affiliation with one of the nation's largest student loan lenders, the program connects you with a resource for the financing you need to reach your educational goals.

You can get information about the Kaplan/American Express Student Loan Program at seminars, in written materials, and through online services. Additional benefits include:

- **Free Assistance Available Toll-Free.** Educational Finance Specialists (EFSs) are availalable 12 hours a day to answer any questions you may have. You can reach an EFS toll-free at (888) KAP-LOAN, Monday through Sunday, from 10:00 A.M. to 10:00 P.M. Eastern time.

- **Money-Saving Features.** Both Federal PLUS and Stafford Loans come with valuable borrower benefits that can save you money at repayment time.

- **Easy Application.** You can access financial aid information, and even apply for a student loan online, at the Kaplan/American Express Student Loan Program Web site (www.kaploan.com).

- **Credit Reevaluation Program.** The Second Review helps previously denied borrowers to reverse their credit-denied status. Borrowers are guided through the process of gathering documentation that might clear up incorrect and/or outdated credit report listings.

Federal Perkins Student Loan

Administered by colleges and universities, the Federal Perkins Student Loan Program is made possible through a combination of resources: an annual allocation from the U.S. Department of Education, a contribution from the participating institution, and repayments by previous borrowers. You may have taken advantage of this program under its previous name, the National Direct Student Loan (NDSL) Program. The program was originally called the National Defense Student Loan Program when it was instituted by the federal government more than thirty years ago. However you read the initials, the NDSL program was one of the first financial aid programs instituted by the U.S. federal government.

Eligibility

As with Federal Work-Study, the college or university determines eligibility for Federal Perkins Loans based on your financial need (calculated through the FAFSA/SAR) and the availability of funds. Besides demonstrating financial need, you have to be enrolled at least half time, and maintain satisfactory progress toward a degree. Keep in mind that Federal Perkins Loans are reserved for the neediest students.

Borrowing Limits

Federal policy allows the maximum annual loan of $5,000 per graduate student. Actually, though, many schools lack the funds to allocate this much to any one student. A graduate student may borrow up to a cumulative total of $30,000, including all outstanding undergraduate and graduate Federal Perkins Loans.

Interest Rate

The terms are very good. The annual interest rate is currently 5 percent. Interest does not accrue while the borrower remains enrolled at least half time.

Fees

Another perk of the Federal Perkins Loan: no fees.

Application Procedures

Usually, you're automatically considered for this loan when you apply for financial aid. If you've been offered and have accepted a Federal Perkins Loan, you'll sign a promissory note for each semester of the loan. The promissory note lists the amount of the loan and states your rights and responsibilities as a borrower. When the signed note is received, either your will be credited for one semester's portion of the loan, or a check will be cut for you directly.

Grace Period

A Federal Perkins Loan has a six-month grace period after a student graduates or drops below half-time attendance. During this period, no repayment is required and no interest accrues. The grace period for a Federal Perkins Loan is six months. If you borrowed under the NDSL Program, you may have a different grace period. You need to check with the school that granted you the loan to find your loan's specific grace period.

Repayment

Borrowers under the Federal Perkins Loan program repay the school, although there may be an intermediary. Many schools contract with outside agencies for billing and collection. Repayment may extend up to ten years, beginning six months (your grace period) after you are enrolled at least half time. The amount of the monthly payment and the maximum number of months allowed for repayment is based on the total amount borrowed. The federal government has set the minimum monthly payment at $40.

Under some special circumstances, borrowers may make arrangements to repay a lower amount or to extend the repayment period. There is no prepayment penalty.

Deferments

You can defer payments of your Federal Perkins loan while you are enrolled until you graduate or drop below half-time. This deferment is not automatic; you must request the deferment forms from either your school or from the billing agency where you are repaying the loan.

Cancellations

This might not make you jump for joy, but it's good to know. The entirety of your Federal Perkins Loans and/or NDSLs will be canceled if you become permanently disabled—or die. You can get a portion of your loans canceled in less drastic circumstances if you:

- Teach handicapped children

- Teach in a designated elementary or secondary school that serves low-income students

- Work in a specified Head Start program or serve as a VISTA or Peace Corps volunteer

Check your promissory note. Your loan may have additional cancellation provisions. Also, if you have "old" Federal Perkins Loans or NDSLs, there may be some different conditions depending on when the original loan was made. Check with your previous school for any special circumstances.

Federal Loan Programs

The two U.S. federal loan programs available to graduate business school students are generally considered the core loan programs, since they carry certain attractive features defined by law. These features include a low interest rate, low fees, and defined deferment provisions. The two programs are:

- Federal Stafford Student Loan Program (part of the Federal Family Education Loan Program)

- William D. Ford Federal Direct Student Loan Program

The terms of these loan programs are similar. The eligibility criteria, interest rates, fees, grace period, deferment and cancellation provisions, and other terms are all basically the same. There are, however, minor differences in the application process and certain repayment options.

The key differences lies in who provides the loan funds. The Federal Stafford Student Loan is part of the Federal Family Education Loan Program (FFELP), through which loans are made by a private lender (such as a bank, a savings and loan association, a credit union, or an insurance company) and are insured by a state or private guarantee agency sponsored by the U.S. federal government. Under the William D. Ford Federal Direct Student Loan Program, the U.S. federal government is the lender.

The school you attend will determine which of these two loans you can apply for. Eligibility for either of these programs is the same. You must:

- Be a citizen, a permanent resident, or eligible noncitizen of the United States

- Be enrolled at least half time (usually six credits)

- Be in good academic standing, be making satisfactory progress toward the degree (as defined by the school)

- Not be in default of any previous loans without being in an approved repayment program

- If you are a male, be registered with, or excused from registering with, the selective service system.

- Show financial need based on the information provided on your FAFSA in order to qualify for the interest subsidy

Federal Stafford Student Loans

The Federal Stafford Student Loan Program provides two types of loans: subsidized and unsubsidized. The subsidized loan are a better deal, but you have to meet the government's financial need criteria. For either type of loan, you may defer payments of principal and interest until you graduate or drop below half-time enrollment. Depending on when you first borrowed, there's a grace period of six or nine months before you'll have to start repayment.

The Federal Stafford Loan Program evolved from the Guaranteed Student Loan Program (GSL) that you may have borrowed under in college. The concept of a federal loan program originated in 1965 as the Federally Insured Student Loan Program (FISL). The Federal Stafford Loan Program has the same purpose as these previous programs—to make loan funds available for students to attend postsecondary school—but the amounts available, interest rates, and deferment provisions have been modified.

Federal Subsidized Stafford Loans are available to all students who meet the financial need criteria. A federally mandated needs analysis, based on information provided on the Federal Application for Federal Student Aid (FAFSA), determines a student's Federal Subsidized Stafford Loan eligibility. Students who don't qualify for the subsidized loan or need to borrow beyond the limit can take out an Unsubsidized Federal Stafford Loan.

Borrowing Limits

Graduate students may borrow up to their demonstrated need with a maximum $8,500 per year in the Federal Subsidized Stafford Loan Program, with a total borrowing limit (including undergraduate Federal Stafford Loans) of $65,500. The Federal Unsubsidized Stafford Loan Program allows an eligible student to borrow up to $18,500 per year, minus any Federal Subsidized Stafford Loan approved. The total cumulative maximum of $138,500 (including the Federal Subsidized Stafford Loans).

Interest Rate

As the programs' name indicates, the federal government subsidizes the interest on the Federal Subsidized Stafford Loan. You're not required to pay interest on these loans until after you leave school. If you have a Federal Unsubsidized Stafford Loan, you're responsible for the interest while you're in school, but most lenders will allow you to capitalize the interest, and not pay it until you leave school. Capitalization means that the interest accrues while you're still in school and is added to the principal at a predetermined time (often at the point of repayment). This means that upon repayment, you will owe more money and pay more interest than you otherwise would have. You should check with your school and/or lender to find out what the interest rates is when you get ready to borrow. Some lenders offer interest "discounts" to students who maintain flawless repayment records. Applications and information about current interest rates and repayment schedules are available at participating lending institutions.

Fees

There's a loan origination fee that is equal to 3 percent of the loan. If you borrow $5,000, for example, the loan origination fee will be $150. The fee, required by law, is sent to the U.S. federal government to offset a portion of the federal interest subsidy. In addition, the guarantee agency may charge you an insurance fee of up to 1 percent of the loan. Both of these fees would be deducted from the loan proceeds when the check is issued. Some lenders reduce this fee as an incentive for borrowers. Shop around for the best deal.

Sources of Federal Stafford Student Loans

Federal Stafford Student Loans are made through participating banks, savings and loan associations, credit unions, pension funds, and insurance companies. You can now arrange a Federal Stafford Student Loan through the Kaplan/American Express Student Loan Program.

Application Procedures

To apply for a Federal Stafford Student Loan, you should follow these procedures.

1. Complete the Free Application for Federal Student Aid (FAFSA) and mail it to the federal processor.

2. Fill out a Common loan application and submit it to the school you plan to attend. Some schools will automatically send you loan applications and instructions that should be followed closely.

Now all you have to do is wait. While you are waiting, the grad school will certify your application and either mail it to the bank or electronically send them the certification information. The bank will electronically forward that information on to the guarantee agency who will approve or deny the loan and send that info back to the bank. The bank will either cut a check made payable to you and the school or will transmit the funds to the school via Electronic Funds Transfer (EFT). Once the funds are available at the school, the funds are credited against any unpaid balance you have and the difference is refunded to you. This whole process can take up to three months so plan for the time lag.

Please take this timetable into account when applying for a Federal Stafford Loan:

* It takes three to four weeks for the federal processor to process your FAFSA.

* Depending on the lender and the time of the year, your may not receive any money until eight to 12 weeks after completing the loan application.

Repayment

The amount of your monthly payment will depend on the total amount you borrowed, the number of months in the repayment schedule, and whether you elected to pay interest on the unsubsidized portion of the loan while in school. The maximum repayment period is usually ten years, with repayment generally in equal monthly installments. You'll have a shorter repayment term if you borrow a small amount, since there's a minimum monthly installment of $50.

If you don't meet the repayment terms of the loan, you go into default and the entire balance of the loan becomes due. If your loan goes into default, your lender may refuse to allow you to borrow again until the entire debt is satisfied. Check with your lender to see if it has developed any innovative ways for you to repay your debt. Lenders are trying to make it possible for students to keep in good standing with their repayments, and they are willing to work with students to help manage their debt.

Deferments

Under certain circumstances you may be able to defer, or postpone, the payments of your Federal Stafford Loan. Deferments are not automatic, you must apply for them.

Forbearance

You can request forbearance in situations that aren't covered by normal deferments. Forbearance means the lender agrees to grant you a temporary suspension of payments, reduced payments, or an extension of the time for your payments.

Federal Direct Loan Program

The Federal Direct Loan Program was authorized by the U.S. Congress in 1993. In this program, the federal government is the lender. Individual schools, rather than banks or other financial institutions, originate the loans. This program includes two types of loans: the Federal Direct Stafford Loan (Subsidized and Unsubsidized) and the Federal PLUS Loan. Since graduate students are considered independent of their parents, their parents are not eligible to borrow PLUS loans.

The eligibility criteria, borrowing limits, interest rate, fees, grace period, and deferment and cancellation provisions for this program are the same as for the Federal Stafford Loan Program, covered above. The Ford Federal Direct Loan Program has different application procedures and repayment options for students.

Application Procedures

The FAFSA and the other required documents that were discussed earlier must be completed. Usually, the Federal Direct Loan will be offered as part of your financial aid package. Once you accept the loan as part of the package, the financial aid officer creates a Loan Origination Record and electronically transmits it to the federal servicer for approval. The approval is transmitted back to the school, and the school produces a promissory note for you to sign. Once the promissory note is signed, the school can disburse the first semester portion of the loan (minus fees) to your student account. Any funds remaining after any unpaid balance you have with the university will be refunded to you. The entire process can take less than a week to complete from the point of loan certification to disbursement of the check. Depending on mailing time and the school's schedule for loan disbursements, it could take longer.

Repayment

Most of the conditions of repayment are the same as for the Federal Stafford Loan Program. Although the same standard repayment plan (fixed payment for up to ten years) is offered in both program, students who participate in the Ford Federal Direct Loan Program have three additional repayment options: the extended repayment plan, the income contingent repayment plan, and the graduated repayment plan.

Option 1: Extended Repayment. Similar to the standard repayment plan, it allows the student to repay a fixed amount over a period longer than ten years.

Option 2: Income Contingent Repayment. You pay a percentage of your salary no matter how much you've borrowed. If you have a high debs, this option could require many more years of repayment than the standard ten years. As your salary increases, so would your loan repayments. The drawback to this option is that the longer you stay in repayment, the more interest you pay on the loan. Indeed, if your payment does not cover the current interest due, unpaid interest will be capitalized, increasing the amount of principal you owe.

Option 3: Graduated Repayment. This allows you to opt for lower payments at the beginning of the repayment cycle when your salary is lower. The payments automatically increase as the years progress. The repayment term remains ten years.

No matter what repayment option you select, the plan will be explained in the promissory note you sign. Repayments will be made to a federal loan servicer contracted by the United States Department of Education.

Federal Loan Consolidation

Federal Loan Consolidation allows students with substantial debt to combine several federal loans into one larger loan with a longer repayment schedule. The new loan has an interest rate based on the weighted average of the rates of the consolidated loans. Students who borrowed under the Federal Stafford Loan (or the earlier Guaranteed Student Loan), the Federal Perkins Loan (or the earlier National Direct Student Loan), the Federal Supplemental Loan for Students, the Auxiliary Loan to Assist Students (ALAS), and the Health Professions Student Loan Program can consolidate all these loans into one new loan.

To qualify for federal loan consolidation, you must be in your grace period or in repayment of your loans, and not be delinquent by more than 90 days. Apply to one of the lenders of your current loans. They'll negotiate to purchase your other loans from the lenders who hold them so your loans will be consolidated. If none of your lenders offers federal loan consolidation, you can go to another lender who does. Arrange to have that lender purchase your loans.

You have the option of consolidating all or only part of your loans. Often, students consolidate their higher interest loans, but keep their Federal Perkins Loans separate since the interest rate is so low. No fees are charged to participate in this program.

You may be eligible for a deferment of principal, but you must continue to pay the interest on your consolidated loan. Deferment of principal is available if you are:

- Enrolled at least half-time in a postsecondary school or graduate program

- Enrolled in an approved graduate fellowship or rehabilitation training program for persons with disabilities

- Temporarily totally disabled, or employed because you're taking care of a temporarily totally disabled dependent

- Unable to find full-time employment

Information about time limitations for repayment is shown in the chart below. Consolidation has several advantages. The monthly payment is reduced while the length of time allowed for repayment is extended. Also, keeping track of payments is easier since there's only one payment for several loans. Prepay all or part of your federal consolidated loan at any time without penalty, reducing the amount of interest you'll end up paying.

Consolidation Federal Loan Repayment	
Total Consolidated Student Loan Debt	**Maximum Repayment Period**
Less than $7,500	10 years
$7,500 to $9,999	12 years
$10,000 to $19,999	15 years
$20,000 to $39,999	20 years
$40,000 to $59,999	25 years
$60,000 or more	30 years

Federal Work-Study Program

The Federal Work-Study (FWS) Program provides financial aid by funding jobs for students. The U.S. federal government gives funds to the school, and the school matches a percentage of these funds. The joint fund pays student salaries for selected jobs. Under this program, you receive a salary or stipend, which usually can't be applied directly to tuition and fee charges. Unfortunately, not all schools have FWS funds for graduate and professional students.

Eligibility

The college or university determines eligibility for FWS funds based on financial need (calculated through the FAFSA/SAR), and the availability of funds. Students must be enrolled at least half time and maintain satisfactory progress toward a degree. Funds from this program often go to undergraduate students first.

Earning limits

Your earnings are limited to the FWS award figure listed in your financial aid package. The figure includes both the federal funds and the school's matching funds. FWS students are eligible for a variety of jobs, both on and off campus. Off-campus jobs usually involve nonprofit institutions. Some schools have work-study agreements with private sector employers, though. Schools might also fund graduate assistantships with FWS money.

Application Procedures

You can sit back and relax on this one. There are generally no separate application procedures for FWS. You'll be automatically considered for FWS when you apply for financial aid. If you've been offered a Federal Work-Study allocation, you select from the variety of approved positions work-study positions available on and off campus.

Private Loan Programs

Many graduate students find that scholarship funds and the federal loan programs are not adequate to meet their expenses in a full-time graduate program. Over the last few years, several private loan programs have emerged to fill the gap. In addition, some schools have customized loan payments to meet their students needs. Check with your school to see what programs they might offer.

As the economic environment changes, new loan private programs are added and some older programs are discontinued. Check with the individual programs for their current provisions.

The TERI Supplemental Loan Program

This is a private educational loan program designed to help students make up the difference between their cost of education and their grants or loans. Approval is based on the creditworthiness of the applicant. For more information, call the toll-free Kaplan/American Express Student Loan Program hotline at (888) KAP-LOAN for more information.

The GradEXCEL Program

This is an education loan program through Nellie Mae, a private loan agency, designed to meet the needs of students enrolled in graduate and professional degree programs. GradEXCEL offers graduate students an educational loan based on projected future earnings rather than on current credit worthiness.

Debt Management

You've read the material on financial aid and loans. You've done the worksheets about paying for your graduate degree. So how much did you calculate you'd need to borrow? This is the time to figure out if you'll actually be able to manage your projected debt. Don't wait until you're in over your head. If your projected indebtedness seems unmanageable, do something now to identify ways to reduce either your borrowing or your payments.

Step 1: Calculate your monthly payments.

Use the following table to calculate your monthly repayments after graduating. In estimating your indebtedness, remember that you're likely to need similar funding for each year you're in school. Multiply all the loan amounts in your financial aid award letter by the number of years you think you'll be in school.

Use the table below to help you calculate most monthly payments on a level-payment plan over five to 30 years. For example, suppose you had a $5,000 loan at 8 percent and a ten-year payment term. As the table shows, the monthly payment for a $1,000 loan would be $12.13. Multiply this by five to get $60.65.

Bear in mind, however, that you may need to calculate several payments. Each lender, under each loan program, should be calculated separately. For example, if you have several Federal Stafford Student Loans issued by a single lender, add them up to arrive at a single balance. But if you have two additional loans issued under a private supplemental loan program, consider them separately. Calculate the payments for the two different programs separately, then add them together to determine your total payment responsibility.

Monthly Loan Payments*

For a $1,000 loan

Rate	60 Months	120 Months	180 Months	240 Months	300 Months
5%	$18.87	$X	$7.91	$6.60	$5.85
6%	19.33	11.10	8.44	7.16	6.44
7%	19.80	11.61	8.99	7.75	7.07
8%	20.28	12.13	9.56	8.36	7.72
9%	20.76	12.67	10.14	9.00	8.39
10%	21.25	13.22	10.75	9.65	9.09
11%	21.74	13.77	11.37	10.32	9.80
12%	22.75	14.35	12.00	11.01	10.53
13%	22.75	14.93	12.65	11.72	11.28
14%	23.27	15.53	13.32	12.44	12.04
16%	24.32	16.75	14.69	13.91	13.59
18%	25.39	18.02	16.10	15.43	15.17
20%	26.49	19.33	17.56	16.99	16.78

*Minimum monthly payment may apply regardless of the loan amount.

Step 2: Estimate Your Starting Salary

You've probably got several schools in mind by now; ask them about starting salaries in your field.

Step 3: Estimate Your Expenses

Be thorough. Include taxes, monthly deductions from salary, student loan payments, living expenses, medical expenses, travel expenses, child care, insurance, gifts, etcetera.

Step 4: Consider Your Financial Options

After comparing your income to your expenses, you'll have a better idea of your postgrad school financial picture. If things look tight, see if you can cut down on your discretionary expenses. Another option is to lower your monthly loan payments. If you wish to adjust your loan payments rather than your living expenses, you must do so before you start your graduate program rather than trying to do it during your schooling or when you graduate. Potential employers won't increase your starting salary to cover your expenses and loan repayments! If your loan repayments are very high, you may have to reevaluate postgraduation job offers strictly in terms of salary.

Your graduate degree is an investment that will produce professional and financial returns. Any investment involves some risk and some level of sacrifice, but you don't want to be paying for it in a reduced living standard for ten years.

When you're projecting your loan repayments, remember this: While the payments will stay relatively stable, your salary will (presumably) increase over the repayment term of the loan. The loan payments will be less onerous as your salary goes up. On the other hand, the longer you're out of school, the more major expenses you're likely to have: a house, car, children, vacations, and so on.

The best strategy is to borrow less while you are in school. Then you won't have as much trouble making ends meet after graduation. Refer to chapter 20, "Planning Your Investment," for suggestions about handling your money now and while you're in school.

Universities with Graduate Programs

For More Information

Alabama

ALABAMA AGRICULTURAL AND MECHANICAL UNIVERSITY

Normal, AL 35762
(205) 851-5266
http://www.aamu.edu

ALABAMA STATE UNIVERSITY

915 South Jackson Street
Montgomery, AL 36101-0271
(334) 229-4275
http://www.alasu.edu

AUBURN UNIVERSITY— AUBURN

Auburn University, AL 36849
(334) 844-4700
http://www.auburn.edu/

AUBURN UNIVERSITY— MONTGOMERY

7300 University Drive
Montgomery, AL 36117-3596
(334) 244-3611
http://www-biz.aum.edu

JACKSONVILLE STATE UNIVERSITY

Jacksonville, AL 36265-9982
(205) 782-5329
http://www.jsucc.jsu.edu

SAMFORD UNIVERSITY

800 Lakeshore Drive
Birmingham, AL 35229
(205) 870-2011
http://www.samford.edu

SPRING HILL COLLEGE

4000 Dauphin Street
Mobile, AL 36608
(334) 380-3094
http://www.shc.edu

TROY STATE UNIVERSITY— DOTHAN

P.O. Box 8368
Dothan, AL 36304-0368
(334) 983-6556
http://www.cybertron.com/~gcb/cis/tsud home.htm

TROY STATE UNIVERSITY— MONTGOMERY

231 Montgomery Street
P.O. Drawer 4419
Montgomery, AL 36103-4419
(800) 355-TSUM
http://www.tsum.edu

TROY STATE UNIVERSITY— TROY

Troy, AL 36082
(334) 670-3000
http://asntsu.asn.net/

TUSKEGEE UNIVERSITY

Tuskegee, AL 36088
(334) 727-8500
http://www.tusk.edu

UNIVERSITY OF ALABAMA— BIRMINGHAM

Birmingham, AL 35294-0104
(205) 934-8221
http://www.uab.edu/

UNIVERSITY OF ALABAMA— HUNTSVILLE

301 Sparkman Drive
Huntsville, AL 35899
(205) 851-5245
http://www.uah.edu

UNIVERSITY OF ALABAMA— TUSCALOOSA

Box 870132
Tuscaloosa, AL 35487-0132
(205) 348-5921
http://ua1vm.ua.edu

UNIVERSITY OF MOBILE

Graduate Admissions
P.O. Box 13220
Mobile, AL 36663-0220
(334) 675-5990
http://www.maf.mobile.al.us/~adminfo/
schools.htm

UNIVERSITY OF MONTEVALLO

Station 6040
Montevallo, AL 35115-6350
(205) 665-6000

UNIVERSITY OF SOUTH ALABAMA

Mobile, AL 36688-0002
(334) 460-6141
http://www.usouthal.edu

Alaska

ALASKA PACIFIC UNIVERSITY

4101 University Drive
Anchorage, AK 99508
(907) 561-1266
http://www.alaska.net/~apu

UNIVERSITY OF ALASKA— ANCHORAGE

3211 Providence Drive
Anchorage, AK 99508
(907) 786-1529
http://www.uaa.alaska.edu/

UNIVERSITY OF ALASKA— FAIRBANKS

Fairbanks, AK 99775-7480
(907) 474-7464
http://zorba.uafadm.alaska.edu/

UNIVERSITY OF ALASKA— SOUTHEAST

11120 Glacier Highway
Juneau, AK 99801
(907) 465-6457

Arizona

ARIZONA STATE UNIVERSITY

Tempe, AZ 85287-1203
(602) 965-7788
http://www.asu.edu/

NORTHERN ARIZONA UNIVERSITY

P.O. Box 4125
Flagstaff, AZ 86011-4125
(520) 523-4348
http://www.nau.edu/

PRESCOTT COLLEGE

220 Grove Avenue
Prescott, AZ 86301
(520) 778-2090
http://www.aztec.asu.edu/prescott.col/

UNIVERSITY OF ARIZONA

Tucson, AZ 85721-0007
(520) 621-3132
http://www.arizona.edu/

UNIVERSITY OF PHOENIX

4615 East Elwood Street
P.O. Box 52069
Phoenix, AZ 85072-2069
(602) 966-9577 ext. customer service
http://www.uophx.edu

Arkansas

ARKANSAS STATE UNIVERSITY

State University, AR 72467
(800) 382-3030
http://www.astate.edu

ARKANSAS TECH UNIVERSITY

Russellville, AR 72801
(501) 968-0343
http://www.atu.edu/

HENDERSON STATE UNIVERSITY

Graduate School Admissions
Arkadelphia, AR 71999-0001
(870) 230-5126
http://www.hsu.edu/

UNIVERSITY OF ARKANSAS—FAYETTEVILLE

200 Silas H. Hunt Hall
Fayetteville, AR 72701
(501) 575-4401
http://www.uark.edu

UNIVERSITY OF ARKANSAS—LITTLE ROCK

2801 South University Avenue
Little Rock, AR 72204
(501) 569-3206
http://www.ualr.edu

UNIVERSITY OF CENTRAL ARKANSAS

Graduate School Admissions
201 Donaghey
Conway, AR 72035-0001
(501) 450-3124
http://www.uca.edu

California

ANTIOCH SOUTHERN CALIFORNIA—LOS ANGELES

13274 Fiji Way
Marina del Ray, CA 90292
(310) 578-1080
http://www.antiochla.edu

ANTIOCH SOUTHERN CALIFORNIA—SANTA BARBARA

801 Garden Street
Santa Barbara, CA 93101
(805) 962-8179

AZUSA PACIFIC UNIVERSITY

901 East Alosta
Azusa, CA 91702-7000
(818) 812-3016
http://apu.edu/

BIOLA UNIVERSITY

13800 Biola Avenue
La Mirada, CA 90639
(562) 903-4752
http://www.biola.edu/

CALIFORNIA INSTITUTE OF INTEGRAL STUDIES

9 Peter Yorke Way
San Francisco, CA 94109
(415) 674-5500

CALIFORNIA INSTITUTE OF TECHNOLOGY

1201 East California Boulevard
Pasadena, CA 91125
(818) 395-6346
http://www.caltech.edu

CALIFORNIA POLYTECHNIC STATE UNIVERSITY—SAN LUIS OBISPO

San Luis Obispo, CA 93407-0005
(805) 756-2311
http://www.calpoly.edu/

CALIFORNIA STATE POLYTECHNIC UNIVERSITY—POMONA

Graduate Admissions
3801 West Temple Avenue
Pomona, CA 91768-4019
(909) 869-7659
http://www.csupomona.edu

CALIFORNIA STATE UNIVERSITY—BAKERSFIELD

9001 Stockdale Highway
Bakersfield, CA 93311-1099
(805) 664-3036
http://www.csubak.edu/

CALIFORNIA STATE UNIVERSITY— CHICO

Chico, CA 95929-0722
(530) 898-5391
http://www.csuchico.edu

CALIFORNIA STATE UNIVERSITY—DOMINGUEZ HILLS

Graduate School Admissions
1000 East Victoria Street
Carson, CA 90747
(310) 243-3600
http://www.csudh.edu

CALIFORNIA STATE UNIVERSITY—FRESNO

5241 North Maple
Fresno, CA 93740-0057
(209) 278-4073
http://www.csufresno.edu/

CALIFORNIA STATE UNIVERSITY—FULLERTON

Fullerton, CA 92634
(714) 278-2370
http://www.fullerton.edu/

CALIFORNIA STATE UNIVERSITY—HAYWARD

Hayward, CA 94542
(510) 885-3822
http://www.mcs.csuhayward.edu/

CALIFORNIA STATE UNIVERSITY—LONG BEACH

1250 Bellflower Boulevard
Long Beach, CA 90840
(562) 985-5471
http://www.csulb.edu/

CALIFORNIA STATE UNIVERSITY—LOS ANGELES

5151 State University Drive
Los Angeles, CA 90032
(213) 343-2752
http://www.calstatela.edu/

CALIFORNIA STATE UNIVERSITY—NORTHRIDGE

18111 Nordhoff Street
Northridge, CA 91330
(818) 677-3786
http://www.csun.edu

CALIFORNIA STATE UNIVERSITY—SACRAMENTO

6000 J Street
Sacramento, CA 95819
(916) 278-3901
http://www.csus.edu/

CALIFORNIA STATE UNIVERSITY—SAN BERNARDINO

Graduate School Admissions
5500 University Parkway
San Bernardino, CA 92407-2397
(909) 880-5000
http://www.csusb.edu/

CALIFORNIA STATE UNIVERSITY— SAN MARCOS

San Marcos, California 92096
(760) 750-4060
http://coyote.csusm.edu/

CALIFORNIA STATE UNIVERSITY—STANISLAUS

801 West Monte Vista Avenue
Turlock, CA 95382
(209) 667-3129
http://www.csustan.edu

CHAPMAN UNIVERSITY

333 North Glassell Street
Orange, CA 92866
(714) 997-6786
http://www.chapman.edu/

CLAREMONT GRADUATE SCHOOL

170 East 10th Street
McManus 131
Claremont, CA 91711-6163
(909) 621-8069
http://www.cgs.edu

COLLEGE OF NOTRE DAME

1500 Ralston Avenue
Belmont, CA 94002
(650) 593-1601
http://www.cnd.edu

FIELDING INSTITUTE

2112 Santa Barbara Street
Santa Barbara, CA 93105-3538
(805) 687-1099

GOLDEN GATE UNIVERSITY

536 Mission Street
San Francisco, CA 94105
(415) 442-7800)
http://www.ggu.edu

HARVEY MUDD COLLEGE

301 East 12th Street
Claremont, CA 91711-5990
(909) 621-8000
http://www.hmc.edu

HUMBOLDT STATE UNIVERSITY

Arcata, CA 95521
(707) 826-4402
http://www.humboldt.edu

JOHN F. KENNEDY UNIVERSITY

12 Altarinda Road
Orinda, CA 94563
(510) 254-0200
http://www.jfku.edu

LOMA LINDA UNIVERSITY

Graduate School Admissions
Loma Linda, CA 92350
(909) 824-4529
http://www.llu.edu/

LaSIERRA UNIVERSITY

4700 Pierce Street
Riverside, CA 92515
(909) 785-2000
http://www.lasierra.edu/

LOYOLA MARYMOUNT UNIVERSITY

7900 Loyola Boulevard
Los Angeles, CA 90045-8350
(310) 338-2721
http://www.lmu.edu/

MASTER'S COLLEGE

21726 Placerita Canyon Road
Santa Clarita, CA 91321-1200
(805) 259-3540
http://www.masters.edu

MILLS COLLEGE

Graduate Admissions
5000 MacArthur Boulevard
Oakland, CA 94613
(510) 430-2255
http://www.mills.edu

MONTEREY INSTITUTE OF INTERNATIONAL STUDIES

425 Van Buren Street
Monterey, CA 93940
(408) 647-4100
http://www.miis.edu

MOUNT ST. MARY'S COLLEGE

10 Chester Place
Los Angeles, CA 90007
(213) 746-0450

NATIONAL UNIVERSITY

4025 Camino del Rio South
San Diego, CA 92108-4194
(619) 563-7305
http://www.nu.edu/

NAVAL POSTGRADUATE SCHOOL

589 Dyer Road
Room 103C
Monterey, CA 93943-5100
(408) 656-3093
http://www.nps.navy.mil

NEW COLLEGE OF CALIFORNIA

50 Fell Street
San Francisco, CA 94131
(415) 241-1300

PACIFIC OAKS COLLEGE

5 Westmoreland Place
Pasadena, CA 91130
(626) 397-1349

PEPPERDINE UNIVERSITY

Malibu, CA 90263-4392
(310) 456-4392
http://www.pepperdine.edu

PHILLIPS GRADUATE INSTITUTE

5445 Balboa Boulevard
Encino, CA 91316-1509
(818) 509-5959

RAND GRADUATE SCHOOL OF POLICY STUDIES

1700 Main Street
Santa Monica, CA 90407-2138
(310) 393-0411

SAN DIEGO STATE UNIVERSITY

5300 Campanile
San Diego, CA 92182-0771
(619) 594-5213
http://www.sdsu.edu

SAN FRANCISCO STATE UNIVERSITY

1600 Holloway Avenue
San Francisco, CA 94132
(415) 338-2233
http://www.sfsu.edu/

SAN JOSE STATE UNIVERSITY

One Washington Square
San Jose, CA 95192-0009
(408) 283-7500
http://www.sjsu.edu

SANTA CLARA UNIVERSITY

Santa Clara, CA 95053
(408) 554-4000
http://www.scu.edu

SAYBROOK INSTITUTE

450 Pacific Avenue
San Francisco, CA 94133
(415) 433-9200
http://www.saybrook.org

SIMPSON COLLEGE

2211 College View Drive
Redding, CA 96003-8606
(530) 224-5600
http://www.simpson.edu/

SONOMA STATE UNIVERSITY

1801 East Cotati Avenue
Rohnert Park, CA 94928
(707) 664-2778
http://www.sonoma.edu/

SOUTHERN CALIFORNIA COLLEGE

55 Fair Drive
Costa Mesa, CA 92626
(714) 556-3610
http://www.admissions@sccu.edu

ST. MARY'S COLLEGE

1928 Saint Mary's Road
Moraga, CA 94556
(510) 631-4000
http://gaelnet.stmarys-ca.edu/

STANFORD UNIVERSITY

Stanford, CA 94305
(415) 723-4291
http://www.stanford.edu

UNITED STATES INTERNATIONAL UNIVERSITY

10455 Pomerado Road
San Diego, CA 92131
(619) 271-4300
http://www.usiu.edu

UNIVERSITY OF CALIFORNIA— BERKELEY

Berkeley, CA 94720
(510) 642-7405
http://www.berkeley.edu/

UNIVERSITY OF CALIFORNIA— DAVIS

Davis, CA 95616-8678
(530) 752-0655
http://www.ucdavis.edu

UNIVERSITY OF CALIFORNIA— IRVINE

Office of Research & Graduate Studies
120 Administration Building
Irvine, CA 92697-3180
(714) 824-6761
http://www.rgs.uci.edu/grad/

UNIVERSITY OF CALIFORNIA—

Los Angeles
Box 951436
Los Angeles, CA 90095-1436
(310) 825-1711 or 4321
http://www.ucla.edu/

UNIVERSITY OF CALIFORNIA— RIVERSIDE

900 University Avenue
Riverside, CA 92521
(909) 787-3313
http://www.ucr.edu

UNIVERSITY OF CALIFORNIA—

San Diego
9500 Gilman Drive
La Jolla, CA 92093-0003
(619) 534-1193
http://www.ucsd.edu

UNIVERSITY OF CALIFORNIA—

San Francisco
P.O. Box 0404
San Francisco, CA 94143
(415) 476-2111
http://www.ucsf.edu/

UNIVERSITY OF CALIFORNIA—SANTA BARBARA

Santa Barbara, CA 93106
(805) 893-2277
http://www.ucsb.edu/

UNIVERSITY OF CALIFORNIA—SANTA CRUZ

Santa Cruz, CA 95064
(408) 459-2301
http://www.ucsc.edu

UNIVERSITY OF LAVERNE

1950 Third Street
LaVerne, CA 91750
(909) 593-3511, ext. 4244
http://www.ulaverne.edu

UNIVERSITY OF REDLANDS

1200 East Colton Avenue
P.O. Box 3080
Redlands, CA 92373-0999
(909) 793-2121
http://www.uor.edu/

UNIVERSITY OF SAN DIEGO

5998 Alcala Park
San Diego, CA 92110-2492
(619) 260-4600
http://www/acusd.edu

UNIVERSITY OF SAN FRANCISCO

2130 Fulton Street
San Francisco, CA 94117-1080
(415) 422-5555
http://www.usfca.edu/

UNIVERSITY OF SOUTHERN CALIFORNIA

University Park
Los Angeles, CA 90089-0913
(213) 740-5683
http://www.usc.edu./

UNIVERSITY OF THE PACIFIC

3601 Pacific Avenue
Stockton, CA 95211
(209) 946-2011
http://www.uop.edu

Colorado

ADAMS STATE COLLEGE

Alamosa, CO 81102
(719) 589-7712

COLORADO STATE UNIVERSITY

Administration Annex
Fort Collins, CO 80523-0015
(970) 491-6817
http://www.colostate.edu/

COLORADO TECHNICAL UNIVERSITY

4435 North Chestnut Street
Colorado Springs, CO 80907
(719) 598-0200

NATIONAL TECHNOLOGICAL UNIVERSITY

700 Centre Avenue
Fort Collins, CO 80526
(970) 495-6400

NATIONAL THEATRE CONSERVATORY

1050 13th Street
Denver, CO 80204
(303) 446-4855

REGIS UNIVERSITY

3333 Regis Boulevard
Denver, CO 80221-1099
(303) 458-4100
http://www.regis.edu/

THE NAROPA INSTITUTE

2130 Arapahoe Avenue
Boulder, CO 80302
(303) 444-0202

UNIVERSITY OF COLORADO—DENVER

Box 173364
Campus Box 167
Denver, CO 80217-3364
(303) 556-2400
http://www.cudenver.edu/

UNIVERSITY OF COLORADO—BOULDER

Campus Box 30
Boulder, CO 80309-0026
(303) 492-7401
http://www.colorado.edu

UNIVERSITY OF COLORADO—COLORADO SPRINGS

Graduate School Admissions
Austin Bluffs Parkway, P.O. Box 7150
Colorado Springs, CO 80933-7150
(719) 262-3121
http://www.uccs.edu

UNIVERSITY OF DENVER

University Park
Denver, CO 80208
(303) 871-2305
http://www.du.edu

UNIVERSITY OF NORTHERN COLORADO

Greeley, CO 80639
(970) 351-2831
http://www.univnorthco.edu

UNIVERSITY OF SOUTHERN COLORADO

2200 Bonforte Boulevard
Pueblo, CO 81001
Systems Engineering:
(719) 549-2889
Applied & Natural Science:
(719) 549-2813
http://www.uscolo.edu/

Connecticut

CENTRAL CONNECTICUT STATE UNIVERSITY

School of Graduate Studies
1615 Stanley Street
New Britain, CT 06050
(860) 832-2278
http://wwwgs.ccsu.ctstateu.edu

CONNECTICUT COLLEGE

270 Mohegan Avenue
New London, CT 06320-4196
(860) 447-1911
http://camel.conncoll.edu

HARTFORD GRADUATE CENTER

275 Windsor Street
Hartford, CT 06120
(860) 548-2421

QUINNIPIAC COLLEGE

Mount Carmel Avenue
Hamden, CT 06518
Education: (203) 228-5420
Computer Science: (203) 228-5385
http://www.quinnipiac.edu

SACRED HEART UNIVERSITY

5151 Park Avenue
Fairfield, CT 06432-1000
(203) 371-7880
http://www.sacredheart.edu

SOUTHERN CONNECTICUT STATE UNIVERSITY

501 Crescent Street
New Haven, CT 06515
(203) 392-5237
http://scwww.ctstateu.edu/

ST. JOSEPH COLLEGE

1678 Asylum Avenue
West Hartford, CT 06117
(860) 232-4571
http://www.sjc.edu/

TRINITY COLLEGE

300 Summit Street
Hartford, CT 06106
(860) 297-2000
http://www.trincoll.edu/homepage.html

UNIVERSITY OF BRIDGEPORT

380 University Avenue
Bridgeport, CT 06601
(203) 576-4558
http://www.bridgeport.edu/

UNIVERSITY OF CONNECTICUT

Storrs, CT 06269
(860) 486-3617
http://www.uconn.edu/

UNIVERSITY OF HARTFORD

200 Bloomfield Avenue
West Hartford, CT 06117
(860) 768-5010
http://www.hartford.edu/

UNIVERSITY OF NEW HAVEN

300 Orange Avenue
West Haven, CT 06516
(203) 932-7133
http://www.newhaven.edu/

WESLEYAN UNIVERSITY

Middletown, CT 06459
(860) 685-2390
http://www.wesleyan.edu

WESTERN CONNECTICUT STATE UNIVERSITY

181 White Street
Danbury, CT 06810
(203) 837-8243
http://www.wcsu.ctstateu.edu

YALE UNIVERSITY

208234 Yale Station
New Haven, CT 06520-8234
(203) 432-2770
http://www.cs.yale.edu/html/yale/
frontdoor.html

Delaware

DELAWARE STATE UNIVERSITY

1200 North DuPont Highway
Dover, DE 19901-2275
(302) 739-5143
http://www.dsc.edu

UNIVERSITY OF DELAWARE

Newark, DE 19716
(302) 831-2129
http://www.udel.edu/

District of Columbia

AMERICAN UNIVERSITY

4400 Massachusetts Avenue, NW
Washington, DC 20016-8001
(202) 885-3406
http://www.american.edu/

CATHOLIC UNIVERSITY OF AMERICA

Cardinal Station Post Office
Washington, DC 20064
(202) 319-5057
http://www.cua.edu

GALLAUDET UNIVERSITY

800 Florida Avenue, NE
Washington, DC 20002
(202) 651-5000
http://www.gallaudet.edu

GEORGE WASHINGTON UNIVERSITY

2121 I Street, NW
Washington, DC 20052
(202) 994-5568
http://gwis.circ.gwu.edu

GEORGETOWN UNIVERSITY

37th and O Streets, NW
Washington, DC 20057
(202) 687-5055
http://www.georgetown.edu

HOWARD UNIVERSITY

2400 Sixth Street, NW
Washington, DC 20059
(202) 806-5805
http://www.howard.edu

MOUNT VERNON COLLEGE

2100 Foxhall Road, NW
Washington, DC 20007
(203) 625-0400
http://www.mvc.edu

OBLATE COLLEGE

391 Michigan Avenue, NE
Washington, DC 20017-1587
(203) 529-6544

UNIVERSITY OF THE DISTRICT OF COLUMBIA

4200 Connecticut Avenue, NW
Washington, DC 20008
(203) 274-5008
http://www.udc.edu

Florida

BARRY UNIVERSITY

11300 N.E. Second Avenue
Miami Shores, FL 33161
(305) 899-3119
http://www.barry.edu/

FLORIDA AGRICULTURAL AND MECHANICAL UNIVERSITY

Tallahassee, FL 32307
(904) 599-3000
http://www.famu.edu

FLORIDA ATLANTIC UNIVERSITY

777 Glades Road
P.O. Box 3091
Boca Raton, FL 33431-0991
(561) 367-3040
http://www.fau.edu

FLORIDA INSTITUTE OF TECHNOLOGY

150 West University Boulevard
Melbourne, FL 32901-6975
(407) 768-8000
http://www.fit.edu

FLORIDA INTERNATIONAL UNIVERSITY

University Park Campus
Miami, FL 33199
(305) 348-2363
http://www.fiu.edu

FLORIDA STATE UNIVERSITY

Tallahassee, FL 32306-1009
(904) 644-2525
http://www.fsu.edu

NOVA SOUTHEASTERN UNIVERSITY

3301 College Avenue
Fort Lauderdale, FL 33314
(954) 475-7300
http://www.nova.edu

ORLANDO COLLEGE

Graduate School Admissions
5421 Diplomat Circle
Orlando, FL 32810
(407) 628-5870

ROLLINS COLLEGE

1000 Holt Avenue
Winter Park, FL 32789
(407) 646-2000
http://www.rollins.edu

ST. THOMAS UNIVERSITY

16400 N.W. 32nd Avenue
Miami, FL 33054
(305) 625-6000
http://www.stu.edu

STETSON UNIVERSITY

DeLand, FL 32720
Arts & Sciences: (904) 822-7410
Counseling: (904) 822-7075
Education: (904) 822-7410
http://www.stetson.edu

UNIVERSITY OF CENTRAL FLORIDA

4000 Central Florida Boulevard
Orlando, FL 32816
(407) 823-2766
http://www.ucf.edu/

UNIVERSITY OF FLORIDA

Gainesville, FL 32611
(352) 392-1365
http://www.ufl.edu

UNIVERSITY OF MIAMI

210 Ferre Building
P.O. Box 248125
Coral Gables, FL 33124-2220
(305) 284-4323
http://www.miami.edu/

UNIVERSITY OF NORTH FLORIDA

4567 St. Johns Bluff Road South
Jacksonville, FL 32224-2645
(904) 646-2666
http://www.unf.edu

UNIVERSITY OF SOUTH FLORIDA

4(203) East Fowler Avenue
Tampa, FL 33620
(813) 974-8800
http://www.usf.edu

UNIVERSITY OF WEST FLORIDA

11000 University Parkway
Pensacola, FL 32514-5750
(904) 474-2230
http://www.uwf.edu

Georgia

ALBANY STATE UNIVERSITY

504 College Drive
Albany, GA 31705
(912) 430-4646
http://www.alsnet.peachnet.edu/
aschome.html

ARMSTRONG STATE COLLEGE

11935 Abercorn Street
Savannah, GA 31419
(912) 927-5275
http://www.armstrong.edu/

AUGUSTA COLLEGE

2500 Walton Way
Augusta, GA 30904-2200
(706) 737-1632
http://www.aug.edu/

CLARK ATLANTA UNIVERSITY

James P. Brawley Drive, SW,
at Fair Street
Atlanta, GA 30314
(404) 880-8765
http://galaxy.eau.edu/cau

EMORY UNIVERSITY

1380 Oxford Road, NE
Atlanta, GA 30322
(404) 727-6123
http://www.emory.edu

GEORGIA COLLEGE

Clark Street
Milledgeville, GA 31061
(912) 453-5004
http://www.gac.peachnet.edu

GEORGIA INSTITUTE OF TECHNOLOGY

225 North Avenue, NW
Atlanta, GA 30332
(404) 894-4612
http://www.gatech.edu

GEORGIA SOUTHERN UNIVERSITY

Landrum Box 8113
Statesboro, GA 30460-8113
(912) 681-5384
http://www.gasou.edu

GEORGIA SOUTHWESTERN COLLEGE

800 Wheatley Street
Americus, GA 31709-4693
(912) 928-1273
http://gswrs6k.1.gsw.peachnet.edu

GEORGIA STATE UNIVERSITY

University Plaza
Atlanta, GA 30303
(404) 651-2000
http://www.gsu.edu

INSTITUTE OF PAPER SCIENCE & TECHNOLOGY

500 10th Street, NW
Atlanta, GA 30318-5794
(404) 894-5700

KENNESAW STATE UNIVERSITY

100 Chastain Road
Kennesaw, GA 30144-5591
(770) 423-6300
http://wwwcoles.kennesaw.edu

MERCER UNIVERSITY

1400 Coleman Avenue
Macon, GA 31207
(912) 752-2700
http://www.mercer.peachnet.edu

MERCER UNIVERSITY— ATLANTA

3001 Mercer University Drive
Atlanta, GA 30341
(770) 986-3000
http://www.mercer.peachnet.edu

OGLETHORPE UNIVERSITY

4484 Peachtree Road Northeast
Atlanta, GA 30319
(404) 364-8307
http://www.oglethorpe.edu/

SHORTER COLLEGE

315 Shorter Avenue
Rome, GA 30165-4298
(706) 291-2121
http://www.shorter.edu

SOUTHERN POLYTECHNIC STATE UNIVERSITY

South Marietta Parkway
Marietta, GA 30060-2896
(770) 528-7281
http://www.sct.edu

STATE UNIVERSITY OF WEST GEORGIA

1600 Maple Street
Carrollton, GA 30118-0001
(770) 836-6500
http://www.westga.edu

UNIVERSITY OF GEORGIA

Athens, GA 30602
(706) 542-1787
http://www.uga.edu

VALDOSTA STATE UNIVERSITY

Valdosta, GA 31698
(912) 333-5694
http://www.valdosta.peachnet.edu

Guam

UNIVERSITY OF GUAM

UOG Station
Mangilao, GU 96923
(671) 735-2202
http://uog2.uog.edu/

Hawaii

CHAMINADE UNIVERSITY OF HONOLULU

Graduate Admissions
3140 Waialae Avenue
Honolulu, HI 96816-1587
Education: (808) 739-4652
Criminal Justice: (808) 739-4705
Public Administration:
(808) 735-4703
http://www.pixie.com/~chaminad/index.html

UNIVERSITY OF HAWAII— MANOA

2600 Campus Road
Room 001
Honolulu, HI 96822
(808) 956-8544
http://www.hawaii.edu/uhinfo.html

Idaho

BOISE STATE UNIVERSITY

1910 University Drive
Boise, ID 83725
(208) 385-3903
http://www.idbsu.edu

IDAHO STATE UNIVERSITY

Pocatello, ID 83209-0009
(208) 236-2150
http://www.isu.edu

NORTHWEST NAZARENE COLLEGE

Dewey at Holly Street
Nampa, ID 83686
(208) 467-8011
http://www.nnc.edu

UNIVERSITY OF IDAHO

Moscow, ID 83844-3017
(208) 885-6111
http://www.uidaho.edu

Illinois

AURORA UNIVERSITY

347 South Gladstone Avenue
Aurora, IL 60506
(630) 896-1975
http://www.aurora.edu

BRADLEY UNIVERSITY

1501 West Bradley Avenue
Peoria, IL 61625
(309) 677-2371
http://www.bradley.edu

CHICAGO STATE UNIVERSITY

95th Street at King Drive
Chicago, IL 60628
(773) 995-2404

COLUMBIA COLLEGE

600 South Michigan Avenue
Chicago, IL 60605-1996
(312) 663-1600
http://www.colum.edu

DEPAUL UNIVERSITY

1 East Jackson Boulevard
Chicago, IL 60604-2287
(312) 362-5367
http://www.depaul.edu/

EASTERN ILLINOIS UNIVERSITY

600 Lincoln Avenue
Charleston, IL 61920
(217) 581-2220
http://www.eiu.edu/

GOVERNORS STATE UNIVERSITY

University Parkway
University Park, IL 60466
(708) 534-5000
http://www.govst.edu

ILLINOIS INSTITUTE OF TECHNOLOGY

3300 South Federal Street
Chicago, IL 60616
(312) 567-3000
http://www.iit.edu

ILLINOIS STATE UNIVERSITY

Normal, IL 61761-6901
(309) 438-2583
http://www.ilstu.edu

LAKE FOREST COLLEGE

Graduate Admissions
555 North Sheridan Road
Lake Forest, IL 60045
(847) 234-3100
http://www.lfc.edu

LEWIS UNIVERSITY

Route 53
Romeoville, IL 60446
(815) 838-0500
http://www.lewisu.edu/

LOYOLA UNIVERSITY—CHICAGO

820 North Michigan Avenue
Chicago, IL 60611
(773) 508-3396
http://www.luc.edu

NATIONAL-LOUIS UNIVERSITY

2840 Sheridan Road
Evanston, IL 60201
(847) 475-1100
http://www.nlu.nl.edu

NORTH CENTRAL COLLEGE

30 North Brainard Street
P.O. Box 3063
Naperville, IL 60566-7063
(630) 637-5840

NORTHEASTERN ILLINOIS UNIVERSITY

5500 North St. Louis Avenue
Chicago, IL 60625
(773) 583-4050 ext. 5133
http://www.neiu.edu/

NORTHERN ILLINOIS UNIVERSITY

DeKalb, IL 60115
(815) 753-0395
http://www.niu.edu

NORTHWESTERN UNIVERSITY

Rebecca Crown Center
633 Clark Street
Evanston, IL 60204-1113
(847) 491-7265
http://nuinfo.nwu.edu/

OLIVET NAZARENE UNIVERSITY

P.O. Box 592
Kankakee, IL 60901
(815) 939-5011
http://www.olivet.edu

QUINCY UNIVERSITY

1800 College Avenue
Quincy, IL 62301
(217) 228-5200
http://www.quincy.edu

ROOSEVELT UNIVERSITY

430 South Michigan Avenue
Chicago, IL 60605
(312) 341-3500

SOUTHERN ILLINOIS UNIVERSITY—CARBONDALE

Carbondale, IL 62901
(618) 536-7791
http://www.siu.edu/cwis/

SOUTHERN ILLINOIS UNIVERSITY—EDWARDSVILLE

Box 1047
Edwardsville, IL 62026-1080
(618) 692-3007
http://www.siue.edu

ST. XAVIER UNIVERSITY

3700 West 103rd Street
Chicago, IL 60655
(773) 298-3050
http://www.sxu.edu

UNIVERSITY OF CHICAGO

5801 South Ellis Avenue, Room 228
Chicago, IL 60637
(773) 702-1234
http://www.uchicago.edu

UNIVERSITY OF ILLINOIS—CHICAGO

P.O. Box 5220
Mail Code 018
Chicago, IL 60680-5220
(312) 996-4350
http://www.uic.edu/

UNIVERSITY OF ILLINOIS—SPRINGFIELD

Shepherd Road
PAC 595
Springfield, IL 62794-9243
(217) 786-6626
http://www.uis.edu

UNIVERSITY OF ILLINOIS—URBANA-CHAMPAIGN

506 South Wright Street
Urbana, IL 61801
(217) 333-0035
http://www.uiuc.edu

WESTERN ILLINOIS UNIVERSITY

Macomb, IL 61455
(309) 298-1806
http://www.wiu.edu/

WHEATON COLLEGE

501 East College Avenue
Wheaton, IL 60187
(630) 752-5195
http://www.wheaton.edu

Indiana

ANDERSON UNIVERSITY

1100 East Fifth Street
Anderson, IN 46012
(765) 641-4080
http://www.anderson.edu/

BALL STATE UNIVERSITY

2100 West Riverside Avenue
Muncie, IN 47306
(765) 285-1287
http://www.bsu.edu/

BETHEL COLLEGE

Graduate Studies Office
1001 West McKinley Avenue
Mishawaka, IN 46545
(219) 257-3343

BUTLER UNIVERSITY

4600 Sunset Avenue
Indianapolis, IN 46208
(317) 940-8100
http://www.butler.edu

EARLHAM COLLEGE

National Road West
Richmond, IN 47374
(765) 983-1200
http://www.earlham.edu/

GRACE COLLEGE

200 Seminary Drive
Winona Lake, IN 46590
(219) 372-5100
http://www.grace.edu

HUNTINGTON COLLEGE

2(303) College Avenue
Huntington, IN 46750
(219) 356-6000
http://www.huntcol.edu

INDIANA STATE UNIVERSITY

217 North Sixth Street
Terre Haute, IN 47809
(812) 237-3111
http://www.indstate.edu/

INDIANA UNIVERSITY— BLOOMINGTON

300 North Jordan Avenue
Bloomington, IN 47405
(812) 855-8931
http://www.indiana.edu/grdschl/

INDIANA UNIVERSITY— NORTHWEST

3400 Broadway
Gary, IN 46408
(219) 980-6991
http://www.iun.indiana.edu/

INDIANA UNIVERSITY—SOUTH BEND

1700 Mishawaka Avenue
P.O. Box 7111
South Bend, IN 46634
(219) 237-4111
http://www.indiana.edu/

INDIANA UNIVERSITY— SOUTHEAST

4201 Grant Line Road
New Albany, IN 47150
(812) 941-2212
http://www.indiana.edu

INDIANA UNIVERSITY—PURDUE UNIVERSITY AT FORT WAYNE

2101 Coliseum Boulevard East
Fort Wayne, IN 46805-1499
(219) 481-6812
http://www.ipfw.indiana.edu/

INDIANA UNIVERSITY— PURDUE UNIVERSITY AT INDIANAPOLIS

Graduate Office, Union Building #518
620 Union Drive
Indianapolis, IN 46202
(317) 274-4023
http://www.iupui.edu

OAKLAND CITY UNIVERSITY

143 Lucretia Street
Oakland City, IN 47660
(812) 749-1231

PURDUE UNIVERSITY

West Lafayette, IN 47907
(765) 494-2600
http://www.purdue.edu

PURDUE UNIVERSITY— CALUMET

Hammond, IN 46323
(219) 989-2257
http://www.purdue.edu

ROSE-HULMAN INSTITUTE OF TECHNOLOGY

5500 Wabash Avenue
Terre Haute, IN 47803
(812) 877-1511
http://www.rose-hulman.edu

ST. JOSEPH'S COLLEGE

P.O. Box 890
Highway 231 South
Rensselaer, IN 47978
(219) 866-6000
http://www.saintjoe.edu

ST. MARY-OF-THE-WOODS COLLEGE

St. Mary-of-the-Woods, IN 47876
(812) 535-5106

ST. MEINRAD COLLEGE

St. Meinrad, IN 47577
(812) 357-6611

UNIVERSITY OF INDIANAPOLIS

1400 East Hanna Avenue
Indianapolis, IN 46227-3697
(317) STU-DENT
http://www.uindy.edu/

UNIVERSITY OF NOTRE DAME

113 Main Building
Notre Dame, IN 46556
(219) 631-7706
http://www.nd.edu/ndhomepage/
ndhomepage.html

UNIVERSITY OF SOUTHERN INDIANA

8600 University Boulevard
Evansville, IN 47712
(812) 465-7015
http://www.usi.edu

VALPARAISO UNIVERSITY

Valparaiso, IN 46383-6493
(219) 464-5313
http://www.valpo.edu

Iowa

DRAKE UNIVERSITY

2507 University Avenue
Des Moines, IA 50311
(515) 271-3871
http://www.drake.edu

IOWA STATE UNIVERSITY

314 Alumni Hall
Ames, IA 50011-2010
(515) 294-0818
http://www.iastate.edu/

LORAS COLLEGE

1450 Alta Vista
Dubuque, IA 52004-0178
(319) 588-7100
http://www.loras.edu

ST. AMBROSE UNIVERSITY

518 West Locust Street
Davenport, IA 52803
(319) 333-3000
http://www.sau.edu/sau.html

UNIVERSITY OF DUBUQUE

2000 University Avenue
Dubuque, IA 52001
(319) 589-3000
http://www.dbq.edu

UNIVERSITY OF IOWA

107 Calvin Hall
Iowa City, IA 52242-1396
(319) 335-1525
http://www.uiowa.edu

UNIVERSITY OF NORTHERN IOWA

1222 West 27th Street
Cedar Falls, IA 50614-0033
(319) 273-2241
http://www.uni.edu

Kansas

BAKER UNIVERSITY

Baldwin City, KS 66006
(800) 955-7747
http://www.bakeru.edu/

EMPORIA STATE UNIVERSITY

1200 Commercial
Emporia, KS 66801
(316) 341-1200
http://www.emporia.edu

FORT HAYS STATE UNIVERSITY

600 Park Street
Hays, KS 67601-4099
(785) 628-4236
http://www.fhsu.edu/

FRIENDS UNIVERSITY

2100 University
Wichita, KS 67213
(800) 577-2233
http://www.friends.edu

KANSAS STATE UNIVERSITY

103 Fairchild Hall
Manhattan, KS 66506-1103
(785) 532-6191
http://www.ksu.edu/

MIDAMERICA NAZARENE COLLEGE

2030 East College Way
Olathe, KS 66062-1899
(913) 782-3750

PITTSBURG STATE UNIVERSITY

1701 South Broadway
Pittsburg, KS 66762
(316) 231-7000
http://www.pittstate.edu/

UNIVERSITY OF KANSAS

Lawrence, KS 66045
(785) 864-4141
http://www.ukans.edu

WASHBURN UNIVERSITY OF TOPEKA

1700 College
Topeka, KS 66621
(785) 231-1010
http://www.wuacc.edu/

WICHITA STATE UNIVERSITY

1845 Fairmount
Wichita, KS 67260-0113
(316) 978-3095
http://twsuvm.uc.twsu.edu

Kentucky

EASTERN KENTUCKY UNIVERSITY

Lancaster Avenue
Richmond, KY 40475-3101
(606) 622-1742
http://www.eku.edu

KENTUCKY STATE UNIVERSITY

East Main Street
Frankfort, KY 40601
(502) 227-6117
http://www.kysu.edu/

MOREHEAD STATE UNIVERSITY

Morehead, KY 40351
(606) 783-2221
http://www.morehead-st.edu/units/
graduate/index.html

MURRAY STATE UNIVERSITY

Sparks Hall
P.O. Box 9
Murray, KY 42071
(800) 272-4678
http://www.mursuky.edu

NORTHERN KENTUCKY UNIVERSITY

LAC 400
Nunn Drive
Highland Heights, KY 41099-7010
(606) 572-6364
http://www.nku.edu

SPALDING UNIVERSITY

851 South Fourth Street
Louisville, KY 40203
(502) 585-9911 ext. 105
http://www.win.net/~spaldingu

UNIVERSITY OF KENTUCKY

100 W.D. Funkhouser Building
Lexington, KY 40506
(606) 257-4615
http://www.uky.edu/

UNIVERSITY OF LOUISVILLE

Houchens Building
Louisville, KY 40292
(800) 852-6525
http://www.louisville.edu

WESTERN KENTUCKY UNIVERSITY

One Big Red Way
Bowling Green, KY 42101
(502) 745-2446
http://www.wku.edu

Louisiana

GRAMBLING STATE UNIVERSITY

100 Main Street
Grambling, LA 71245
(318) 274-2457

LOUISIANA STATE UNIVERSITY—SHREVEPORT

One University Place
Shreveport, LA 71115
(318) 797-5061
http://www.lsus.edu

LOUISIANA STATE UNIVERSITY AND AGRICULTURAL AND MECHANICAL COLLEGE

Baton Rouge, LA 70803-2750
(504) 388-3203
http://www.lsu.edu

LOUISIANA TECH UNIVERSITY

Box 3178 Tech Station
Ruston, LA 71272
(318) 257-0211
http://www.latech.edu

LOYOLA UNIVERSITY—NEW ORLEANS

6363 St. Charles Avenue
New Orleans, LA 70118
(504) 865-3240
http://www.loyno.edu

MCNEESE STATE UNIVERSITY

4100 Ryan Street
Lake Charles, LA 70609-2495
(318) 475-5000
http://www.mcneese.edu

NORTHEAST LOUISIANA UNIVERSITY

Monroe, LA 71209
(318) 342-5252
http://www.nlu.edu

NORTHWESTERN STATE UNIVERSITY OF LOUISIANA

Natchitoches, LA 71497
(318) 357-6361
http://www.nsula.edu

SOUTHEASTERN LOUISIANA UNIVERSITY

SLU 752
Hammond, LA 70402
(504) 549-2062
http://www.selu.edu

SOUTHERN UNIVERSITY

Agricultural and
Mechanical College
Baton Rouge, LA 70813
(504) 771-5390
http://www.subr.edu/

SOUTHERN UNIVERSITY AT NEW ORLEANS

New Orleans, LA 70126
(504) 286-5314
Criminal Justice: (504) 286-5174
Social Work: (504) 286-5376

TULANE UNIVERSITY

6823 St. Charles Avenue
New Orleans, LA 70118
(504) 865-5100
http://www.tulane.edu/

UNIVERSITY OF NEW ORLEANS

New Orleans, LA 70148
(504) 280-6676
http://www.uno.edu

UNIVERSITY OF SOUTHWESTERN LOUISIANA

East University Avenue
Lafayette, LA 70504
(318) 482-6965
http://www.usl.edu

XAVIER UNIVERSITY OF LOUISIANA

7325 Palmetto Street
New Orleans, LA 70125
(504) 483-7487
http://www.xula.edu

Maine

COLLEGE OF THE ATLANTIC

105 Eden Street
Bar Harbor, ME 04609
(207) 288-5015 or (800) 528-0025
http://www.coa.edu

UNIVERSITY OF MAINE

Orono, ME 04469
(207) 581-3218
http://www.ume.maine.edu

UNIVERSITY OF NEW ENGLAND

Hills Beach Road
Biddeford, ME 04005
(207) 283-0171
http://www.une.edu

UNIVERSITY OF SOUTHERN MAINE

Office of Graduate Studies
96 Falmouth Street, P.O. Box 9300
Portland, ME 04104-9300
(207) 780-4386
http://www.usm.maine.edu/

Maryland

BOWIE STATE UNIVERSITY

Bowie, MD 20715-9465
(301) 464-6561
http://www.bowiestate.edu

COLLEGE OF NOTRE DAME OF MARYLAND

4701 North Charles Street
Baltimore, MD 21210
(410) 435-0100

COPPIN STATE COLLEGE

Graduate Admissions
2500 West North Avenue
Baltimore, MD 21216
(410) 383-5990
http://coeacl.coppin.umd.edu

FROSTBURG STATE UNIVERSITY

Frostburg, MD 21532
(301) 687-7053
http://www.fsu.umd.edu

HOOD COLLEGE

Frederick, MD 21701-8575
(301) 696-3400
http://www.hood.edu/

JOHNS HOPKINS UNIVERSITY

3400 North Charles Street
Baltimore, MD 21218
(410) 516-8174
http://www.jhu.edu

LOYOLA COLLEGE

4501 North Charles Street
Baltimore, MD 21210-2699
(800) 221-9107
http://www.loyola.edu

MORGAN STATE UNIVERSITY

Cold Spring Lane and Hillen Road
Baltimore, MD 21239
(410) 319-3185
http://www.morgan.edu

MOUNT SAINT MARY'S COLLEGE

16300 Old Emmitsburg Road
Emmitsburg, MD 21727
(301) 447-5326
http://www.msmary.edu

ST. JOHN'S COLLEGE

P.O. Box 2800
Annapolis, MD 21404
(410) 263-2371
http://www.sjca.edu

TOWSON STATE UNIVERSITY

800 York Road
Towson, MD 21204-7097
(410) 830-2501
http://www.towson.edu

UNIVERSITY OF BALTIMORE

1420 North Charles Street
Baltimore, MD 21201
(410) 837-4777
http://www.ubalt.edu

UNIVERSITY OF MARYLAND— COLLEGE PARK

College Park, MD 20742
(301) 405-4198
http://www.umcp.umd.edu

UNIVERSITY OF MARYLAND— BALTIMORE COUNTY

1000 Hilltop Circle
Baltimore, MD 21250
(410) 455-2537
http://www.umbc.edu

UNIVERSITY OF MARYLAND— EASTERN SHORE

Princess Anne, MD 21853
(410) 651-6507
http://www.umd.edu/

UNIVERSITY OF MARYLAND—UNIVERSITY COLLEGE

University Boulevard at Adelphi Road
College Park, MD 20742
(301) 985-7155

WASHINGTON COLLEGE

300 Washington Avenue
Chestertown, MD 21620
(410) 778-2800
http://www.washcoll.edu

WESTERN MARYLAND COLLEGE

2 College Hill
Westminster, MD 21157
(410) 848-7000
http://www.wmc.car.md.us

Massachusetts

AMERICAN INTERNATIONAL COLLEGE

1000 State Street
Springfield, MA 01109
(413) 737-7000
http://www.aic.edu

ANNA MARIA COLLEGE

Graduate Admissions
Sunset Lane Box #O
Paxton, MA 01612
(508) 849-3360
http://www.anna-maria.edu/
amcpage/amchead.htm

ASSUMPTION COLLEGE

500 Salisbury Street
Worcester, MA 01615-0005
(508) 767-7000

BOSTON COLLEGE

140 Commonwealth Avenue
Chestnut Hill, MA 02167
(617) 552-3265
http://www.infoeagle.bc.edu

BOSTON UNIVERSITY

121 Bay State Road
Boston, MA 02215
(617) 353-2696
http://web.bu.edu

BRANDEIS UNIVERSITY

South Street
P.O. Box 9110
Waltham, MA 02254-9110
(617) 736-3410
http://www.brandeis.edu

BRIDGEWATER STATE COLLEGE

Gates House
Bridgewater, MA 02325
(508) 697-1237
http://www.bridgew.edu

CLARK UNIVERSITY

950 Main Street
Worcester, MA 01610-1477
(508) 793-7676
http://www.clarku.edu

ELMS COLLEGE

291 Springfield Street
Chicopee, MA 01013
413 594-2761

EMERSON COLLEGE

100 Beacon Street
Boston, MA 02116
(617) 824-8610
http://www.emerson.edu/

EMMANUEL COLLEGE

400 The Fenway
Boston, MA 02115
(617) 735-9715
http://www.emmanuel.edu

FITCHBURG STATE COLLEGE

160 Pearl Street
Fitchburg, MA 01420-2697
(978) 345-2151
http://www.fsc.edu

HARVARD UNIVERSITY

Byerly Hall
8 Garden Street
Cambridge, MA 02138
(617) 495-5315
http://www.harvard.edu

HELLENIC COLLEGE

50 Goddard Avenue
Brookline, MA 02146
(617) 731-3500

LESLEY COLLEGE

Institutional Research
29 Everett Street
Cambridge, MA 02138-2790
(617) 868-9600
http://www.lesley.edu

MASSACHUSETTS INSTITUTE OF TECHNOLOGY

77 Massachusetts Avenue
Cambridge, MA 02139
(617) 253-4791
http://web.mit.edu/

MOUNT HOLYOKE COLLEGE

College Street
South Hadley, MA 01075-1488
(413) 538-2000
http://www.mtholyoke.edu

NORTHEASTERN UNIVERSITY

360 Huntington Avenue
Boston, MA 02115
(617) 373-2170
http://www.neu.edu

SALEM STATE COLLEGE

352 Lafayette Street
Salem, MA 01970
(508) 741-6000

SIMMONS COLLEGE

300 The Fenway
Boston, MA 02115
(617) 521-2000
http://www.simmons.edu

SMITH COLLEGE

Northampton, MA 01063
(413) 584-2700
http://www.smith.edu

SPRINGFIELD COLLEGE

263 Alden Street
Springfield, MA 01109-3797
(413) 748-3729
http://www.springfieldcollege.edu/

SUFFOLK UNIVERSITY

8 Ashburton Place
Boston, MA 02108
(617) 573-8000
http://www.suffolk.edu

TUFTS UNIVERSITY

Medford, MA 02155
(617) 627-3395
http://www.tufts.edu

UNIVERSITY OF MASSACHUSETTS—AMHERST

Whitmore Building
Amherst, MA 01003
(413) 545-0721
http://www.umass.edu

UNIVERSITY OF MASSACHUSETTS—DARTMOUTH

285 Old Westport Road
North Dartmouth, MA 02747-2300
(508) 999-8604
http://www.umassd.edu/welcome.html

UNIVERSITY OF MASSACHUSETTS—LOWELL

One University Avenue
Lowell, MA 01854
(978) 934-2380
http://www.uml.edu

UNIVERSITY OF MASSACHUSETTS—BOSTON

100 Morrissey Boulevard
Boston, MA 02125-3393
http://www.umb.edu

WESTERN NEW ENGLAND COLLEGE

1215 Wilbraham Road
Springfield, MA 01119
Engineering: (413) 782-1249
http://www.wnec.edu

WESTFIELD STATE COLLEGE

Western Avenue
Westfield, MA 01086
(413) 568-3311

WHEELOCK COLLEGE

200 The Riverway
Boston, MA 02215-4176
(617) 734-5200 ext. 195

WILLIAMS COLLEGE

Williamstown, MA 01267
(413) 597-3131
http://www.williams.edu/

WORCESTER POLYTECHNIC INSTITUTE

100 Institute Road
Worcester, MA 01609
(508) 831-5000
http://www.wpi.edu

Michigan

ANDREWS UNIVERSITY

Admissions
Berrien Springs, MI 49104
(616) 471-3303
(800) 253-2874
http://www.andrews.edu/

CENTRAL MICHIGAN UNIVERSITY

College of Graduate Studies
200 IET
Mount Pleasant, MI 48859
(517) 774-4723
http://www.cmich.edu

CRANBROOK ACADEMY OF ART

1221 Woodward Avenue
Box 801
Bloomfield Hills, MI 48303-0801
(248) 645-3300

EASTERN MICHIGAN UNIVERSITY

Ypsilanti, MI 48197
(734) 487-3400
http://www.emich.edu

GMI ENGINEERING & MANAGEMENT INSTITUTE

1700 West Third Avenue
Flint, MI 48504-4898
(800) 955-4464
http://www.gmi.edu

GRAND VALLEY STATE UNIVERSITY

Allendale, MI 49401
(616) 895-2025
http://www.gvsu.edu

LAWRENCE TECHNOLOGICAL UNIVERSITY

21000 West Ten Mile Road
Southfield, MI 48075
(248) 204-4000

MARYGROVE COLLEGE

8425 West McNichols
Detroit, MI 48221-2599
(313) 927-1200

MICHIGAN STATE UNIVERSITY

East Lansing, MI 48824-0590
(517) 355-8332
http://www.msu.edu/

MICHIGAN TECHNOLOGICAL UNIVERSITY

1400 Townsend Drive
Houghton, MI 49931-1295
(906) 487-1885
http://www.mtu.edu/

NORTHERN MICHIGAN UNIVERSITY

1401 Presque Isle
Marquette, MI 49855
(906) 227-2300
http://www.nmu.edu

OAKLAND UNIVERSITY

The Graduate School
Rochester, MI 48309-4401
(248) 370-3168
http://www.acs.oakland.edu/

SAGINAW VALLEY STATE UNIVERSITY

University Center, MI 48710
(517) 790-4000
http://www.svsu.edu

SIENA HEIGHTS COLLEGE

1247 East Siena Heights Drive
Adrian, MI 49221
(517) 264-7665

UNIVERSITY OF DETROIT MERCY

4001 West McNichols Road
Detroit, MI 48221
(313) 993-1245
http://www.udmercy.edu/

UNIVERSITY OF MICHIGAN— FLINT

303 East Kearsley
Flint, MI 48502-2186
(810) 762-3171
http://www.flint.umich.edu

UNIVERSITY OF MICHIGAN— ANN ARBOR

Ann Arbor, MI 48109
(313) 764-8129
http://www.umich.edu/

UNIVERSITY OF MICHIGAN— DEARBORN

4901 Evergreen Road
1080 AB
Dearborn, MI 48128-1491
Education: (313) 593-5090
Engineering: (313) 593-5241
Public Administration:
(313) 436-9135
http://www.umd.umich.edu/

WAYNE STATE UNIVERSITY

Detroit, MI 48202
(313) 577-2424
http://www.wayne.edu

WESTERN MICHIGAN UNIVERSITY

Kalamazoo, MI 49008
(616) 387-2000
http://www.wmich.edu

Minnesota

AUGSBURG COLLEGE

2211 Riverside Avenue
Minneapolis, MN 55454
(612) 330-1001
http://www.augsburg.edu/

BEMIDJI STATE UNIVERSITY

1500 Birchmont Drive, NE
Bemidji, MN 56601
(218) 755-2040

COLLEGE OF ST. CATHERINE

2004 Randolph Avenue
St. Paul, MN 55105
(612) 690-6000
http://www.stkate.edu/

HAMLINE UNIVERSITY

1536 Hewitt Avenue
St. Paul, MN 55101
(800) 888-2182
http://www.hamline.edu

MANKATO STATE UNIVERSITY

MSU 55
Mankato, MN 56002-8400
(507) 389-2321
http://www.mankato.edu/

MOORHEAD STATE UNIVERSITY

1104 Seventh Avenue South
Moorhead, MN 56563
(218) 236-2182
http://www.moorhead.msus.edu

ST. CLOUD STATE UNIVERSITY

720 Fourth Avenue South
St. Cloud, MN 56301
(320) 255-2113
http://www.stcloud.msus.edu

ST. MARY'S UNIVERSITY OF MINNESOTA

2510 Park Avenue South
Minneapolis, MN 55404
(612) 874-9877
http://www.smumn.edu

UNIVERSITY OF MINNESOTA— DULUTH

Duluth, MN 55812
(218) 726-7523
http://www.d.um.edu

UNIVERSITY OF MINNESOTA— TWIN CITIES

231 Pillsbury Drive, SE
Minneapolis, MN 55455-0213
(612) 625-3014
http://www.umn.edu/

UNIVERSITY OF ST. THOMAS

2115 Summit Avenue
St. Paul, MN 55105
(612) 962-5000
http://www.stthomas.edu

WINONA STATE UNIVERSITY

Winona, MN 55987
(507) 457-5000
http://www.winona.msus.edu

Mississippi

JACKSON STATE UNIVERSITY

Jackson, MS 39217
(601) 968-2455
http://ccaix.jsums.edu/

MISSISSIPPI COLLEGE

200 West College Street
Clinton, MS 39058
(601) 925-3000
http://www.mc.edu

MISSISSIPPI STATE UNIVERSITY

Mississippi State, MS 39762
(601) 325-7474
http://www.msstate.edu

UNIVERSITY OF MISSISSIPPI

University, MS 38677
(601) 232-7111
http://www.olemiss.edu

UNIVERSITY OF SOUTHERN MISSISSIPPI

Southern Station
Hattiesburg, MS 39406
(601) 266-4369
http://www.usm.edu

Missouri

AVILA COLLEGE

11901 Wornall Road
Kansas City, MO 64145-1698
(816) 942-8400
http://www.avila.edu

CENTRAL MISSOURI STATE UNIVERSITY

Warrensburg, MO 64093
(816) 543-4677
In April 1998: (660) 543-4677
http://www.cmsuvmb.cmsu.edu

FONTBONNE COLLEGE

6800 Wydown Boulevard
St. Louis, MO 63105
(314) 862-3456
http://www.fontbonne.edu

LINCOLN UNIVERSITY

820 Chestnut
Jefferson City, MO 65102-0029
(573) 681-5000

LINDENWOOD COLLEGE

St. Charles, MO 63301
(314) 949-2000

NORTHWEST MISSOURI STATE UNIVERSITY

800 University Drive
Maryville, MO 64468
(660) 562-1145
http://www.nwmissouri.edu

PARK COLLEGE

8700 River Park Drive
Parkville, MO 64152
(816) 741-2000

SAINT LOUIS UNIVERSITY

221 North Grand Boulevard
St. Louis, MO 63103-2097
(314) 977-2222
http://www.slu.edu

SOUTHEAST MISSOURI STATE UNIVERSITY

One University Plaza
Cape Girardeau, MO 63701
(573) 651-2192
http://www.semo.edu/

SOUTHWEST MISSOURI STATE UNIVERSITY

901 South National
Springfield, MO 65804
(417) 836-5335
http://www.smsu.edu/

TRUMAN STATE UNIVERSITY

Kirksville, MO 63501
(660) 785-4000

UNIVERSITY OF MISSOURI— COLUMBIA

Columbia, MO 65211
(573) 882-6311
http://www.missouri.edu/alt_index.html

UNIVERSITY OF MISSOURI— KANSAS CITY

Kansas City, MO 64110
(816) 235-1111
http://www.umkc.edu

UNIVERSITY OF MISSOURI— ROLLA

1890 Miner Circle
Rolla, MO 65401-0910
(573) 341-4315
http://www.umr.edu

UNIVERSITY OF MISSOURI— ST. LOUIS

Graduate School Admissions
8001 Natural Bridge Road
St. Louis, MO 63121-4499
(314) 516-5458
http://www.umsl.edu

WASHINGTON UNIVERSITY

One Brookings Drive
Box 1089
St. Louis, MO 63130
(314) 935-6880
http://www.wustl.edu

WEBSTER UNIVERSITY

470 East Lockwood
St. Louis, MO 63119-3194
(314) 968-7462
http://www.websteruniv.edu

Montana

MONTANA STATE UNIVERSITY—BOZEMAN

Bozeman, MT 59717
(406) 994-4145
http://www.montana.edu

MONTANA TECH OF THE UNIVERSITY OF MONTANA

1300 West Park Street
Butte, MT 59701-8997
(406) 496-4128
http://www.mtech.edu

UNIVERSITY OF GREAT FALLS

(formerly College of Great Falls)
1301 20th Street South
Great Falls, MT 59405
(406) 761-8210

UNIVERSITY OF MONTANA

Missoula, MT 59812
(406) 243-2572
http://www.umt.edu/

Nebraska

CHADRON STATE COLLEGE

Graduate School Admissions
Chadron, NE 69337-2690
(308) 432-6000
http://www.csc.edu

CONCORDIA COLLEGE

800 North Columbia Avenue
Seward, NE 68434
(402) 643-7377
http://www.cus.edu/cunb.html

CREIGHTON UNIVERSITY

Graduate School Admissions
2500 California
Omaha, NE 68178
(402) 280-2870
http://bluejay-creighton.edu/

UNIVERSITY OF NEBRASKA— LINCOLN

14th and R Streets
Lincoln, NE 68588
(402) 472-2878
http://www.unl.edu/index.html

UNIVERSITY OF NEBRASKA— KEARNEY

905 West 25th
Kearney, NE 68849-0661
(308) 865-8500
http://www.betty_boop.unk.edu

UNIVERSITY OF NEBRASKA— OMAHA

60th and Dodge Streets
Omaha, NE 68182-0005
(402) 554-2393
http://www.unomaha.edu/

Nevada

UNIVERSITY OF NEVADA— RENO

Mail Stop 110
Reno, NV 89557-0002
(702) 784-6869
http://www.unr.edu/

UNIVERSITY OF NEVADA—LAS VEGAS

4505 South Maryland Parkway
Las Vegas, NV 89154
(702) 895-4391
http://www.unlv.edu

New Hampshire

ANTIOCH NEW ENGLAND GRADUATE SCHOOL

Roxbury Street
Keene, NH 03431
(603) 357-6265
http://sparc.antiochne.edu/

DARTMOUTH COLLEGE

Graduate School Admissions
Hanover, NH 03755
(603) 646-1110
http://www.dartmouth.edu

KEENE STATE COLLEGE

229 Main Street
Keene, NH 03435-2604
(603) 352-1909
http://www.keene.edu

NEW ENGLAND COLLEGE

Henniker, NH 03242
(603) 428-2211

PLYMOUTH STATE COLLEGE OF THE UNIVERSITY SYSTEM OF NEW HAMPSHIRE

15 Halderness Road
Plymouth, NH 03264
(603) 535-2735
http://www.plymouth.edu/

RIVIER COLLEGE

420 Main Street
Nashua, NH 03060-5086
(603) 888-1311
http://www.riv.edu/

UNIVERSITY OF NEW HAMPSHIRE

Thompson Hall, Room 109
105 Main Street
Durham, NH 03824
(603) 862-3000
http://unhinfo.unh.edu

New Jersey

COLLEGE OF NEW JERSEY

(formerly Trenton State College)
Hillwood Lakes
CN 4700
Trenton, NJ 08650-4700
(609) 771-1855
http://www.trenton.edu

DREW UNIVERSITY

Graduate School Admissions
36 Madison Avenue
Madison, NJ 07940
(973) 408-3110
http://www.drew.edu

FAIRLEIGH DICKINSON UNIVERSITY

Graduate Admissions
1000 River Road
Teaneck, NJ 07666
(201) 692-2554
http://www.fdu.edu

JERSEY CITY STATE COLLEGE

2039 Kennedy Boulevard
Jersey City, NJ 07305
(201) 200-2000
http://www.jcstate.edu/

KEAN COLLEGE OF NEW JERSEY

P.O. Box 411
Union, NJ 07083-0411
(908) 527-2000
http://www.kean.edu

MONMOUTH UNIVERSITY

Cedar Avenue
West Long Branch, NJ 07764-1898
(732) 571-3452
http://www.monmouth.edu

MONTCLAIR STATE UNIVERSITY

Valley Road and Normal Avenue
Upper Montclair, NJ 07043-1624
(973) 655-5147
http://www.montclair.edu

NEW JERSEY INSTITUTE OF TECHNOLOGY

University Heights
Newark, NJ 07102-1982
(973) 596-3000
http://www.njit.edu

PRINCETON UNIVERSITY

Princeton, NJ 08544
(609) 258-3034
http://www.princeton.edu

RIDER UNIVERSITY

2083 Lawrenceville Road
Lawrenceville, NJ 08648-3099
(609) 896-5036
http://www.rider.edu

ROWAN COLLEGE OF NEW JERSEY

Glassboro, NJ 08028
(609) 256-4000
http://www.rowan.edu

RUTGERS UNIVERSITY— CAMDEN COLLEGE OF ARTS AND SCIENCE

Camden, NJ 08102
(609) 225-1766
http://www.rutgers.edu

RUTGERS UNIVERSITY— MASON GROSS SCHOOL OF THE ARTS

New Brunswick, NJ 08903
(732) 932-1766
http://www.rutgers.edu

RUTGERS UNIVERSITY—NEW BRUNSWICK

College Avenue
New Brunswick, NJ 08903
(732) 932-1766
http://www.rutgers.edu

RUTGERS UNIVERSITY— NEWARK

Graduate and Professional Admissions
249 University Avenue
Blumenthal Hall
Newark, NJ 07102
(973) 353-5205
http://www.rutgers.edu

SETON HALL UNIVERSITY

400 South Orange Avenue
South Orange, NJ 07079-2689
(973) 761-9332
http://www.shu.edu/

STEVENS INSTITUTE OF TECHNOLOGY

Castle Point on Hudson
Hoboken, NJ 07030
(201) 216-5234
http://www.stevens-tech.edu

WILLIAM PATERSON COLLEGE OF NEW JERSEY

300 Pompton Road
Wayne, NJ 07470
(973) 595-2000
http://pioneer.wilpaterson.edu/

New Mexico

EASTERN NEW MEXICO UNIVERSITY

Portales, NM 88130
(505) 562-1011
http://www.enmu.edu

NEW MEXICO HIGHLANDS UNIVERSITY

Las Vegas, NM 87701
(505) 425-7511
http://www.nmhu.edu

NEW MEXICO STATE UNIVERSITY

Box 30001
Dept. 3A
Las Cruces, NM 88003-8001
(505) 646-2736
http://www.nmsu.edu/

ST. JOHN'S COLLEGE

1160 Camino Cruz Blanca
Santa Fe, NM 87501
(505) 984-6083
http://www.sjca.edu/

UNIVERSITY OF NEW MEXICO

107 Humanities Building
Albuquerque, NM 87131-1041
(505) 277-2711
http://www.unm.edu

WESTERN NEW MEXICO UNIVERSITY

1000 College Avenue
Silver City, NM 88062
(505) 538-6317
http://www.wnmu.edu

New York

ADELPHI UNIVERSITY

South Avenue
Garden City, NY 11530
(516) 877-3000
http://www.adelphi.edu/

ALFRED UNIVERSITY

Saxon Drive
Alfred, NY 14802-1205
(607) 871-2115
http://www.alfred.edu

BARD COLLEGE

Graduate School Admissions
P.O. Box 5000
Annandale-on-Hudson, NY
12504-5000
Main Graduate: (914) 758-6822
Fine Arts: (914) 758-7481
Curatorial Studies: (914) 758-7588
Bard Graduate: (212) 501-3051
http://www.bard.edu

CLARKSON UNIVERSITY

Box 5625
Potsdam, NY 13699
315 268-6442
http://www.clarkson.edu

COLGATE UNIVERSITY

13 Oak Drive
Hamilton, NY 13346
315 824-7401
http://www.colgate.edu

COLLEGE OF NEW ROCHELLE

29 Castle Place
New Rochelle, NY 10805
Education: (914) 632-5330
Human Sciences: (914) 654-5561
Art & Commercial Arts:
(914) 654-5279

COLLEGE OF ST. ROSE

432 Western Avenue
Albany, NY 12203
518 454-5111
http://www.strose.edu

COLUMBIA UNIVERSITY

School of Arts and Sciences
109 Low Memorial Library
New York, NY 10027
(212) 854-4737
http://www.columbia.edu

COLUMBIA UNIVERSITY

School of Engineering and
Applied Science
530 Seely Mudd Hall
New York, NY 10027
(212) 854-2931

CORNELL UNIVERSITY

Graduate School
Ithaca, NY 14853
(607) 255-4884
http://www.cornell.edu

CITY UNIVERSITY OF NEW YORK—BARUCH COLLEGE

17 Lexington Avenue
New York, NY 10010
(212) 802-2000
http://www.baruch.cuny.edu

CITY UNIVERSITY OF NEW YORK—BROOKLYN COLLEGE

2900 Bedford Avenue
Brooklyn, NY 11210
(718) 951-5914
http://www.brooklyn.cuny.edu

CITY UNIVERSITY OF NEW YORK—CITY COLLEGE

Graduate School Admissions
Convent Avenue and 138th Street
New York, NY 10031
(212) 650-6236
http://www.ccny.cuny.edu

CITY UNIVERSITY OF NEW YORK—LEHMAN COLLEGE

250 Bedford Park Boulevard West
Bronx, NY 10468
(718) 960-7276
http://www.cuny.edu

CITY UNIVERSITY OF NEW YORK—THE COLLEGE OF STATEN ISLAND

2800 Victory Boulevard
Staten Island, NY 10314
(718) 982-2013
http://www.cuny.edu/

CITY UNIVERSITY OF NEW YORK—GRADUATE SCHOOL AND UNIVERSITY CENTER

33 West 42nd Street
New York, NY 10036-8099
(212) 642-2812
http://www.cuny.edu/

CITY UNIVERSITY OF NEW YORK—HUNTER COLLEGE

695 Park Avenue
New York, NY 10021
(212) 772-4490
http://www.hunter.cuny.edu

CITY UNIVERSITY OF NEW YORK—QUEENS COLLEGE

65-30 Kissena Boulevard
Flushing, NY 11367
(718) 997-5200
http://www.qc.edu

COOPER UNION

41 Cooper Square
New York, NY 10003
(212) 353-4120
http://www.cooper.edu

EUGENE LANG COLLEGE OF THE NEW SCHOOL FOR SOCIAL RESEARCH

65 West 11th Street
New York, NY 10011
(212) 229-5665
http://www.newschool.edu

FASHION INSTITUTE OF TECHNOLOGY

Seventh Avenue at 27th Street
New York, NY 10001-5992
(212) 760-7675

FORDHAM UNIVERSITY

441 East Fordham Road
New York, NY 10458
(718) 817-4415
http://www.fordham.edu

HOFSTRA UNIVERSITY

Hempstead, NY 11550
(516) 463-6707
http://www.hofstra.edu

IONA COLLEGE

715 North Avenue
New Rochelle, NY 10801
(914) 633-2000
http://www.iona.edu

ITHACA COLLEGE

111 Towers Concourse
Ithaca, NY 14850-7142
(607) 274-3527
http://www.ithaca.edu

LONG ISLAND UNIVERSITY—BROOKLYN CAMPUS

One University Plaza
Brooklyn, NY 11201
(718) 488-1011
http://www.liunet.edu

LONG ISLAND UNIVERSITY—C.W. POST CAMPUS

Graduate School Admissions
720 Northern Boulevard
Brookville, NY 11548-1300
(800) 548-7526
(516) 299-2417

MANHATTAN COLLEGE

Manhattan College Parkway
Riverdale, NY 10471
(718) 862-7200
http://www.mancol.edu

MANHATTANVILLE COLLEGE

2900 Purchase Street
Purchase, NY 10577
(914) 694-5300
http://www.manhattanville.edu

MARIST COLLEGE

290 North Road
Poughkeepsie, NY 12601-1387
(914) 575-3530
http://www.marist.edu

NEW YORK INSTITUTE OF TECHNOLOGY

P.O. Box 8000
Old Westbury, NY 11568-8000
(516) 686-7519
http://www.nyit.edu

NEW YORK UNIVERSITY

22 Washington Square North
New York, NY 10011
(212) 998-1212
http://www.nyu.edu/

NYACK COLLEGE

1 South Boulevard
Nyack, NY 10960-3698
(914) 358-1710

PACE UNIVERSITY

1 Pace Plaza
New York, NY 10038
(212) 346-1531
http://www.pace.edu

PARSONS SCHOOL OF DESIGN

66 Fifth Avenue
New York, NY 10011
(212) 229-8900
http://www.parsons.newschool.edu

POLYTECHNIC UNIVERSITY

6 MetroTech Center
Brooklyn, NY 11201
(718) 260-3600
http://www.poly.edu

POLYTECHNIC UNIVERSITY— WESTCHESTER GRADUATE CENTER

36 Saw Mill River Road
Hawthorne, NY 10532
(914) 323-2000

PRATT INSTITUTE

200 Willoughby Avenue
Brooklyn, NY 11205
(718) 636-3600
http://www.pratt.edu

RENSSELAER POLYTECHNIC INSTITUTE

Troy, NY 12180
(518) 276-6789
http://www.rpi.edu

ROCHESTER INSTITUTE OF TECHNOLOGY

60 Lomb Memorial Drive
Rochester, NY 14623
(716) 475-6631
http://www.rit.edu

SAGE COLLEGES

45 Ferry Street
Troy, NY 12180
(518) 270-2000
http://www.sage.edu/html/rsc/
welcome.html

SARAH LAWRENCE COLLEGE

One Meadway
Bronxville, NY 10708
(914) 337-0700
http://www.slc.edu

ST. BERNARD'S INSTITUTE

1100 South Goodman Street
Rochester, NY 14620
(716) 271-1320

ST. BONAVENTURE UNIVERSITY

P.O. Box D
St. Bonaventure, NY 14778-2284
(716) 375-2202
http://www.cs.sbu.edu/index.html

ST. JOHN'S UNIVERSITY

8000 Utopia Parkway
Jamaica, NY 11439
(718) 990-6161
http://foghorn.stjohns.edu/

STATE UNIVERSITY OF NEW YORK—ALBANY

1400 Washington Avenue
Albany, NY 12222
(518) 442-3980
http://www.albany.edu

STATE UNIVERSITY OF NEW YORK—BINGHAMTON

P.O. Box 6000
Binghamton, NY 13902-6000
(607) 777-2284
http://www.binghamton.edu

STATE UNIVERSITY OF NEW YORK—BUFFALO

Buffalo, NY 14260
(716) 645-5601
http://www.buffalo.edu

STATE UNIVERSITY OF NEW YORK—BUFFALO STATE COLLEGE

1300 Elmwood Avenue
Buffalo, NY 14222
(716) 645-2939
http://www.snybuf.edu

STATE UNIVERSITY OF NEW YORK—COLLEGE AT BROCKPORT

Brockport, NY 14420-2915
(716) 395-5456
http://www.acs.brockport.edu

STATE UNIVERSITY OF NEW YORK—COLLEGE AT CORTLAND

P.O. Box 2000
Cortland, NY 13045
(607) 753-4712
http://www.cortland.edu/

STATE UNIVERSITY OF NEW YORK—COLLEGE AT FREDONIA

Fredonia, NY 14063
(716) 673-3251
http://www.fredonia.edu

STATE UNIVERSITY OF NEW YORK—COLLEGE AT ONEONTA

Oneonta, NY 13820
(607) 436-2524
http://www.oneonta.edu

STATE UNIVERSITY OF NEW YORK—COLLEGE AT OSWEGO

602 Culkin Hall
Oswego, NY 13126
(315) 341-3152
http://www.oswego.edu/

STATE UNIVERSITY OF NEW YORK—COLLEGE AT PLATTSBURGH

101 Broad Street
Plattsburgh, NY 12901
(518) 564-2040
http://www.plattsburgh.edu

STATE UNIVERSITY OF NEW YORK—COLLEGE AT POTSDAM

Potsdam, NY 13676-2294
(315) 267-2165
http://www.potsdam.edu

STATE UNIVERSITY OF NEW YORK—COLLEGE OF ENVIRONMENTAL SCIENCE AND FORESTRY

Syracuse, NY 13210
(315) 470-6500
http://www.esf.edu

STATE UNIVERSITY OF NEW YORK—EMPIRE STATE COLLEGE

One Union Avenue
Saratoga Springs, NY 12866
(518) 587-2100
http://www.esc.edu

STATE UNIVERSITY OF NEW YORK—GENESEO

1 College Circle
Geneseo, NY 14454
(716) 245-5571
http://www.geneseo.edu/

STATE UNIVERSITY OF NEW YORK—INSTITUTE OF

Technology at Utica/Rome
P.O. Box 3050
Utica, NY 13504-3050
(315) 792-7208
http://www.sunyit.edu

STATE UNIVERSITY OF NEW YORK—NEW PALTZ

(formerly SUNY College at New Paltz)
75 South Manheim Boulevard
New Paltz, NY 12561-2499
(914) 257-3285 or (914) 257-3286
http://www.newpaltz.edu/

STATE UNIVERSITY OF NEW YORK—PURCHASE COLLEGE

735 Anderson Hill Road
Purchase, NY 10577
(914) 251-6300
http://www.purchase.edu

STATE UNIVERSITY OF NEW YORK—STONY BROOK

Stony Brook, NY 11794
(516) 689-7040
http://www.sunysb.edu/

SYRACUSE UNIVERSITY

303 Bowne Hall
Syracuse, NY 13244
(315) 443-4492
http://www.syr.edu

TOURO COLLEGE

27-33 West 23rd Street
New York, NY 10010-4202
(212) 463-0400

UNION COLLEGE

Schenectady, NY 12308
(518) 388-6288
http://www.union.edu

UNIVERSITY OF ROCHESTER

Rochester, NY 14627
(716) 275-2121
http://www.rochester.edu

VASSAR COLLEGE

Raymond Avenue
Poughkeepsie, NY 12601
(914) 437-7000
http://www.vassar.edu

YESHIVA UNIVERSITY

Main Campus
500 West 185th Street
New York, NY 10033-3201
(212) 960-5277
http://www.yu.edu

North Carolina

APPALACHIAN STATE UNIVERSITY

Cratis D. Williams Graduate School
Walker Hall
Boone, NC 28608
(704) 262-2130
http://www.acs.appstate.edu/

DUKE UNIVERSITY

2138 Campus Drive
Box 90586
Durham, NC 27708
(919) 684-3913
http://www.duke.edu/duke.html

EAST CAROLINA UNIVERSITY

East Fifth Street
Greenville, NC 27858-4353
(919) 328-6012
http://ecuvax.cis.edu/

GARDNER-WEBB UNIVERSITY

Boiling Springs, NC 28017-9980
(704) 434-2361

MEREDITH COLLEGE

Graduate Admissions
3800 Hillsborough Street
Raleigh, NC 27607-5298
(919) 829-8600
http://www.meredith.edu/meredith

NORTH CAROLINA A&T STATE UNIVERSITY

1601 East Market Street
Greensboro, NC 27411
(910) 334-7920
http://www.ncat.edu

NORTH CAROLINA CENTRAL UNIVERSITY

P.O. Box 19717
Durham, NC 27707
(919) 560-6100
http://www.nccu.edu

NORTH CAROLINA STATE UNIVERSITY

Box 7103
Raleigh, NC 27695-7103
(919) 515-2872
http://www.ncsu.edu

UNIVERSITY OF NORTH CAROLINA—ASHEVILLE

One University Heights
Asheville, NC 28804-3299
(704) 251-6481
http://www.unca.edu

UNIVERSITY OF NORTH CAROLINA—CHAPEL HILL

Chapel Hill, NC 27599-2200
(919) 962-2611
http://www.unc.edu

UNIVERSITY OF NORTH CAROLINA—CHARLOTTE

9201 University City Boulevard
Charlotte, NC 28223-0001
(704) 547-3371
http://www.unccvm.uncc.edu

UNIVERSITY OF NORTH CAROLINA—GREENSBORO

1000 Spring Garden Street
Greensboro, NC 27412
(910) 334-5596
http://www.uncg.edu

UNIVERSITY OF NORTH CAROLINA—WILMINGTON

601 South College Road
Wilmington, NC 28403-3297
(910) 962-3135
http://www.uncwil.edu/

WAKE FOREST UNIVERSITY

Box 7305 Reynolda Station
Winston-Salem, NC 27109
(910) 759-5301
http://www.wfu.edu

WARREN WILSON COLLEGE

P.O. Box 9000
Asheville, NC 28815
(704) 298-3325
http://www.warren-wilson.edu

WESTERN CAROLINA UNIVERSITY

Cullowhee, NC 28723
Before June 1998: (704) 227-7398
After June 1998: (828) 227-7398
http://www.wcu.edu

North Dakota

MINOT STATE UNIVERSITY

Graduate Studies
500 University Avenue West
Minot, ND 58707
(701) 858-3250
http://warp6.cs.misu.nodak.edu/

NORTH DAKOTA STATE UNIVERSITY

P.O. Box 5790
Fargo, ND 58105
(701) 231-7033
http://www.ndsu.nodak.edu/

UNIVERSITY OF NORTH DAKOTA

University Station
Grand Forks, ND 58202-8172
(701) 777-2784
http://www.nodak.edu

Ohio

AIR FORCE INSTITUTE OF TECHNOLOGY

AFIT/RP, Building 125
2950 P Street
Wright-Patterson AFB
OH 45433-7765
(937) 255-7168
http://www.afit.af.mil

ASHLAND UNIVERSITY

401 College Avenue
Ashland, OH 44805
(419) 289-5977
http://www.ashland.edu

ATHENAEUM OF OHIO

6616 Beechmont Avenue
Cincinnati, OH 45230-2091
(513) 231-2223

BOWLING GREEN STATE UNIVERSITY

Bowling Green, OH 43403
(419) 372-2791
http://www.bgsu.edu/

CASE WESTERN RESERVE UNIVERSITY

10900 Euclid Avenue
Cleveland, OH 44106
(216) 368-4390
http://www.cwru.edu

CLEVELAND STATE UNIVERSITY

1983 East 24th Street
Cleveland, OH 44115
(216) 687-3593
http://www.csuohio.edu

FRANCISCAN UNIVERSITY OF STEUBENVILLE

University Boulevard
Steubenville, OH 43952-6701
(800) 783-6220
http://www.franuniv.edu/

HEIDELBERG COLLEGE

310 East Market Street
Tiffin, OH 44883
(419) 448-2000
http://www.heidelberg.edu

JOHN CARROLL UNIVERSITY

20700 North Park Boulevard
Cleveland, OH 44118
(216) 397-1886
http://www.jcu.edu

KENT STATE UNIVERSITY

P.O. Box 5190
Kent, OH 44242-0001
(330) 672-2660
http://www.kent.edu

MALONE COLLEGE

515 25th Street, NW
Canton, OH 44709
(330) 471-8210
http://www.malone.edu

MIAMI UNIVERSITY

102 Roudebush Hall
Oxford, OH 45056
(513) 529-4125
http://www.muohio.edu/

MOUNT VERNON NAZARENE COLLEGE

800 Martinsburg Road
Mount Vernon, OH 43050
Before June 1998: (614) 397-1244
After June 1998: (740) 397-1244

OBERLIN CONSERVATORY

77 West College Street
Oberlin, OH 44074
(440) 775-8413
http://www.oberlin.edu

OHIO STATE UNIVERSITY—COLUMBUS

3rd Floor Lincoln Tower
1800 Cannon Drive
Columbus, OH 43210-1200
(614) 292-3980
http://www.acs.ohio-state.edu

OHIO UNIVERSITY

Athens, OH 45701-2979
Before June 1998: (614) 593-2800
After June 1998: (740) 593-2800
http://www.ohiou.edu/

PONTIFICAL COLLEGE JOSEPHINUM

7625 North High Street
Columbus, OH 43235
(614) 885-5585

THE UNION INSTITUTE

440 East McMillan Street
Cincinnati, OH 45206-1925
(513) 861-6400
http://www.tui.edu

UNIVERSITY OF AKRON

302 Buchtel Common
Akron, OH 44325
(330) 972-7663
http://www.uakron.edu

UNIVERSITY OF CINCINNATI

Cincinnati, OH 45221-0127
(513) 556-4335
http://www.uc.edu/

UNIVERSITY OF DAYTON

300 College Park
Dayton, OH 45469-1620
(937) 229-2343
http://www.udayton.edu

UNIVERSITY OF TOLEDO

2801 West Bancroft Street
Toledo, OH 43606
(419) 530-4242
http://www.utoledo.edu/

URSULINE COLLEGE

2550 Lander Road
Pepper Pike, OH 44124
(440) 449-4200

WALSH UNIVERSITY

2020 Easton Street, NW
North Canton, OH 44720
(330) 499-7090
http://www.walsh.edu

WRIGHT STATE UNIVERSITY

Dayton, OH 45435
(937) 873-2976
http://www.wright.edu/

XAVIER UNIVERSITY

3800 Victory Parkway
Cincinnati, OH 45207-5311
Education Arts & Criminal Justice: (513) 745-3360
Health Services Administration:
(513) 745-1912
http://www.xu.edu

YOUNGSTOWN STATE UNIVERSITY

One University Plaza
Youngstown, OH 44555-0001
(330) 742-3091
http://www.ysu.edu

Oklahoma

EAST CENTRAL UNIVERSITY

Ada, OK 74820-6899
(580) 332-8000
http://student.ecok.edu/

NORTHEASTERN STATE UNIVERSITY

Tahlequah, OK 74464
(918) 456-5511 ext. 3690
http://www.nsuok.edu

OKLAHOMA CITY UNIVERSITY

2501 North Blackwelder
Oklahoma City, OK 73106
(405) 521-5000
http://frodo.okcu.edu/

OKLAHOMA STATE UNIVERSITY

Stillwater, OK 74078
(405) 744-6368
http://www.okstate.edu

ORAL ROBERTS UNIVERSITY

7777 South Lewis Avenue
Tulsa, OK 74171
(918) 495-6518
http://www.oru.edu

PHILLIPS UNIVERSITY

100 South University Avenue
Enid, OK 73701-6439
(580) 548-2316
http://www.phillips.edu

SOUTHERN NAZARENE UNIVERSITY

6729 N.W. 39th Expressway
Bethany, OK 73008
(405) 789-6400

SOUTHWESTERN OKLAHOMA STATE UNIVERSITY

100 Campus Drive
Weatherford, OK 73096-3098
(580) 774-3769
http://www.swosu.edu

UNIVERSITY OF CENTRAL OKLAHOMA

100 North University
Edmond, OK 73034
(405) 341-2980 ext. 3341
http://www.ucok.edu/

UNIVERSITY OF OKLAHOMA

Norman, OK 73019
(405) 325-3811
http://www.uoknor.edu

UNIVERSITY OF TULSA

600 South College Avenue
Tulsa, OK 74104
(918) 631-2336
http://www.utulsa.edu

Oregon

GEORGE FOX COLLEGE

414 North Meridian
Newberg, OR 97132
(503) 538-8383, ext.2260 or
(800) 631-0921
http://www.gfc.edu

LEWIS & CLARK COLLEGE

Graduate School Admissions
0615 S.W. Palatine Hill Road
Portland, OR 97219-7899
(503) 768-7700
http://www.lclark.edu

OREGON GRADUATE INSTITUTE OF SCIENCE AND TECHNOLOGY

P.O. Box 91000
Portland, OR 97291-1000
(503) 690-1121
http://www.ogi.edu

OREGON STATE UNIVERSITY

Corvallis, OR 97331
(541) 737-3201
http://orst.edu/

PACIFIC UNIVERSITY

2043 College Way
Forest Grove, OR 97116
(800) 933-9308
http://www.pacificu.edu

PORTLAND STATE UNIVERSITY

P.O. Box 751
Portland, OR 97207-0751
(503) 725-3511
http://www.pdx.edu/

REED COLLEGE

3203 S.E. Woodstock Boulevard
Portland, OR 97202-8199
(503) 777-7259
http://www.reed.edu

SOUTHERN OREGON STATE COLLEGE

Ashland, OR 97520
(541) 552-6203
http://www.sosc.osshe.edu

UNIVERSITY OF OREGON

Eugene, OR 97403-1217
(541) 346-3201
http://www.uoregon.edu/

UNIVERSITY OF PORTLAND

5000 North Willamette Boulevard
Portland, OR 97203-5798
(800) 227-4568
http://www.uofport.edu/

WARNER PACIFIC COLLEGE

2219 S.E. 68th Avenue
Portland, OR 97215
(503) 775-4366

WESTERN OREGON STATE COLLEGE

345 North Monmouth Avenue
Monmouth, OR 97361
(503) 838-8492
http://www.wosc.osshe.edu

Pennsylvania

ALLENTOWN COLLEGE OF ST. FRANCIS DE SALES

2755 Station Avenue
Center Valley, PA 18034-9568
(610) 282-1100
http://www.allencol.edu

BEAVER COLLEGE

450 South Easton Road
Glenside, PA 19038-3295
(215) 572-2900

BLOOMSBURG UNIVERSITY OF PENNSYLVANIA

400 East Second Street
Bloomsburg, PA 17815
(717) 389-4317
http://www.bloomu.edu

BRYN MAWR COLLEGE

101 North Merion Avenue
Bryn Mawr, PA 19010-2899
(610) 526-5075
http://www.brynmawr.edu

BUCKNELL UNIVERSITY

Lewisburg, PA 17837
(717) 524-1304
http://www.bucknell.edu

CALIFORNIA UNIVERSITY OF PENNSYLVANIA

250 University Drive
California, PA 15419
(412) 938-4404
http://www.cup.edu/

CARNEGIE MELLON UNIVERSITY

5000 Forbes Avenue
Pittsburgh, PA 15213
(412) 268-2000
http://www.cmu.edu

CHESTNUT HILL COLLEGE

9601 Germantown Avenue
Philadelphia, PA 19118-2695
(215) 248-7001

CLARION UNIVERSITY OF PENNSYLVANIA

Clarion, PA 16214
(814) 226-2337
http://www.clarion.edu

DREXEL UNIVERSITY

3141 Chestnut Street
Philadelphia, PA 19104
(800) 2-DREXEL
http://www.drexel.edu/

DUQUESNE UNIVERSITY

600 Forbes Avenue
Pittsburgh, PA 15282
(412) 396-6400
http://www.duq.edu/

EAST STROUDSBURG UNIVERSITY OF PENNSYLVANIA

East Stroudsburg, PA 18301
(717) 422-3211
http://www.esu.edu/

EDINBORO UNIVERSITY OF PENNSYLVANIA

Edinboro, PA 16444
(814) 732-2000
http://www.edinboro.edu/

GANNON UNIVERSITY

University Square
Erie, PA 16541
(814) 871-7000
http://www.gannon.edu

GENEVA COLLEGE

3200 College Avenue
Beaver Falls, PA 15010
(412) 847-6500
http://www.geneva.edu

IMMACULATA COLLEGE

Box 901
Immaculata, PA 19345
(610) 647-4400
http://www.immaculata.edu

INDIANA UNIVERSITY OF PENNSYLVANIA

101 Stright Hall
Indiana, PA 15705-1088
(412) 357-2222
http://www.iup.edu

KUTZTOWN UNIVERSITY OF PENNSYLVANIA

College Hill
Kutztown, PA 19530
(610) 683-4000
http://www.kutztown.edu

LaSALLE UNIVERSITY

Graduate School Admissions
1900 West Olney Avenue
Philadelphia, PA 19141-1199
(215) 951-1057
http://www.lasalle.edu/academ/
grad/grad.html

LEHIGH UNIVERSITY

Bethlehem, PA 18015-3035
(610) 758-4500
http://www.lehigh.edu

LINCOLN UNIVERSITY

P.O. Box 179
Lincoln University, PA 19352
(610) 932-8300
http://www.lincoln.edu

LOCK HAVEN UNIVERSITY OF PENNSYLVANIA

Akeley Building
Lock Haven, PA 17745
(717) 893-2547
http://www.lhup.edu/

MANSFIELD UNIVERSITY OF PENNSYLVANIA

Mansfield, PA 16933
(717) 662-4000
http://www.mnsfld.edu

MARYWOOD COLLEGE

2300 Adams Avenue
Scranton, PA 185091598
(717) 340-6002
http://www.marywood.edu

MERCYHURST COLLEGE

Glenwood Hills
Erie, PA 16546
(814) 824-2202
http://utopia.mercy.edu

MILLERSVILLE UNIVERSITY OF PENNSYLVANIA

P.O. Box 1002
Millersville, PA 17551-0302
(717) 872-3011
http://marauder.millsv.edu

NEUMANN COLLEGE

One Neumann Drive
Aston, PA 19014-1297
(610) 459-0905
http://www.neumann.edu

PENNSYLVANIA

State University
University Park, PA 16802
(814) 865-1795
http://www.psu.edu/

PENNSYLVANIA STATE UNIVERSITY—ERIE

The Behrend College
Station Road
Erie, PA 16563-0105
(814) 898-6000
http://euler.bd.psu.edu

PENNSYLVANIA STATE UNIVERSITY—HARRISBURG

Middletown, PA 17057
(717) 948-6000
http://hbg.psu.edu

PENNSYLVANIA STATE UNIVERSITY—GREAT VALLEY

Graduate Center
30 East Swedesford Road
Malvern, PA 19355
(610) 648-3200

POINT PARK COLLEGE

201 Wood Street
Pittsburgh, PA 15222
(412) 391-4100

ROBERT MORRIS COLLEGE

Narrows Run Road
Coraopolis, PA 15108-1189
(412) 262-8200
http://www.robert-morris.edu

SAINT JOSEPH'S UNIVERSITY

5600 City Avenue
Philadelphia, PA 19131
(610) 660-1289
http://www.sju.edu

SHIPPENSBURG UNIVERSITY OF PENNSYLVANIA

1871 Old Main Drive
Shippensburg, PA 17257-2299
(717) 532-1213
http://www.ship.edu

SLIPPERY ROCK UNIVERSITY OF PENNSYLVANIA

Slippery Rock, PA 16057
(412) 738-2051
http://www.sru.edu

ST. FRANCIS COLLEGE

Loretto, PA 15940
(814) 472-3000

TEMPLE UNIVERSITY

1801 North Broad Street
Philadelphia, PA 19122-1803
(215) 204-1380
http://www.temple.edu

UNIVERSITY OF PENNSYLVANIA

Philadelphia, PA 19104
(215) 898-5720
http://www.upenn.edu:80/

UNIVERSITY OF PITTSBURGH

4200 Fifth Avenue
Pittsburgh, PA 15260
(412) 624-0790
http://www.pitt.edu/

UNIVERSITY OF SCRANTON

800 Linden Street
Scranton, PA 18510-4632
(717) 941-7400
http://www.uofs.edu

UNIVERSITY OF THE ARTS

Broad and Pine Streets
Philadelphia, PA 19102
(215) 732-4832

VILLANOVA UNIVERSITY

800 Lancaster Avenue
Villanova, PA 19085
(610) 519-7090
http://www.vill.edu

WEST CHESTER UNIVERSITY OF PENNSYLVANIA

High Street and University Avenue
West Chester, PA 19383
(610) 436-1000
http://www.wcupa.edu

WIDENER UNIVERSITY

One University Place
Chester, PA 19013
(610) 499-4372
http://www.widener.edu

WILKES UNIVERSITY

P.O. Box 111
Wilkes-Barre, PA 18766
(717) 831-4415
http://www.wilkes.edu/

Puerto Rico

CARIBBEAN CENTER FOR ADVANCED STUDIES

Apartado 3711
Old San Juan Station
San Juan, PR 00904-3711
(787) 725-6500

CENTRO DE ESTUDIOS AVANZADOS DE PUERTO RICO Y EL CARIB

Del Cristo Street, No. 52
Box S 4467
San Juan, PR 00904
(787) 723-4481

INTER-AMERICAN UNIVERSITY OF PUERTO RICO

P.O. Box 5100
San German, PR 00683
(787) 264-1912
http://metro.inter.edu/

PONTIFICAL CATHOLIC UNIVERSITY OF PUERTO

2250 Las Americas Avenue
Suite 563
Ponce, PR 00731-6382
(787) 841-2000

UNIVERSITY OF PUERTO RICO—MAYAGUEZ

P.O. Box 5000
Mayaguez, PR 00681-5000
(787) 832-4040 ext.2400
http://mayaweb.upr.clu.edu/rum/
acad_aff/graduate

UNIVERSITY OF PUERTO RICO—RIO PIEDRAS CAMPUS

P.O. Box 21790, UPR Station
Rio Piedras, PR 00931-1790
(787) 764-0000 ext. 3410 or 5659
http://lambda.upr.clu.edu/degi/html

UNIVERSITY OF THE SACRED HEART

Box 12383 Loiza Station
Santurce, PR 00914
(787) 728-1515

Rhode Island

BROWN UNIVERSITY

45 Prospect Street
Box 1876
Providence, RI 02912
(401) 863-2600
http://www.brown.edu/

PROVIDENCE COLLEGE

549 River Avenue
Providence, RI 02918-0001
(401) 865-2274
http://www.providence.edu

RHODE ISLAND COLLEGE

Providence, RI 02908
(401) 456-8117
http://www.ric.edu

SALVE REGINA UNIVERSITY

100 Ochre Point Avenue
Newport, RI 02840-4192
(401) 847-6650
http://www.salve.edu/~walsh/
salvehp.html

UNIVERSITY OF RHODE ISLAND

Kingston, RI 02881
(401) 874-2872
http://www.uri.edu/

South Carolina

CLEMSON UNIVERSITY

E-106 Martin Hall
Clemson, SC 29634-5120
(864) 656-3195
http://www.clemson.edu

COLLEGE OF CHARLESTON

66 George Street
Charleston, SC 29424
(803) 953-5670
http://www.cofc.edu

CONVERSE COLLEGE

580 East Main Street
Spartanburg, SC 29302
(864) 596-9000
http://www.icusc.org/converse/
cchome.htm

FRANCIS MARION UNIVERSITY

P.O. Box 100547
Florence, SC 29501-0547
(803) 661-1231
http://swampfox.fmarion.edu

SOUTH CAROLINA STATE UNIVERSITY

300 College Street, NE
P.O. Box 7127
Orangeburg, SC 29117-7127
(803) 536-7064
http://192.231.63.160/scsu/state.
htm

SOUTHERN WESLEYAN UNIVERSITY

Wesleyan Drive
Central, SC 29630
(864) 639-2453
http://www.icusc.eog/s_wesley/
swhome.htm

UNIVERSITY OF SOUTH CAROLINA

901 Sumter Street
Suite 304
Columbia, SC 29208
(803) 777-4243
http://www.scarolina.edu/admissions/
grad/index.htm

WINTHROP UNIVERSITY

(701) Oakland Avenue
Rock Hill, SC 29733
(803) 323-2204
http://lurch.winthrop.edu/

South Dakota

AUGUSTANA COLLEGE

2001 South Summit
Sioux Falls, SD 57197
(605) 336-5516
http://www.augie.edu/

SOUTH DAKOTA STATE UNIVERSITY

Box 2201
Brookings, SD 57007
(605) 688-4181
http://www.sdstate.edu

UNIVERSITY OF SOUTH DAKOTA—VERMILLION

414 East Clark Street
Vermillion, SD 57069
(605) 677-6498
http://www.usd.edu

Tennessee

AUSTIN PEAY STATE UNIVERSITY

Clarksville, TN 37044
(931) 648-7414
http://www.apsu.edu

DAVID LIPSCOMB UNIVERSITY

3901 Granny White Pike
Nashville, TN 37204-3951
(615) 269-1000

EAST TENNESSEE STATE UNIVERSITY

Johnson City, TN 37614-0002
(423) 929-4221
http://www.east-tenn-st.edu

FISK UNIVERSITY

1000 17th Avenue North
Nashville, TN 37208
(615) 329-8500
http://www.fisk.edu

FREED-HARDEMAN UNIVERSITY

158 East Main Street
Henderson, TN 38340
(901) 989-6000
http://www.fhu.edu/

MIDDLE TENNESSEE STATE UNIVERSITY

114 Cope Administration Building
Murfreesboro, TN 37132
(615) 898-2840
http://www.mtsu.edu

TENNESSEE STATE UNIVERSITY

3500 John A. Merritt Boulevard
Nashville, TN 37209-1561
(615) 963-5901
http://www.tnstate.edu/

TENNESSEE TECHNOLOGICAL UNIVERSITY

Box 5006 T.T.U.
Cookeville, TN 38505
(800) 255-8881
http://www.tntech.edu

TREVECCA NAZARENE UNIVERSITY

333 Murfreesboro Road
Nashville, TN 37210
(615) 248-1200

UNIVERSITY OF MEMPHIS

The Graduate School
Administration Building #317
Memphis, TN 38152
(901) 678-2911
http://www.memphis.edu

UNIVERSITY OF TENNESSEE— CHATTANOOGA

615 McCallie Avenue
Chattanooga, TN 37403
(423) 755-4667
http://www.utc.edu

UNIVERSITY OF TENNESSEE— MARTIN

309 Administration Building
Martin, TN 38238
(901) 587-7012
http://www.utm.edu

UNIVERSITY OF TENNESSEE— KNOXVILLE

Graduate Admissions and Records
218 Student Services Building
Knoxville, TN 37996-0220
(423) 974-3251
http://www.utk.edu

UNIVERSITY OF THE SOUTH

335 Tennessee Avenue
Sewanee, TN 37383-1000
(931) 598-1000
http://www.sewanee.edu

VANDERBILT UNIVERSITY

2305 West End Avenue
Nashville, TN 37203-1700
(615) 322-2651
http://www.vanderbilt.edu

Texas

ANGELO STATE UNIVERSITY

2601 West Avenue North
San Angelo, TX 76909
(915) 942-2041 or (915) 942-2058
http://www.angelo.edu

BAYLOR UNIVERSITY

Graduate School
P.O. Box 97032
Waco, TX 76798-7032
(254) 755-3588
http://www.baylor.edu

CRISWELL COLLEGE

Graduate Admissions
4010 Gaston Avenue
Dallas, TX 75246
(214) 821-5433
http://www.criswell.edu

EAST TEXAS STATE UNIVERSITY—TEXARKANA

2600 North Robison Road
P.O. Box 5518
Texarkana, TX 75505-5518
(903) 838-6514

HARDIN-SIMMONS UNIVERSITY

Box 16210
Abilene, TX 79698
(915) 670-1298
http://www.hsutx.edu

INCARNATE WORD COLLEGE

4301 Broadway
San Antonio, TX 78209-6397
(210) 829-6000
http://www.iwctx.edu/

LAMAR UNIVERSITY

Beaumont, TX 77710
(409) 880-8345
http://www.lamar.edu

MIDWESTERN STATE UNIVERSITY

3410 Taft Boulevard
Wichita Falls, TX 76308
(940) 689-4000
http://www.mwsu.edu

PRAIRIE VIEW A&M UNIVERSITY

P.O. Box 3089
Prairie View, TX 77446
(409) 857-2315
http://www.pvamu.edu/

RICE UNIVERSITY

6100 Main Street MS13
Houston, TX 77005
(713) 527-4002
http://www.rice.edu

SAM HOUSTON STATE UNIVERSITY

P.O. Box 2448
Huntsville, TX 77341
(409) 294-1111
http://oliver.shsu.edu/

SOUTHWEST TEXAS STATE UNIVERSITY

601 University Drive
San Marcos, TX 78666-5709
(512) 245-2581
http://www.swt.edu

ST. MARY'S UNIVERSITY

One Camino Santa Maria
San Antonio, TX 78228-8503
(210) 436-3101

STEPHEN F. AUSTIN STATE UNIVERSITY

Graduate School
Box 13024
Nacogdoches, TX 75962-3024
(409) 468-2807
http://www.research.sfasu.edu/

SOUTHERN METHODIST UNIVERSITY

6422 Boaz Street
P.O. Box 296
Dallas, TX 75275
Engineering: (214) 768-3042
Media Arts: (214) 768-3765
Theology: (214) 768-2432
http://www.smu.edu

SUL ROSS STATE UNIVERSITY

Alpine, TX 79832
(915) 837-8011

TARLETON STATE UNIVERSITY

Tarleton Station
Stephenville, TX 76402
(254) 968-9000
http://www.tarleton.edu/

TEXAS A&M INTERNATIONAL UNIVERSITY

5201 University Boulevard
Laredo, TX 78041
(956) 722-8001
http://www.tamiu.edu/.

TEXAS A&M UNIVERSITY— COLLEGE STATION

College Station, TX 77843-1265
(409) 845-1044
http://www.tamu.edu/

TEXAS A&M UNIVERSITY— COMMERCE

East Texas Station
Commerce, TX 75429
(903) 886-5167
http://www.tamu.edu

TEXAS A&M UNIVERSITY— CORPUS CHRISTI

6300 Ocean Drive
Corpus Christi, TX 78412
(512) 994-2624
http://www.tamucc.edu

TEXAS A&M UNIVERSITY— KINGSVILLE

Campus Box 215
Kingsville, TX 78363
(512) 593-2315
http://www.tamuk.edu/

TEXAS CHRISTIAN UNIVERSITY

2800 South University Drive
Fort Worth, TX 76129
(817) 921-7000
http://www.tcu.edu

TEXAS SOUTHERN UNIVERSITY

3100 Cleburne
Houston, TX 77004
(713) 313-7233

TEXAS TECH UNIVERSITY

Box 45005
Lubbock, TX 79409-2017
(806) 742-2787
http://www.ttu.edu

TEXAS WOMAN'S UNIVERSITY

P.O. Box 425589
Denton, TX 76204-5589
(940) 898-3073
http://www.twu.edu

TRINITY UNIVERSITY

715 Stadium Drive
San Antonio, TX 78212-7200
(210) 736-7011
http://www.trinity.edu/

UNIVERSITY OF CENTRAL TEXAS

Graduate Admissions
1901 South Clear Creek Road
P.O. Box 1416
Killeen, TX 76540-1416
(254) 526-8262
http://www.vvm.com/uct/graduate.htm

UNIVERSITY OF DALLAS

1845 East Northgate Drive
Irving, TX 75062-4799
Liberal Arts: (214) 721-5106
http://www.udallas.edu

UNIVERSITY OF HOUSTON

4800 Calhoun
Houston, TX 77004
(713) 743-1000
http://www.uh.edu

UNIVERSITY OF HOUSTON— VICTORIA

2506 East Red River
Victoria, TX 77901-4450
(512) 788-6222

UNIVERSITY OF HOUSTON— CLEAR LAKE

2700 Bay Area Boulevard
Houston, TX 77058
(713) 283-2518
http://www.129.7.160.115/

UNIVERSITY OF MARY HARDIN-BAYLOR

P.O. Box 8004
Belton, TX 76513
(254) 939-4521
http://www.umhd.edu

UNIVERSITY OF NORTH TEXAS

Box 13797
Denton, TX 76203-3797
(940) 565-2636
http://www.unt.edu/

UNIVERSITY OF ST. THOMAS

3800 Montrose Boulevard
Houston, TX 77006
(713) 522-7911
http://basil.stthom.edu/home

UNIVERSITY OF TEXAS— AUSTIN

Austin, TX 78712-1157
(512) 471-6500
http://www.utexas.edu

UNIVERSITY OF TEXAS— ARLINGTON

701 South Nedderman, Suite 241
P.O. Box 19088-A
Arlington, TX 76019
(817) 273-2681
http://www.uta.edu

UNIVERSITY OF TEXAS— DALLAS

P.O. Box 830688, AD 27
Richardson, TX 75083-0688
(972) 883-2270
http://www.utdallas.edu

UNIVERSITY OF TEXAS— EL PASO

500 West University Avenue
El Paso, TX 79968
(915) 747-5582
http://www.utep.edu/

UNIVERSITY OF TEXAS— PAN AMERICAN

1201 West University Drive
Edinburg, TX 78539
(956) 381-2207
http://www.panam.edu/

UNIVERSITY OF TEXAS— SAN ANTONIO

6900 North Loop 1604 West
San Antonio, TX 78249
(800) 669-0919
http://www.utsa.edu

UNIVERSITY OF TEXAS— TYLER

3900 University Boulevard
Tyler, TX 75701
(903) 566-7000
http://www.uttyl.edu/

UNIVERSITY OF TEXAS OF THE PERMIAN BASIN

4901 East University
Odessa, TX 79762
(915) 552-2020

WEST TEXAS A&M UNIVERSITY

2501 Fourth Avenue
Canyon, TX 79016
(806) 656-2730
http://www.wtamu.edu/

Utah

BRIGHAM YOUNG UNIVERSITY

B-356 ASB
Provo, UT 84602-1339
(801) 378-4091
http://www.byu.edu/

SOUTHERN UTAH UNIVERSITY

351 West Center Street
Cedar City, UT 84720
(435) 586-7740
http://www.suu.edu/

UNIVERSITY OF UTAH

110 Park
Salt Lake City, UT 84112
(801) 581-7200
http://www.utah.edu

UTAH STATE UNIVERSITY

Logan, UT 84322-0900
(435) 797-1189
http://www.usu.edu

WESTMINSTER COLLEGE OF SALT LAKE CITY

1840 South 1300 East
Salt Lake City, UT 84105-3697
(801) 484-7651
http://www.wcslc.edu

Vermont

BENNINGTON COLLEGE

Bennington, VT 05201
(802) 442-5401 ext. 255
http://www.bennington.edu

GODDARD COLLEGE

Plainfield, VT 05667
(802) 454-8311
http://sun.goddard.edu

MIDDLEBURY COLLEGE

Language Schools
Middlebury, VT 05753
(802) 443-5510
http://www.middlebury.edu/

NORWICH UNIVERSITY

65 South Main Street
Northfield, VT 05663
(802) 485-2000
http://www.norwich.edu/

ST. MICHAEL'S COLLEGE

Winooski Park
Colchester, VT 05439
(802) 654-2000
http://www.smcvt.edu

UNIVERSITY OF VERMONT

194 South Prospect Street
Burlington, VT 05405-3596
(802) 656-2699
http://www.uvm.edu/

Virgin Islands

UNIVERSITY OF THE VIRGIN ISLANDS

Charlotte Amalie, VI 00802
(809) 776-9200
http://mola.uvi.edu:7000/

Virginia

COLLEGE OF WILLIAM AND MARY

Williamsburg, VA 23187-8795
(757) 221-4000
http://www.wm.edu

EASTERN MENNONITE UNIVERSITY

Harrisonburg, VA 22801-2462
(540) 432-4000
http://www.emu.edu

GEORGE MASON UNIVERSITY

4400 University Drive
Fairfax, VA 22030
(703) 993-2400
http://www.gmu.edu/

HOLLINS COLLEGE

P.O. Box 9707
Roanoke, VA 24020
(540) 362-6000
http://www.hollins.edu

JAMES MADISON UNIVERSITY

Harrisonburg, VA 22807
(540) 568-6211
http://www.jmu.edu

LIBERTY UNIVERSITY

P.O. Box 20000
Lynchburg, VA 24506-8001
(804) 582-2000
http://www.liberty.edu

LONGWOOD COLLEGE

Graduate Admissions
201 High Street
Farmville, VA 23909
(804) 395-2000
http://www.lwc.edu

MARY WASHINGTON COLLEGE

1301 College Avenue
Fredericksburg, VA 22401-5358
(540) 654-1000
http://www.mwc.edu

MARYMOUNT UNIVERSITY

2807 North Glebe Road
Arlington, VA 22207-4299
(703) 284-1500
http://www.marymount.edu

NORFOLK STATE UNIVERSITY

2401 Corprew Avenue
Norfolk, VA 23504
(757) 683-8015
http://cyclops.nsu.edu

OLD DOMINION UNIVERSITY

Hampton Boulevard
Norfolk, VA 23529-0050
(757) 683-3637
http://www.odu.edu

RADFORD UNIVERSITY

Radford, VA 24142
(540) 831-5000
http://www.runet.edu

REGENT UNIVERSITY

1000 Regent University Drive
Virginia Beach, VA 23464
(757) 579-4014
http://www.regent.edu

SHENANDOAH UNIVERSITY

1460 University Drive
Winchester, VA 22601
(540) 665-4581
http://www.su.edu

UNIVERSITY OF RICHMOND

Richmond, VA 23173
(804) 289-8000
http://www.urich.edu

UNIVERSITY OF VIRGINIA

1939 Ivy Road
Charlottesville, VA 22903-1711
(804) 924-0311
http://www.virginia.edu

VIRGINIA COMMONWEALTH UNIVERSITY

901 West Franklin Street
Richmond, VA 23284-9005
(800) 841-3638
http://www.vcu.edu

VIRGINIA POLYTECHNIC INSTITUTE AND STATE UNIVERSITY

Virginia Tech Graduate School
Blacksburg, VA 24061-0202
(540) 231-6691
http://www.vt.edu

VIRGINIA STATE UNIVERSITY

Petersburg, VA 23806-2096
(804) 524-5984
http://www.vsu.edu

VIRGINIA UNION UNIVERSITY

Richmond, VA 23220
(804) 257-5600

Washington

ANTIOCH UNIVERSITY— SEATTLE

2607 Second Avenue
Seattle, WA 98121
(206) 441-5352, ext.5201
www.seattleantioch.edu

CENTRAL WASHINGTON UNIVERSITY

400 East Eighth
Ellensburg, WA 98926-7510
(509) 963-1211
http://www.cwu.edu

CITY UNIVERSITY

335-116th Avenue SE
Bellevue, WA 98004
(425) 637-1010
http://www.cityu.edu/inroads/
welcome1.html

EASTERN WASHINGTON UNIVERSITY

MS 12
526 5th Street
Cheney, WA 99004-2496
(509) 359-2296
http://www.ewu.edu

EVERGREEN STATE COLLEGE

Olympia, WA 98505
(360) 866-6000
http://www.evergreen.edu

GONZAGA UNIVERSITY

East 502 Boone Avenue
Spokane, WA 99258-0001
(509) 328-5546
http://www.gonzaga.edu

SAINT MARTIN'S COLLEGE

Lacey, WA 98503
(360) 491-4700

SEATTLE PACIFIC UNIVERSITY

3307 Third Avenue West
Seattle, WA 98119
(206) 281-2021
http://www/spu.edu

SEATTLE UNIVERSITY

Broadway and Madison
Seattle, WA 98122-4460
(206) 296-5900
http://www.seattleu.edu/

UNIVERSITY OF WASHINGTON

1400 N.E. Campus Parkway
Seattle, WA 98195
(206) 543-5929
http://www.washington.edu/

WALLA WALLA COLLEGE

204 South College Avenue
College Place, WA 99324
(509) 527-2421
http://www.wwc.edu

WASHINGTON STATE UNIVERSITY

342 French Administration Building
Pullman, WA 99164-1036
(509) 335-3535
http://www.wsu.edu/

WESTERN WASHINGTON UNIVERSITY

516 High Street
Bellingham, WA 98225-9009
(360) 650 3170
http://www.wwu.edu/

Wisconsin

EDGEWOOD COLLEGE

855 Woodrow Street
Madison, WI 53711
(608) 257-4861
http://www.edgewood.edu

MARQUETTE UNIVERSITY

517 North 14th Street
Milwaukee, WI 53233
(414) 288-7137
http://www.mu.edu

MILWAUKEE SCHOOL OF ENGINEERING

1025 North Broadway
Milwaukee, WI 53202-3109
(800) 332-6763
http://www.msoe.edu

NASHOTAH HOUSE

2777 Mission Road
Nashotah, WI 53058-9793
(414) 646-3371

SILVER LAKE COLLEGE

2406 South Alverno Road
Manitowoc, WI 54220-9319
(920) 684-6691

ST. NORBERT COLLEGE

100 Grant Street
DePere, WI 54115
(920) 403-3103
http://www.snc.edu/

UNIVERSITY OF WISCONSIN—

Eau Claire
105 Garfield Avenue
Eau Claire, WI 54701
(715) 836-5415
http://www.uwec.edu

UNIVERSITY OF WISCONSIN— LA CROSSE

1725 State Street
La Crosse, WI 54601
(608) 785-8067
http://www.uwlax.edu/

UNIVERSITY OF WISCONSIN— MADISON

750 University Avenue
Madison, WI 53706
(608) 262-2433
http://www.wisc.edu/

UNIVERSITY OF WISCONSIN—MILWAUKEE

P.O. Box 749
Milwaukee, WI 53201-0749
(414) 229-4982
http://www.uwm.edu/

UNIVERSITY OF WISCONSIN—SUPERIOR

Superior, WI 54880
(715) 394-8295
http://www.uwsuper.edu/

UNIVERSITY OF WISCONSIN—WHITEWATER

800 West Main Street
Whitewater, WI 53190
(414) 472-1006
http://www.uww.edu

UNIVERSITY OF WISCONSIN—GREEN BAY

2420 Nicolet Drive
Green Bay, WI 54311
(920) 465-2111
http://www.uwgb.edu/

UNIVERSITY OF WISCONSIN—OSHKOSH

800 Algoma Boulevard
Oshkosh, WI 54901
(920) 424-1223
http://www.uwosh.edu/

UNIVERSITY OF WISCONSIN—PLATTEVILLE

1 University Plaza
Platteville, WI 53818
(608) 342-1263
http://www.uwplatt.edu/

UNIVERSITY OF WISCONSIN—RIVER FALLS

104 North Hall
River Falls, WI 54022
(715) 425-3843
http://www.uwrf.edu/

UNIVERSITY OF WISCONSIN—STEVENS POINT

Stevens Point, WI 54481
(715) 346-2441
http://www.uwsp.edu/

UNIVERSITY OF WISCONSIN—STOUT

Menomonie, WI 54751
(715) 232-2452
http://www.uwstout.edu

West Virginia

MARSHALL UNIVERSITY

400 Hal Greer Boulevard
Huntington, WV 25755
(304) 696-2243
http://www.marshall.edu/

WEST VIRGINIA GRADUATE COLLEGE

100 A.E. Peyton Drive
South Charleston, WV 25303
(304) 746-2500
http://www.wvgc.edu

WEST VIRGINIA UNIVERSITY

P.O. Box 6009
Morgantown, WV 26506-6009
(304) 293-2121
http://www.wvu.edu

WEST VIRGINIA UNIVERSITY INSTITUTE OF TECHNOLOGY

Montgomery, WV 25136
(304) 442-3024

WHEELING JESUIT COLLEGE

316 Washington Avenue
Wheeling, WV 26003
(304) 243-2000
http://www.wjc.edu

Wyoming

UNIVERSITY OF WYOMING

Laramie, WY 82071
(307) 766-2287
http://www.uwyo.edu/

How Did We Do? Grade Us.

Thank you for choosing a Kaplan book. Your comments and suggestions are very useful to us. Please answer the following questions to assist us in our continued development of high-quality resources to meet your needs.

The Kaplan book I read was: _____

My name is: _____

My address is: _____

_____

My e-mail address is: _____

What overall grade would you give this book? Ⓐ Ⓑ Ⓒ Ⓓ Ⓕ

How relevant was the information to your goals? Ⓐ Ⓑ Ⓒ Ⓓ Ⓕ

How comprehensive was the information in this book? Ⓐ Ⓑ Ⓒ Ⓓ Ⓕ

How accurate was the information in this book? Ⓐ Ⓑ Ⓒ Ⓓ Ⓕ

How easy was the book to use? Ⓐ Ⓑ Ⓒ Ⓓ Ⓕ

How appealing was the book's design? Ⓐ Ⓑ Ⓒ Ⓓ Ⓕ

What were the book's strong points? _____

How could this book be improved? _____

Is there anything that we left out that you wanted to know more about?

Would you recommend this book to others? ☐ YES ☐ NO

Other comments: _____

_____

_____

Do we have permission to quote you? ☐ YES ☐ NO

Thank you for your help. Please tear out this page and mail it to:

Dave Chipps, Managing Editor
Kaplan Educational Centers
888 Seventh Avenue
New York, NY 10106

Or, you can answer these questions online at www.kaplan.com/talkback.

Thanks!

About
KAPLAN®
Educational Centers

Kaplan Educational Centers is one of the nation's premier education companies, providing individuals with a full range of resources to achieve their educational and career goals. Kaplan, celebrating its 60th anniversary, is a wholly-owned subsidiary of The Washington Post Company.

TEST PREPARATION & ADMISSIONS

Kaplan's nationally-recognized test prep courses cover more than 20 standardized tests, including entrance exams for secondary school, college and graduate school as well as foreign language and professional licensing exams. In addition, Kaplan offers private tutoring and comprehensive, one-to-one admissions and application advice for students applying to graduate school.

SCORE! EDUCATIONAL CENTERS

SCORE! after-school learning centers help students in grades K-8 build academic skills, confidence and goal-setting skills in a motivating, sports-oriented environment. Kids use a cutting-edge, interactive curriculum that continually assesses and adapts to their academic needs and learning style. Enthusiastic Academic Coaches serve as positive role models, creating a high-energy atmosphere where learning is exciting and fun for kids.With nearly 40 centers today, new centers continue to open nationwide.

KAPLAN LEARNING SERVICES

Kaplan Learning Services provides customized assessment, education and training programs to K-12 schools, universities and businesses to help students and employees reach their educational and career goals.

KAPLAN INTERNATIONAL

Kaplan serves international students and professionals in the U.S. through Access America, a series of intensive English language programs, and LCP International Institute, a leading provider of intensive English language programs at on-campus centers in California, Washington and New York. Kaplan and LCP offer specialized services to sponsors including placement at top American universities, fellowship management, academic monitoring and reporting and financial administration.

KAPLOAN

Students can get key information and advice about educational loans for college and graduate school through **KapLoan** (Kaplan Student Loan Information Program). Through an affiliation with one of the nation's largest student loan providers, **KapLoan** helps direct students and their families through the often bewildering financial aid process.

KAPLAN PUBLISHING

Kaplan Books, a joint imprint with Simon & Schuster, publishes titles in test preparation, admissions, education, career development and life skills; Kaplan and *Newsweek* jointly publish the highly successful guides, **How to Get Into College** and **How to Choose a Career & Graduate School**. *SCORE!* and *Newsweek* have teamed up to publish **How to Help Your Child Suceed in School**.

Kaplan InterActive delivers award-winning, high quality educational products and services including Kaplan's best-selling **Higher Score** test-prep software and sites on the internet **(http://www.kaplan.com)** and America Online. Kaplan and Cendant Software are jointly developing, marketing and distributing educational software for the kindergarten through twelfth grade retail and school markets.

KAPLAN CAREER SERVICES

Kaplan helps students and graduates find jobs through Kaplan Career Services, the leading provider of career fairs in North America. The division includes **Crimson & Brown Associates**, the nation's leading diversity recruiting and publishing firm, **The Lendman Group and Career Expo**, both of which help clients identify highly sought-after technical personnel, and sales and marketing professionals.

COMMUNITY OUTREACH

Kaplan provides educational resources to thousands of financially disadvantaged students annually, working closely with educational institutions, not-for-profit groups, government agencies and other grass roots organizations on a variety of national and local support programs. Also, Kaplan centers enrich local communities by employing high school, college and graduate students, creating valuable work experiences for vast numbers of young people each year.

Want more information about our services, products, or the nearest Kaplan center?

Call our nationwide toll-free numbers:

 1-800-KAP-TEST for information on our live courses, private tutoring and admissions consulting
1-800-KAP-ITEM for information on our products
1-888-KAP-LOAN* for information on student loans

Connect with us in cyberspace:

 On AOL, keyword:"Kaplan"
On the World Wide Web, go to: http://www.kaplan.com
Via e-mail: info@kaplan.com

Write to:

Kaplan Educational Centers
888 Seventh Avenue
New York, NY 10106

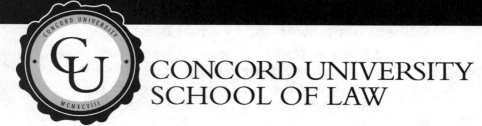